SECOND EDITION

ISSUES

a course book for
Advanced Level
English Language

PETER TURNER

Hodder & Stoughton

A MEMBER OF THE HODDER HEADLINE GROUP

British Library Cataloguing in Publication Data

Turner, Peter
  Issues. – 2nd ed.
  I. Title
  808.4

  ISBN 0 340 55631 5

First published 1987
Impression number   10 9 8 7 6 5 4
Year   1999   1998   1997   1996

Typeset by Litho Link Limited, Welshpool, Powys.
Printed in Great Britain for Hodder & Stoughton Educational,
a division of Hodder Headline Plc, 338 Euston Road,
London NW1 3BH by Redwood Books, Trowbridge, Wiltshire.

Contents

Acknowledgements

The publishers would like to thank the following for permission to reproduce copyright material in this volume:

The extract from Alfred Davey, *Learning to be prejudiced* reproduced by permission of Edward Arnold (1983); the extract from Brian Inglis, *The Forbidden Game* reproduced by permission of Curtis Brown Ltd on behalf of Brian Inglis. Copyright Brian Inglis 1975; the Associated Examining Board for the extract from D W Winnicott, *The Child, the Family and the Outside World*; Andre Deutsch Ltd for the extract from Norman Mailer, *The Presidential Papers* (1968); BBC Enterprises Ltd for the extracts from Rex Moorfoot, *Television in the eighties* (1982), Peter Black, *The Biggest Aspidistra in the World* (1972) and Janet Cohen, *File on Four*; Basil Blackwell for the extracts from Anthony Giddens, *Sociology* (Polity Press, 1990) and Kathy Myers, *Understanding Advertisers* (in *Language, Image, Media*, eds. Davis and Walton, 1983); extracts from the Authorized Version of the Bible (The King James Bible), the rights in which are vested in the Crown, are reproduced by permission of the Crown's patentee, Cambridge University Press; Faber and Faber Ltd for the extract from Robert Harris, *Gotcha! The Media, the Government and the Falklands Crisis* (1983); Gower Publishing Group for the extracts from Dennie Briggs, *In Place of Prison* (Temple Smith, 1975) and Thomas J Cottle, *Black Testimony: the voices of Britain's West Indians* (Wildwood House Ltd, 1978); Hamish Hamilton for the extract from Leon Radzinovicz and Joan King, *The Growth of Crime* (1977); Her Majesty's Stationery Office for the extracts from *Half Our Future: A Report of the Central Advisory Council for Education*, 1963 and The Official Report of the House of Lords and House of Commons Debates (Hansard); Ellis Horwood for the extract from Alan Burns, *The Microchip: Appropriate or inappropriate technology* (1981); John Wiley & Sons Ltd for the extract from Barrie Sherman, *The New Revolution* (1985); Kogan Page Limited for the extracts from Robert Allen, *How to save the world* (1980); the extracts from Tony Parker, *The Man Inside*, Betty Friedan, *The Second Stage*, and Betty Friedan, *The Feminine Mystique* reproduced by permission of Michael Joseph Ltd; the articles by Buchi Emecheta (1985), Anuradha Vittachi (1980) and Judy Gahagan, *Science on the Couch* (1988), New Internationalist; the extract from Michael Shallis, *The Silicon Idol*, reproduced by permission of Oxford University Press (1984); the extracts from Susan George, *How the Other Half Dies* (1976), Edward Blishen, *The School that I'd like* (1969), David J Smith, *Racial Disadvantage in Britain: The PEP Report* (1977), and 'Advertising' by Frank Whitebread, in *Discrimination and Popular Culture* (ed. Denys Thompson, 1964), all reproduced by permission of Penguin Books Ltd; the extracts from Teresa Hayter, *The Creation of World Poverty* (1981) and Peter Fryer, *Staying Power* (1984) reproduced by permission of Drake Marketing Services on behalf of Pluto Press; Routledge, for the extracts from Janet Radcliffe Richards, *The Sceptical Feminist* (1980), Peter Conrad, *Television: The medium and its manners* (1982) and E Ellis Cashmore, *A dictionary of Race & Ethnic Relations*; SCM Press Ltd for the extract from

David Bleakley, *In Place of Work* (1981); Screen for the extract from Beverley Brown, *British film censorship: an interview with James Ferman* (23:5, 1982); The Observer for H G Wells, *Our World in 50 years' time* and the front page of The Observer 9.12.90; Mirror Group Newspapers for the article by Frank Corless, *Brady's Xmas Feast;* The Spectator, for Peter Ackroyd, *Pictures from Italy* (19.4.86); The Sunday Telegraph Ltd, for the front page of The Sunday Telegraph (9.12.90); Victor Gollancz Ltd, for the extract from Christopher Evans, *The Mighty Micro* (1979); Guardian News Service Ltd, for the articles *Rainforest Factfile*, and *Still Papering Over the Cracks* by Yasmin Alibhai; Professor David Pearce for his article, *Options for the Forest* (in the Guardian, 8.12.89); Bryan Magee, for the extracts from his article *Women's Rights and Wrongs* (in the Guardian, 12.11.89); Manchester University Press for the extract from John Whale, *The Politics of the Media* (1977); Edward Arnold Publishers, for the extract from E M Forster, *Two Cheers for Democracy* (1972); News of the World, for the front page from The News of the World (9.12.90) and the extract from Sunday magazine; Random Century for the extracts from Benjamin Spock, *Baby and Child Care* (The Bodley Head, 1979), Jonathan Gathorne-Hardy, *Love, Sex, Marriage and Divorce* (Jonathan Cape, 1981), Naomi Wolf, *The Beauty Myth* (Chatto & Windus, 1990); Random House Inc, for the extract from Paul Ehrlich, *The Population Bomb* (Ballantine Books, 1968); Times Newspapers for the extracts from The Times and the Sunday Times. Copyright Times Newspapers.

The publishers would like to thank the following for giving permission to reproduce copyright photographic material in this book:

Cover, Richard Smith/Katz Pictures; p 56, Colin Taylor Productions; p 81, Topham Picture Source; p 105, Ecoscene; p 125 left, John Birdsall Photography; p 125 right, Andes Press Agency; p 154/5, Topham Picture Source; p 176 top left, © John P Cavanagh/The Women's Press; p 176 bottom left, © Colin Tromp/Chatto and Windus; p 176 right, Topham Picture Source; p 198, © David Simmonds; p 227, Ford Motor Company Limited.

I would like to thank my colleagues at Bournemouth and Poole College of Further Education for their advice and assistance in preparing the two editions of this book, in particular Bob Baker, Irene Bee, Nicky Burgess, Dave Cook, Andrea Etherington, Martin Price, Jim Watson and Mike Wedge, and also Stuart Holloway at Bankstown College of TAFE, Sydney, Australia. For their cheerful willingness to act as guinea-pigs and critics, my thanks are due in addition to my A level English students at Bournemouth and Poole College from 1982–90, and my HSC English students at Bankstown College in 1991. Thanks for their help and encouragement also go to my friends Jim Hall, Lorie Harding, Julie Matthews, Mikki Nanowski and John Randall, and for their assistance with the final preparation of the manuscript to Robyne Boyle, Melissa Brock, Marian Lorrison and Robyn Smiley.

Preface

The essential idea of this book is to provide a thematically integrated approach to advanced level English studies. It aims to cover some of the major social, political and cultural issues of the late 20th century, in a way which would be of value both for post–GCSE English examination work, and for general and social studies discussion, with or without written work to follow.

The book is most specifically directed towards the AEB A and AS level English (Language and Literature) syllabuses, and the themes chosen are ones that appear frequently on the A-level Language exam essay paper. The discussion material may also be of value for sixth form and FE college Social/Liberal/General Studies sessions.

Part I concentrates on techniques and practice in discussion essay and narrative writing, summary and comprehension, and exercises are set in the current format of the AEB English examination.

Each chapter in Part II, except for the last, covers a single issue, providing a comprehension or summary exercise, a series of extracts designed to present a wide range of viewpoints and information, with suggestions for discussion, research and further written work, and lists of essay titles and additional stimulus material. Each thematic chapter also contains a final section dealing with problems inherent in some aspect of written work. The last chapter deals with four additional issues more briefly, providing, overall, for two full-scale discussion and writing sessions per term over a two-year course.

The essay questions are generally taken from AEB A level examination papers, with a few also taken from AEB Use of English and O/A level English Language – Professional and Business Use papers.

THE DISCUSSION ESSAY

General preparation for essay writing

Essay writing is an ancient art, practised by many great writers of the past. If you want to read written English at its most lucid, you cannot do better than to turn to the essays of George Orwell. The essay is also, of course, the essential vehicle for testing academic subjects at Advanced level. At this level, as practised by people like you, it is a formal exercise, with relatively rigid conventions. The purpose of this chapter is to explore the conventions and offer advice on essay preparation.

Let us begin, then, with some general approaches to preparation for advanced English discussion essay writing. A study of past examination papers over the previous few years will give you a good idea of the kinds of topics favoured by the examination board with which you are concerned. You will probably find that most of the issues covered in this book feature in past examination papers. During your course you will almost certainly be involved in class discussions or debates on the issues, and jotting down ideas which interest you from these sessions is a start. But the material contained in the book is obviously not intended to provide the last word on any topic. To be adequately informed you must read further into the topic before the discussion takes place, and each chapter contains suggestions for preparatory reading.

Early on in your course, it would be advisable to make a list of the most important issues which recur in past examination essay questions. This should guide your reading. It is not enough, of course, if you are preparing for an examination which includes questions requiring analysis of current issues, simply to learn about the topics covered in this book. The examination paper you eventually sit may include none of them. Wider reading is therefore essential. A quality Sunday newspaper is a valuable source of information, and periodicals and good daily papers can also be useful. Simply *reading* informed analysis is bound to develop your own ideas and understanding, but newspapers and magazines are by nature ephemeral; before they reach the waste bin you are likely to have forgotten the details. If you cut out and keep useful articles and collect them, perhaps in the form of a scrapbook, then you will be able to *learn* some of their contents and to refer back to them as you would to books. You could draw up a list of 20 or more themes and make a collection of pieces relating to each.

If you follow this advice, you should find at least one question on your examination paper about which you have prepared some material. But there is no guarantee. It is quite possible that none of the topics you have researched will appear in any form at all on your final examination paper. Will it matter? It may, or it may not. You cannot be expected to have a specialist knowledge of any subject area on the language essay paper, so a carefully thought out argument, with only a few 'hard' facts to back it up, can form a perfectly adequate essay. Much depends on whether you have thought about the issue on which you choose to write before you start writing. Working out your ideas as you go along almost inevitably results in a laboured and unconvincing essay. Thus, breadth of reading and thinking is the only certain safeguard in examinations which are as unpredictable as general English essay papers.

Planning and writing a discussion essay

Let's look at a hypothetical situation. You are faced with an examination paper which contains no topic on which you are specifically prepared. You therefore choose the question with which you feel most comfortable. Let us imagine that the title you have chosen is: ' "Cars are not a blessing but a curse!" What are your views?' Let's now go back a little to fundamentals.

You will almost certainly have been told to make notes and a plan before beginning an English essay. The same principle applies to more advanced essay work. But if you have only got an hour, or less, for an essay, you can't devote much of it to detailed planning. The examination for which you are now preparing, however, may well allow you more time for your essay. If you are advised to spend an hour and a half on the essay, for example, you can afford to spend up to 20 minutes on planning and making quite detailed notes. The examiner will expect to see them. Admittedly there can be no scheme for essay writing which suits everyone, but probably the most useful approach for most people is simply to sit and think about the subject, and jot down ideas as they come into your mind. They may or may not follow a logical pattern of development, and at the initial planning stage it does not matter. An overall approach to the topic will probably occur to you after a few minutes, and the more-or-less random notes can be organised into a paragraph scheme, once you have worked out a sufficient range of ideas. Some people seem to be able to write well-balanced and logically-developed essays off the top of their heads, but for the majority, detailed planning makes a crucial difference.

Specimen answer

Here is an example of an essay planned and written in an hour and a half. You should perhaps be warned that the viewpoint it adopts is deliberately provocative!

'Cars are not a blessing but a curse!' What are your views?

Random notes

2 Convenience – buses take longer in and between towns
        – annoyance of using buses when car breaks down
2 Reorganised public transport system
3 Using up world's scarce oil
3 Need to do without petrol-driven car if oil gives out
3 Noise pollution
3 Greenhouse Effect
3 Ozone layer
4 Accidents – major cause of death
        – drain on Health Service
        – danger to cyclists/puts people off cycling
5 Garage bills and other costs
4 Motorways – pollution of environment
        – destroy countryside
3 Air pollution – carbon monoxide, especially Tokyo and Los Angeles
4 Destruction of towns – flyovers and bypasses
        – motorways go right into cities
1 Intro. – origins of car
     – are cars a blessing?
4 Effects on people – adds to isolation
        – stress: traffic jams/rushing through traffic
5 Conclusion: main advantage – speed and convenience
      could cars be done away with?
      effect on unemployment

Plan

1 Intro. – history of car
2 Advantages: convenience → reorganisation of transport system
3 Disadvantages: pollution and depletion of resources
4 Disadvantages: destructive effect on people and places
5 Conclusion: cost and summing up

Essay

In 1885 a German, Carl Benz, produced the first petrol-driven vehicle, which proved to be the forerunner of the modern car. Few people in those days realised what a monster had been spawned. If they had foreseen the extent to which the automobile has come to dominate life in the Western world a century later, would they have looked on Herr Benz's achievement with approval?

To many people in the 1990s a car has come to seem an indispensable part of daily life. The extent to which I myself have become dependent on my car is highlighted whenever it breaks down and I have to use buses. By the time I have walked to the bus stop, which is some distance from my house, and waited for twenty minutes in the pouring rain for a bus which leaves me with a twenty-minute walk the other end, the car does indeed seem a blessing. In a town like Bournemouth, the public transport system is so run-down that cars tend to be the only comfortable and efficient mode of travel. Does this have to be the case?

Many people feel that the days of the car are numbered, that the world's reserves of oil will be exhausted within a generation, and the petrol-driven car will have to be phased off the roads. What will happen then? The answer which many have suggested, a full-scale reorganisation of the public transport system, shows that the car is not necessarily such an indispensable asset as we tend to assume. If everyone used buses instead of cars, then public transport could be run efficiently, with a regular, rapid network of routes in every town and city in the country, and with no traffic jams! There could be express buses, stopping only at major points along the route, even within cities. However, cars are fast and efficient, except in rush hours, so what, apart from slowing down the depletion of oil reserves, would mankind gain from the loss of the motor car? Is it really a curse?

You have only to travel to Tokyo or Los Angeles to realise the appalling effects of cars on the environment. Traffic police in Tokyo have to wear masks and carry oxygen, or they would collapse because the air is so polluted with carbon monoxide from cars. Cars produce other more insidious types of pollution. Perhaps the most deadly threat facing mankind is the global warming resulting from the Greenhouse Effect and the destruction of the ozone layer. Cars are considered by scientists to be the major contributors to this potential catastrophe. On a less cataclysmic scale, noise pollution, caused by the ceaseless roar of engines and honking of horns, is a further cause of stress in major cities. Actual death from these causes at the moment, however, is rare. The car is, nevertheless, a major killer.

One of the principal causes of premature death in the Western world is from car accidents. Thousands of people are killed on the roads every year in Britain. Thousands more are injured and maimed, which results not only in indescribable suffering, but also in a serious drain on the resources of the National Health Service, with precious space in hospital wards taken up, for months or years, by the car's victims. Not only human life is destroyed by the ubiquitous car. Towns and cities are ruthlessly knocked about to build flyovers and bypasses which destroy the character of our urban areas; motorways destroy the peace and beauty of the countryside.

6

Clearly the car has come to dominate human life to an unhealthy extent. Can the monster be killed off, without too much pain? Car workers will say 'no'. Unemployment would soar if the motor industry folded up. But is the saving of jobs a strong enough reason for the destruction of human life and the environment? With an efficient public transport system, the only real blessings of the car – speed and convenience – would be rendered insignificant, and the death of the private car would make the world altogether safer and less stressful.

Technical analysis of the specimen answer

This would gain a high grade as a general English language essay, despite the fact that, as you can see, it contains little 'hard' factual information. One of its advantages, of course, is that it contains no errors of spelling, punctuation or grammar! Perfection in the essentials of written English is not expected, even for an *A* grade at A level, but an examiner will not give an essay a top grade without a high level of formal accuracy. However, our concern in this chapter is with content and presentation of ideas. Let's analyse the content.

How many 'hard' facts does the essay actually contain? The opening sentence presents precise historical detail, and the argument of paragraph 4 is backed up by references to problems in particular cities. Are even these facts absolutely necessary? The first adds elegance to the opening. It gets the essay off to a stylish start, but has no particular value as information. What about paragraph 4? If you knew generally about the problems of atmospheric pollution, but could not give any specific details, would the argument be weakened? Such facts certainly add colour and an air of authority to the arguments, but the points could be made without them. The essential requirement is that you have thought about the issues themselves. Paragraph 5, in fact, conspicuously fails to provide any precise facts and figures. The vague 'thousands' is not particularly convincing; exact figures would add potency to the argument. But the analysis is still valid, despite the vagueness in the details.

The one crucial feature of any successful discussion essay is a coherent argument, and for this, obviously enough, you must have a definite viewpoint. The key idea of this essay is developed in paragraph 3 – it does not have to be stated immediately. A careful build-up to the central argument is always more effective than a bald statement of attitude at the beginning, which tends in any case to pre-empt the argument. You will, what is more, be expected to show that you realise that there are two sides to any argument, and at least passing reference to the opposing point of view is essential.

Paragraph 2, the first main paragraph after the brief introduction, develops one of the major arguments *in favour* of private cars. It leads, in the last sentence, directly into the central argument about the reorganisation of public transport. Thereafter, the essay concentrates on arguments against the use of private cars. There is nothing wrong with such heavy weighting of your argument. In fact, one common weakness of discussion essays is a lack of direction, presenting first one side of the case, then the other, and leading nowhere. Showing that you understand the opposition's case does not mean that you have to be unbiased, unless the question specifically asks you to 'discuss arguments for *and* against' something. Careful organisation of your ideas into paragraphs, however, is essential. Let's look in more detail at the planning of essays.

If you look at the random notes for the essay above, you will notice numbers before each point. The numbers are written in *after* the paragraph plan has been worked out, and refer to the paragraph into which each point will fit. This is simply a convenient way of picking out the ideas which are relevant to a particular paragraph, swiftly working out the order in which they are to be used, and checking that you have not missed any points. You may find the technique useful if you have not tried it before.

As stated earlier, the actual paragraph plan will probably not fit into place in your mind until after you have started making random notes. Similarly, the plan may well be modified when you actually begin writing your essay. There is no need at all to feel that you must follow your plan. It is, after all, for your benefit. If you look again at the essay you will notice that it does not even contain the same number of paragraphs as the plan indicates. What in fact occurred when the essay was being written was that the argument about the reorganisation of public transport assumed a greater importance after the essay had been started than had been envisaged at the planning stage, and instead of being incorporated into the discussion of the advantages of private motorised transport, it earned a paragraph for itself. If the original paragraph scheme had been followed, paragraph 2 would have been twice as long as the others, which is, in any case, structurally unsatisfactory. New ideas will always come to you when you start writing, and as long as they are directly relevant to the paragraph on which you are working, they can be accommodated perfectly easily. If they are not immediately relevant, they can be added to the random notes and incorporated where they do fit in.

If you do think of new ideas as you go along, however, you may come up against the eternal bugbear of examinations – time. Trying to develop every idea that occurs to you can result in your running out of time before you have managed to follow through your prepared structure properly. Therefore, it is essential to *pace* yourself. Good ideas may have to be discarded if time is getting short; other ideas, which you would like to develop, may have to be stated much more briefly than they might be. The final sentence of paragraph 5, for instance, glosses very briefly over two ideas which could have been embellished and made much more compelling with examples. However, this would have been at the expense of an adequate conclusion, which is an essential requirement of a properly constructed essay.

Not all the random notes are included in the essay. The point about individual isolation and stress caused by queues of cars with single occupants was left out. The ideas are just as valid as many that *are* included, and might have been illustrated interestingly by referring, for instance, to a Ray Bradbury science fiction story about a time in the near future when pedestrians in the Western world are almost unknown and everybody uses cars. But it would have taken too long to explain the point of the story. The reference to bicycles is also missing. When ideas are flowing freely, self-discipline is sometimes required! No illustration of a single idea should, in any case, take up too much space, and more crucially, you should *never* include ideas just because you have thought of them. Your essay must have direction, and every idea must be plainly relevant to the theme of the paragraph in which it appears.

So, although there is no need to adhere rigidly to your original plan, it should provide a clear overall structure for your essay, and a reasonably full set of random notes to refer back to will almost certainly make the writing of the essay much easier. As well as achieving coherence within paragraphs, you should try to dovetail neatly from one paragraph to the next. If you look once more at the essay, you will notice that the first three paragraphs all end with a question. As long as it is not overused, this can be a reasonably simple and effective technique by which to achieve links between paragraphs. The final sentence of paragraph 4 also leads, by a statement this time, directly into the theme of paragraph 5. Thus the argument develops with an air of naturalness and inevitability. The conclusion, though quite short, is firmly stated; this too is essential. It must also, however, like the introduction, be interesting, which a bald statement of opinion, or a brief rehash of some of the earlier arguments would not. Before the final statement of opinion in this essay, reference is made to an argument against the abolition of private cars, which was not mentioned earlier. There is no reason why you should not include new material in your concluding paragraph, provided it does not obscure the conclusion itself.

Additional points

Finally, a few general questions that often arise about discussion essay writing. Should you refer to yourself and your own experience in a formal discussion essay? Again, if you look back at the essay, you will notice that paragraph 2 draws entirely on personal experience to elaborate the point. As long as you do not fall into the classic logical flaw of arguing from the particular to the general, a personal anecdote can add interest and variety to an essay (though it must be added here that some teachers disapprove of the use of the personal pronoun in any but a personal essay). Secondly, will it jeopardise your chances if you adopt an unconventional viewpoint with which the examiner is likely to disagree? The answer to this question is again illustrated by the essay. Most people, examiners included, would probably disagree with its viewpoint. Perhaps even the writer was playing devil's advocate to some extent, for the sake of producing an interesting discussion! This would certainly not prevent the essay from gaining a high grade. The examiner is not looking for the 'right' answer, but for clarity of expression, of ideas and of organisation, and these are the qualities which you must strive to develop as you progress through your course.

Lastly, do the introduction and conclusion need to be the same length as the other paragraphs? The short answer to this is 'no'. The main purpose of the introduction is to define the terms of the question, if necessary, and to explain the approach you are taking to it. It only needs to be a few lines long. The same applies to the conclusion, the purpose of which is to round off your argument with a final definitive statement. Much time can be lost trying and failing to get started on an essay. The great majority of your time should be spent on the main paragraphs, which form the 'body' of the essay.

NARRATIVE WRITING

2

If the choice of titles for continuous writing contains a narrative option, this can be a good alternative to the conventional essay for students with a flair for creative writing and a vivid imagination. In examinations which contain both essay and story questions, the highest marks are often gained by those who choose to write a story. However, there tend to be more pitfalls in narrative than in essay writing, and the lowest marks also tend to be scored by story writers.

Before we look at some of the common ingredients of successful narrative writing, then, we shall look at some of the dangers of choosing the story option.

Pitfalls of narrative writing

Probably the main reason why students score particularly badly when they attempt a story is that there is a tendency to treat it as a 'soft option'. You don't have to *know* anything to write a story! A student who decides that he or she does not have enough ideas or information about a discussion or personal essay topic, and chooses the story out of desperation, has every chance of failure. Rambling and incoherent stories score very low marks.

A story *has* to capture the reader's interest and appeal to his or her imagination from the start. It has, therefore, to have a structure: it must develop towards some kind of coherent climax. Probably the major pitfall of examination story writing is the failure to map out the storyline in your mind before you start writing. If you think the story out as you go along, without knowing how the plot is going to unfold and how the story is going to end, you are likely to end up with a weak and shapeless narrative.

The most damaging pitfall of all is the failure to make clear the relevance of the narrative to the question. The title theme *must* be an integral part of the story, and must not just be loosely fitted in somewhere. However effective a story may be otherwise, if the reader cannot work out fairly early on how it relates to the title, it will fail badly.

Even if the story is well thought out and interesting, there is another pitfall which is peculiar to narrative writing. The time limitation of the examination is much more of a potential problem with narrative than with any other kind of writing. If a story is developing effectively and convincingly, you cannot simply 'wind it up' in the last ten minutes if you find yourself running out of time. A rushed ending can be disastrous in a story, and pacing yourself is therefore especially important. Too much incidental detail can slow the story down fatally. Stories do tend to need time to unfold, and an examination room is not the ideal setting for an exercise of the creative imagination.

Dullness is, of course, a fatal flaw in a narrative piece. You cannot hope to gain a high mark if your storyline, characters and descriptions fail to capture the reader's interest. For example, a simple story, based on a personal experience which is of no particular intrinsic interest, with a straightforward linear structure and characters who are impossible to visualise or relate to, and in which the ending is an anticlimax, is likely to be marked down more than a pedestrian answer to a discussion topic. Conversely, an unconvincing adventure story, packed with detail, but with little structure, with cardboard characters and a contrived ending, is likely to score even fewer marks.

Nevertheless, if you find you have a good idea for a story when you read through the titles in the examination, and you possess some flair for creative writing, the story can be an excellent choice.

Let us look now at some of the common features of effective short stories.

Narrative writing technique

To talk of rules for short story writing is, in a sense, absurd. Truly creative writing cannot be circumscribed by convention. The only meaningful test of the success or otherwise of a piece of narrative writing is whether or not it *works*; if it arouses and sustains the interest of the reader, then it has succeeded. A story can work brilliantly with or without dialogue, with or without detailed setting and characterisation, and so on. The vogue towards the end of the 1980s for 50-word mini-sagas clearly illustrated the fact that none of the conventional features of narrative writing are actually necessary for stories to be effective.

However, it is possible to talk of features or techniques which are *commonly* found in successful short stories, and which *tend* to add interest and effectiveness to narrative writing.

We will look at the most important of these techniques or features, and then see how they work in an actual story.

An arresting start

A lengthy introductory explanation of the situation and the main characters in the story is generally a poor way to start. The opening of a story is more likely to capture the reader's interest if it is arresting.

If the story begins with an actual incident, rather than an explanation, the reader is involved from the start. A passage of dialogue inevitably creates immediacy, and can make an effective opening. Another generally effective technique is to open with an incident some way into the actual story, followed by an explanation of how the situation arose and who the characters are, possibly dealt with through flashbacks as the story unfolds.

Here is a very basic example of a story opening which is immediately arresting. These are the opening few lines of a story called *The Five-Forty-Eight* by John Cheever:

> When Blake stepped out of the elevator, he saw her. A few people, mostly men waiting for girls, stood in the lobby watching the elevator doors. She was among them. As he saw her, her face took on a look of such loathing and purpose that he realised she had been waiting for him.

The story is immediately under way: we want to read on!

Suspense or surprise

The essence of most successful narrative writing is to keep the reader wanting to know what is going to happen. There are two ways of structuring a story in order to do this: suspense and surprise. The technique of suspense means that the writer drops hints that something is going to happen to one or more of the characters of which they themselves are ignorant; the reader is therefore more aware of what is going on than the characters, but is nevertheless kept guessing as to exactly *what* is going to happen. Surprise means that reader and characters are equally unaware of how the story is going to end.

It is difficult to maintain the reader's interest in a story if you make it obvious what is going to happen. If the climax is too predictable, it becomes an anticlimax.

A powerful climax

The focal point of most successful stories is the climax, towards which everything has been leading. It normally comes close to the end of the story, and is followed by a brief 'dénouement' in which the loose ends are tied up. A well-constructed story usually has a single climax, which clearly stands out as the major incident. Too many dramatic events earlier in the story can, in fact, reduce the impact of the climax, and damage the story. There is certainly no need to write complicated plots with a wealth of incident; a simple storyline, with a powerful climax, can make a perfectly effective story.

The 'twist' or shock ending

A popular narrative technique is that of the final, unexpected 'twist' at the very end of the story. The technique was developed to the point of becoming a formula by the American comic story writer O. Henry, and tends nowadays to be somewhat derided. However, a skilfully handled 'twist' can create a very memorable ending.

The ultimate expression of this technique is to leave the 'twist' or revelation until the very last sentence. A good illustration of the technique at its most gruesomely dramatic is *The Boarded Window*, a short story by the late 19th-century American writer, Ambrose Bierce. A brief summary of the story is needed for the twist to be appreciated:

The wife of an American frontiersman of the early 19th century has just died of a fever. The couple had lived contentedly in a lonely cabin in the woods, and the man is described preparing his wife's body for burial. His task finally completed, he lays the body out on the kitchen table and falls asleep, exhausted, as a long wailing sound is heard in the woods surrounding the cabin. He awakes, hours later, in pitch darkness, as the table, on which he is slumped, shakes, and he hears the sound of bare feet on the floor. A heavy body appears to be hurled against the table, which seems to be empty. The man grabs his rifle and fires randomly into the darkness. This is how the story ends:

> By the flash which lit up the room with a vivid illumination, he saw an enormous panther dragging the dead woman towards the window, its teeth fixed in her throat! Then there was darkness blacker than before, and silence; and when he returned to consciousness the sun was high and the wood was vocal with songs of birds.
>
> The body lay near the window where the beast had left it when frightened away by the flash and report of the rifle. The clothing was deranged, the long hair in disorder, the limbs lay anyhow. From the throat, dreadfully lacerated, had issued a pool of blood not yet entirely coagulated. The ribbon with which he had bound the wrists was broken; the hands were tightly clenched. Between the teeth was a fragment of the animal's ear.

Bringing people and places to life

A more-or-less essential feature of effective narrative writing is the ability to capture the essence of a character or location in a few words. If the reader cannot visualise characters and places, his or her interest in them is considerably lessened. Detailed descriptions are generally unnecessary, and excessive detail is likely merely to clog up the story. But one or two well-chosen phrases, creating a visual impression of the appearance of a person or place, generally increase the reader's involvement in the story considerably.

Here are two examples of how a skilful writer can create a vivid picture of a character in a few words.

In the story *Eli, the Fanatic*, the American writer, Philip Roth, introduces a character with this sentence: 'Tzuref, a bald, shaggy-browed man who looked as if he'd once been fat, sat back on an empty chair, halfway hidden, as though he were settled on the floor.'

Another American writer, F. Scott Fitzgerald, in his story *Babylon Revisited*, introduces a new character, Charlie, thus: 'He was thirty-five, and good to look at. The Irish nobility of his face was sobered by a deep wrinkle between his eyes.'

We have an instant visual impression of these characters, and thus they become three-dimensional for us.

The use of dialogue

Perhaps the simplest way to bring an incident to life and create immediacy is by the use of dialogue. The way people talk gives strong character clues, and inventing conversations for your characters is a more effective way of conveying an impression of them than by definitive statements.

One of the cardinal rules of creative writing is 'showing, rather than telling'. Instead of simply making statements about people, situations and events, it is always more subtle and interesting to *reveal* them to the reader, by incident and dialogue.

One danger should be mentioned here, though. Dialogue is notoriously difficult to punctuate accurately. You should make sure that you check carefully how dialogue is punctuated before you use it in a story.

Choosing evocative words

In all forms of writing it is necessary to choose your words with care. This is particularly true of creative and narrative writing. Although adjectives should not be overworked – if every noun has an accompanying adjective the result is likely to be a feeling of artificiality and stiffness – well-chosen and colourful adjectives and adverbs can add greatly to the effectiveness of your writing. The use of imagery, especially of the figures of meaning and sound analysed in the next chapter, can enhance the vividness of your writing still further, though again, such techniques should not be overworked.

An example of a short story

The story which follows illustrates most of the features which we have just considered. It is a horror story, and the grotesque ending will not be to everyone's taste. But it is a fine example of how to make even the most bizarre story realistic and believable. It was written in 1988 by a 17-year-old college GCSE student, Kim Carty.

Three Little Piggies

Andrea flopped down, relieved, into a welcoming armchair. The Wilsons had just left and now she was all alone, save for the two sleeping children upstairs. She smiled secretly to herself as she pictured Helen Wilson, still looking fabulous at 38, fussing with her hair in the hallway mirror.

'The children are already asleep, so help yourself to anything you want to eat,' Helen said, trying to find her lipstick.

'Hurry along Helen!' Mr Wilson called, as he started up the engine.

'How do I look?' Helen asked, turning to face Andrea.

'You look wonderful,' Andrea replied.

Helen smiled thankfully. 'Right, where's my coat?'

'Here,' Andrea answered, laughing. Mr Wilson sounded his horn in annoyance.

'Better go. Oh, by the way, I've left a number by the phone upstairs and in the lounge in case you get into any difficulties.'

Andrea smiled and nodded. She had heard these instructions at least a thousand times!

'We should be back at half-past-one,' Helen confirmed, as she stepped out into the cold night.

'Have a good time,' Andrea called. She watched silently as the large estate car pulled away. Turning around, she entered the house, shutting the huge oak door.

Stepping out of her high red shoes, she padded into the kitchen. It took her a good ten minutes to find the jar of coffee. As usual, it was in the place she was least expecting. Armed with a mug of steaming coffee and a packet of 'Hob-nobs', she headed towards the lounge, switching off the light with some difficulty.

The kitchen was immediately shrouded in darkness. Outside, the moon shone bright and clear, sending ominous shadows dancing across the driveway. No one, including Andrea, noticed the enormous, slightly stooped figure of a man. Nor did they notice him moving slowly towards the house, holding something large, which gleamed in the moonlight.

She sat, relaxed by the warmth of the fire, sipping her drink. For some reason she began to feel incredibly tired.

No, she thought, she must not give in to the welcoming, slowly enclosing blackness, she must . . . The sudden shrill ring of the phone jolted her to her senses.

'Damn it!' she thought, as she pulled herself up to answer it. 'Hello,' she answered, hoping it was a wrong number. The phone went dead.

'How funny!' she thought, as she replaced the receiver. She no longer felt like sleeping; instead she reached for the remote control and switched on the television. The room seemed to come to life, and feel more cheery. This made her feel safe and not quite so alone.

Changing channels, she settled down to watch a film, starring Kirk Douglas. It was not even ten minutes before the phone rang again. Placing down her mug, she answered the phone.

'Hello. This is five-seven-four-double-two . . .'

The sudden insane laugh made her nearly drop the phone.

'Who is this?' she asked, startled and annoyed.

'There were three little piggies. Oh what fun! Two were disembowelled, then there was one.'

The voice, cracking in places, sounded evil and menacing. Again the insane and hysterical laughing commenced.

'Go to hell!' Andrea yelled, slamming down the receiver. She searchd frantically for her cigarettes. The calls had made her nervous and she desperately needed a cigarette to calm her down.

The slow entry of nicotine in her lungs helped to soothe her fraught nerves.

Luckily, the children had not been awoken by the phone or her raised voice. How strange! she thought. Feeling a sudden boldness, she strode towards the kitchen in order to make herself another coffee. The fearful ring stopped her dead in her tracks. It was almost a mixture of instinct and habit now which made her raise the receiver.

This time she did not recite the number or say hello; instead she listened as the slow, gruff voice commenced. 'I know you're alone, and I'm gonna get you! You hear? Get you, get y . . .'. She slammed the hand set down before he had time to finish. Who the hell was it? she thought. A drunkard, a pervert? Picking back up the receiver she dialled the operator. The voice sounded distant but reassuring.

'Hello, can I help you?'

'Yes,' Andrea answered. Her body heaved, and she was close to tears. 'Could you trace an outside call for me? The number is five-seven-four-two-two-five.'

'Are you alright?' the lady asked, concerned.

'I'm fine. It's just a drunk keeps ringing me up and making threats,' Andrea replied.

'I see. If he rings again keep him talking. This will enable me to trace the call quickly. I'll ring you back if there are any results.'

Feeling relieved, Andrea settled back into the chair and began watching the film. The phone came to life almost immediately. Panic gripped her as she gingerly reached towards the phone. The man's voice sounded frightful to her ears.

'There was one little piggy, oh what fun!

Her throat was slit, then there was none.'

'You're nothing but a pervert, a damn pervert!' she screamed, as she let the receiver fall back into place.

Lighting up a cigarette, she paced the room, watching the phone. Suddenly it came alive, filling the room and her ears with its persistent call for attention.

She grabbed the hand-set ready to listen, again, to the abuse.

'Listen quickly.' The operator's voice sounded disturbing.

'Tell me,' the operator continued, 'do you have another phone in the house?' Andrea, confused, could not think for a minute.

'Why yes, there's a phone upstairs with the children.' Her voice was awkward and slow.

'Whoever has been calling you has been using the phone upstairs. For heaven's sake, get out quickly!'

The phone went dead. Sobbing, she stumbled towards the door. Opening it, she ran quickly towards the stairs and front door.

The sight which met her bulging eyes sent her vomiting into the corner. On the middle part of the stairs stood a huge and grotesque-looking man. His eyes, filled with mad frenzy, bore down on her. His clothes and face were drenched in blood, and in his right hand he held a blood-splattered chopper. It was what the man held in his left hand that made her faint. It steamed slowly, giving off a hot and sickly smell. The children, or what was left of them, were lying at the top of the stairs. They had been disembowelled and their insides completely 'cleaned' out. Slowly he let the warm, soft, glistening entrail slip from his hand as he made his way towards Andrea.

Analysis of 'Three Little Piggies'

One of the interesting features of this story is that, although the climax is dramatic and even lurid in the extreme, the opening is extremely leisurely and uneventful. This contrast goes a long way towards explaining the success of the story. The simple domestic details of the opening create a sense of normality and everyday reality to which almost anyone could relate. When the phone starts ringing and the panic begins, the reader believes completely in the character and situation, and the steady build-up towards the ghastly climax is entirely convincing.

The dialogue at the beginning of the story is, in fact, a flashback to what happened just before the story opened. It could hardly be less dramatic. What it does is to establish a realistic, utterly ordinary domestic situation, and an impression of both the central character, Andrea, and the children's parents. Natural dialogue such as this is far more effective in conveying a sense of character than statements telling us *about* the characters. Tiny details, such as the line: 'Mr Wilson sounded his horn in annoyance', add greatly to the sense of everyday reality and the illusion that we are reading about real people. The dialogue serves another important function: it enables us to share Andrea's impressions of the Wilsons, and thus we are able to identify more easily with her. The ability to create identification with and concern for a story's central character is a crucial aspect of the story-teller's art. It might be a useful exercise to try rewriting the second paragraph of the story without using any dialogue, and compare the two versions.

Once the Wilsons have left, a series of very precise details is given of Andrea preparing to settle down for the evening. They do nothing in particular to advance the plot, but are of great importance in increasing our identification with the character. Tiny details like her search for the coffee, and her choice of 'Hob-nobs', make her seem entirely believable. These are things with which everyone can identify. Similarly, her sudden sleepiness just before the phone rings for the first time, and her switching of the channels afterwards, and selecting a Kirk Douglas film, all help us to visualise the situation. It is surprising how much difference even the simplest use of precise details, such as the mention of Kirk Douglas, makes to the aura of realism in a story. You could perhaps find other examples, and try reading the passages in which they feature, with the details left out to show the difference.

Between the description of Andrea switching off the light and of her relaxing in front of the fire, a paragraph is included which suddenly changes the nature of the story, with the approach towards the house of the shadowy figure with the gleaming implement. From this point on, the story becomes one of suspense. We know something awful is going to happen to Andrea, and she does not. It might be interesting to consider whether the introduction of suspense at this point is successful: might the story have had even more impact if surprise had been employed instead of suspense, so that we have no more idea than Andrea that there is an intruder?

Once the first 'three little piggies' message has been given, the pace of the story picks up considerably, and the events move rapidly towards the climax. It is even more important now to use convincing details of everyday life, to prevent a sense of unreality creeping in. The writer does this through the description, for instance, of Andrea's frantic search for her cigarettes after the first horrible shock, followed by the sentence: 'The slow entry of nicotine in her lungs helped to soothe her fraught nerves.' This sentence is in fact a complete paragraph. It is worth noting the effect of the paragraphing here. By placing this sentence apart, Kim Carty has actually captured a sense of the soothing, slowing-down effect of the nicotine. In narrative writing, the rules of paragraphing which were analysed in Chapter 1 do not apply. In a story, paragraphing can be used purely for effect, as this one-sentence paragraph illustrates.

Andrea's reactions to the insane telephone calls are once again entirely believable; we can identify completely with her, in her panic and anger. The excitement builds up rapidly, and the syntax adds to the sense of tension: just before the final, climactic paragraph, a sequence of three short, dramatic sentences vividly captures the panic and desperation of the terrified girl.

Then comes the climax. We may well feel that the grotesquerie is gratuitous, but we cannot feel that the ending is in any way contrived; the story has been building up inexorably towards some sort of horrific culmination, however distasteful we may find it.

A final comment on the style of the story. It is written in a very natural way, but this does not mean that the words are not chosen with care and conscious effect. A sentence near the beginning will illustrate this: 'Stepping out of her high red shoes, she padded into the kitchen.' From this description we can picture exactly not only what she was wearing but also how she walked; it is the choice of precise verbs in this case which creates the sense impression. It might be worth reading through the story again and picking out phrases which capture a sense of people, atmosphere and incident particularly vividly.

One final, general point. The inspiration for this story was a film, *The Babysitter*, which has a similar story-line. There is absolutely nothing wrong with such mild plagiarism. You will not be marked on the basis of your story being entirely original; what is being tested is your ability to write an interesting story, convincingly and well.

Narrative titles

a   Leaving.
b   A grain of sand.
c   Paradise.
d   The grass is always greener on the other side.
e   Innocence is best.
f   Write a story involving a family, a foreigner, a boat, a horse and sunflowers.
g   Envy.
h   Write a fairy tale about growing up.
i   Swimming against the current.
j   Silence

LITERARY STYLE

3

In this chapter we will look at imagery, concentrating on the essential techniques by which special vividness and resonance can be achieved in writing. Narrative, and in particular descriptive and dramatic writing, can be greatly enlivened by imagery. The techniques of comparison and sound colouring analysed in this chapter have been used for thousands of years to bring such writing to life.

An understanding of the various figures of meaning and sound which are explained and illustrated in this chapter is essential for students who are intending to produce narrative or descriptive writing of their own, and for those who are likely to be called on to analyse the style of others' writing, both in language comprehension exercises and in the study of literary texts.

The main techniques are explained and illustrated first, and then passages from works of literature by three modern writers are offered for further exploration.

Figures of meaning

Simile

A comparison between two distinctly different things indicated by the word 'like' or 'as':

e.g.   Sometimes I might get drunk,
        Walk like a duck and smell like a skunk.

> BOB DYLAN (*I shall Be Free*)

The child was like ice in her womb.

> D. H. LAWRENCE (*Odour of Chrysanthemums*)

Comparisons are used to clarify ideas by appealing to our imagination. The similes in the Bob Dylan song appeal directly to our senses, creating a vivid momentary picture in our mind's eye. The line from the D.H. Lawrence story also creates a powerful sense impression, of extreme physical coldness, capturing a sense of the mother's emotional coldness towards the baby inside her, far more vividly than any literal explanation could.

Metaphor

A direct statement of identity between two distinctly different things, *without* using 'like' or 'as':

> e.g. But at my back I always hear
> Time's wingèd chariot hurrying near;
> And yonder all before use lie
> Deserts of vast eternity.
>
> ANDREW MARVELL (*To his Coy Mistress*)

> Life's a long song,
> But the tune
> Ends too soon
> For us all.
>
> IAN ANDERSON (*Life's a Long Song*)

The pair of metaphors in the Marvell extract heighten, and make more imaginatively compelling, the contrast between the intensity and brevity of earthly life, and the infinite nothingness of death. By comparing the rapid movement of earthly time with a 'winged chariot hurrying near', a powerful sense of speed and urgency is created, and this forms a vivid contrast with the impression of everlasting barrenness captured by the metaphor of 'deserts'. The images are largely visual. The idea of the shortness of life is also suggested in the lines from the Ian Anderson song, though here the metaphorical comparison of life with a song which 'ends too soon' has a direct, non-visual appeal.

Personification

An inanimate object or an abstract concept is spoken of as though it were endowed with life or with human attributes or feelings:

> e.g. The yellow fog that rubs its back upon the window-panes
> T.S. ELIOT (*The Love Song of J. Alfred Prufrock*)

> Pale flakes with fingering stealth come feeling for our faces
> WILFRED OWEN (*Exposure*)

In these two images, fog and snow are given the force of living presences by the use of personification. A gentle, quite benign quality is given to Eliot's 'yellow fog' by the human comparison, whereas Owen's 'pale flakes', though also gentle, are made to seem much more sinister and malign, by the comparison with a blind person's fingers feeling for the faces of the soldiers in a First World War trench.

Though not strictly personification according to the conventional definition, the attribution of human qualities to non-human living creatures has much the same effect:

e.g.   . . . the hens twitch and grieve for their tea – soaked sops
DYLAN THOMAS (Under Milk Wood)

Thomas's description of the hens in terms of human beings in a state of nervous anxiety might well be considered to be an example of personification.

Symbol

A word or object which is both literal and which also signifies something beyond itself.

Some symbols are widely recognised in Western culture, for example, the peacock as a symbol of pride and vanity, the eagle as a symbol of heroic endeavour. Leonard Cohen uses the former in this symbolic sense in *Story of Isaac*, a song about the dangers of self-glorification, which ends:

The peacock spreads his fan.

Other symbols are more personal to a particular writer and work. The old priest in James Joyce's story *The Sisters*, for instance, is literally paralysed, but he also becomes, in his *physical* paralysis, a symbol of the *spiritual* paralysis of Ireland's religious life, of which he is a representative. Whether or not symbolism is present in a work depends on personal interpretation; sometimes it is obvious, sometimes subtle and uncertain.

Figures of sound

Alliteration

The repetition of consonants in a sequence of words:

e.g.   Only the stuttering rifles' rapid rattle
Can patter out their hasty orisons.
WILFRED OWEN (Anthem for Doomed Youth)

Figures of sound produce sound colouring, designed to add emphasis to ideas and emotions, and to create and reinforce tone and feeling.

The lines from *Anthem for Doomed Youth* capture the sound and rapidity of rifle fire in wartime, an effect which is created partly by the repeated, relatively harsh 'r' consonant. The line from *Exposure*, by the same poet, quoted in the section on personification, also employs alliteration. The effect here is quite the opposite. The repeated soft 'f' sounds help to capture a sense impression of the gentle, slow, unremitting, deathly penetration of snowflakes in a trench in wartime, killing the soldiers who are exposed to them more slowly, but more certainly, than bullets.

Sibilants

Alliteration using 's' sounds:

>e.g.   And as he slowly drew up, snake-easing his shoulders
>
>D.H. LAWRENCE (*Snake*)

The sound and motion of an uncoiling snake, lithe and leisurely and hissing, is here captured partly by the use of repeated 's' sounds.

Assonance

The repetition of vowel sounds in a sequence of words:

>e.g.   Heaps of entangled weeds that slowly float
>
>GEORGE CRABBE (*Peter Grimes*)

The sound colouring of a passage is largely dependent on the juxtaposition of vowel sounds. If a particular vowel is repeated, it gains special emphasis, and tends therefore to be the dominant sound. In the line from *Peter Grimes* there are two pairs of identical vowel sounds. Both are long vowels, helping to emphasise the impression of slow, meandering movement of the 'heaps of . . . weeds'; the repeated long 'o' sound at the end of the line creates an especially heavy, sombre effect. The sentence from the D.H. Lawrence story, quoted in the section on simile, also employs assonance. The key word 'ice' receives great emphasis from the repetition of the same long 'i' sound in the words 'child' and 'like', investing the line with an 'icy' feel. The chilling effect of the line is enhanced still further by the dark, heavy sound of the final word, 'womb'. In the line from *Anthem for Doomed Youth*, which is quoted above to illustrate alliteration, assonance is also used, in the words 'rapid rattle/can patter', the sharp, hard, short 'a' sounds adding to the violent, mechanical impression of rapid gunfire.

Onomatopoeia

A word, or sequence of words, whose sound seems to resemble the sound it denotes:

>e.g.   And *droning* shells *burst* with a *hollow bang*.
>
>SIEGFRIED SASSOON (*The Redeemer*)

The line is intended to capture the sound of shells in flight, and exploding. A similar onomatopoeic effect is created by the lines from Owen's *Anthem for Doomed Youth*, in the word 'stuttering' and in the cluster of words discussed in the section on assonance.

Passages for literary analysis

Let us now see how these techniques can be used by a skilful writer for atmospheric and dramatic effect.

The Birds

The passages which follow are from *The Birds*, a short story by Daphne du Maurier. *The Birds* is a horror story (which was freely adapted by Alfred Hitchcock for his famous film). It explores the reactions of a Cornish farm labourer, Nat Hocken, and his family and neighbours, to regular, concerted attacks on people and their homes by birds, whose aim, as the story gradually reveals, is the destruction of the human race!

The first three passages illustrate the use of literary devices to create atmosphere: the first, of the restless movement and the abnormality of the birds' behaviour, at the beginning of the story; the second, of cold and desolation, and the third, of a more relaxed atmosphere, as normality seems to have returned. The fourth passage is both atmospheric and dramatic, as Nat watches the birds mass over the sea for an attack, and the final passage is a climactic description of birds swooping down on Nat as he rushes across the fields towards his home.

I

Black and white, jackdaw and gull, mingled in strange partnership, seeking some sort of liberation, never satisfied, never still. Flocks of starlings, rustling like silk, flew to fresh pasture, driven by the same necessity of movement, and the smaller birds, the finches and the larks, scattered from tree to hedge as if compelled. Nat watched them, and he watched the sea-birds, too. Down in the bay they waited for the tide. They had more patience. Oyster-catchers, redshank, sanderling and curlew watched by the water's edge; as the slow sea sucked at the shore and then withdrew, leaving the strip of seaweed bare and the shingle churned, the sea-birds raced and ran upon the beaches. Then that same impulse to flight seized upon them too. Crying, whistling, calling, they skimmed the placid sea and left the shore. Make haste, make speed, hurry and begone; yet where, and to what purpose? The restless urge of autumn, unsatisfying, sad, had put a spell upon them and they must flock, and wheel, and cry; they must spill themselves of motion before winter came.

2

The sky was hard and leaden, and the brown hills that had gleamed in the sun the day before looked dark and bare. The east wind, like a razor, stripped the trees, and the leaves, crackling and dry, shivered and scattered with the wind's blast. Nat stubbed the earth with his boot. It was frozen hard. He had never known a change so swift and sudden. Black winter had descended in a single night.

3

She said nothing of the birds. She began to push and struggle with another little girl. The bus came ambling up the hill. Nat saw her on to it, then turned and walked back towards the farm. It was not his day for work, but he wanted to satisfy himself that all was well. Jim, the cowman, was clattering in the yard.

4

He got up and went out of the back door and stood in the garden, looking down towards the sea. There had been no sun all day, and now, at barely three o'clock, a kind of darkness had already come, the sky sullen, heavy, colourless like salt. He could hear the vicious sea drumming on the rocks. He walked down the path, half-way to the beach. And then he stopped. He could see the tide had turned. The rock that had shown in mid-morning was now covered, but it was not the sea that held his eyes. The gulls had risen. They were circling, hundreds of them, thousands of them, lifting their wings against the wind. It was the gulls that made the darkening of the sky. And they were silent. They made not a sound. They just went on soaring and circling, rising, falling, trying their strength against the wind.

5

As he jumped the stile he heard the whirr of wings. A black-backed gull dived down at him from the sky, missed, swerved in flight, and rose to dive again. In a moment it was joined by others, six, seven, a dozen, black-backed and herring mixed. Nat dropped his hoe. The hoe was useless. Covering his head with his arms he ran towards the cottage. They kept coming at him from the air, silent save for the beating wings. The terrible, fluttering wings. He could feel the blood on his hands, his wrists, his neck. Each stab of a swooping beak tore his flesh. If only he could keep them from his eyes. Nothing else mattered. He must keep them from his eyes. They had not learnt yet how to cling to a shoulder, how to rip clothing, how to dive in mass upon the head, upon the body. But with each dive, with each attack, they became bolder. And they had no thought for themselves. When they dived low and missed, they crashed, bruised and broken, on the ground. As Nat ran he stumbled, kicking their spent bodies in front of him. He found the door, he hammered upon it with his bleeding hands. Because of the boarded windows no light shone. Everything was dark. 'Let me in,' he shouted, 'it's Nat. Let me in.' He shouted loud to make himself heard above the whirr of the gulls' wings. Then he saw the gannet, poised for the dive, above him in the sky. The gulls circled, retired, soared, one with another, against the wind. Only the gannet remained. One single gannet, above him in the sky. The wings folded suddenly to its body. It dropped, like a stone. Nat screamed, and the door opened. He stumbled across the threshold, and his wife threw her weight against the door. They heard the thud of the gannet as it fell.

DAPHNE DU MAURIER

Analysis of *The Birds* passages

Let us look in detail at passage 1, and see how Daphne du Maurier creates atmosphere in the extract through figures of meaning and sound, and through the rhythm of her prose.

The predominant consonant in the first two sentences is 's', the sibilants emphasising the restlessness and nervous energy of the birds. The simile 'rustling like silk' in the second sentence reinforces this sensation. The sibilants here, together with the simile, add to the onomatopoeic effect of 'rustling'. The sentence as a whole is broken up into a sequence of short phrases, which in itself adds to the sense of agitation. This is then followed by three short, fairly dramatic sentences, the last of which consists of only four words, which reinforces the sense of tense expectancy.

In the long sixth sentence, sibilants again feature prominently. The sound of the words is combined with the rhythm of the prose to suggest an impression of the sound and movement of the sea: the separated monosyllables of 'the slow sea sucked' create a slow rhythm which is enhanced by the 's' consonants and the long, heavy vowel sounds; but the rhythm of 'at the shore and then withdrew' is faster, and the whole effect is to suggest the movement of a wave itself, rolling in, and rushing out again. Similarly, rhythm and sound combine in the last part of the sentence, the alliteration of 'raced and ran' adding emphasis to the rushing rhythm of the words.

Onomatopoeia is used again in the eighth sentence, in the word 'whistling', and the effect is enhanced by the assonance in 'whistling . . . skimmed'. The sea is here personified in the phrase 'the placid sea', and personification is used again in the final sentence, as 'Autumn' is described as putting 'a spell upon' the birds, with its 'restless urge'. The last two sentences also display the technique of rhetorical repetition, in the phrases 'Make haste, make speed' and 'they must flock . . .they must spill', adding again to the intensity of the writing, and the sense of restlessness and agitation which du Maurier is trying to convey.

Some of the sound colouring and the rhythmic movement of this passage are, in fact, too subtle for simple analysis in terms of recognisable techniques to be possible. The extent to which the use of the techniques analysed is deliberate, and how much of it is instinctive is, of course, impossible to tell.

Now attempt a similar analysis of the other four passages from *The Birds*. You should comment on the syntax as well as on the figures of speech.

ISSUES

The Village By The Sea

In her novel *The Village By The Sea*, the Indian writer Anita Desai focuses
on a small fishing village in rural India, and the struggle of a poor family to
come to terms with the changes which are overtaking the ancient, settled
ways of village life. Part of her purpose in writing the novel was to capture
for the reader a sense of the atmosphere of a place and a life-style which is
disappearing.

The two extracts which follow are from the first three pages of the novel.
Lila, a teenage Hindu girl from the village, is described going down to the
seashore in the early morning.

The writing is highly atmospheric and evocative. Try to define the
atmosphere, and explain how Anita Desai creates it.

I

When she came to the edge of the sea, she lifted the folds of her sari and tucked
them up at her waist, then waded out into the waves that came rushing up over her
feet and swirling about her ankles in creamy foam. She waded in till she came to a
cluster of three rocks. One of them was daubed with red and white powder. It was
the sacred rock, a kind of temple in the sea. At high tide it would be inundated but
now, at low tide, it could be freshly consecrated. Lila took the flowers from her
basket and scattered them about the rock, then folded her hands and bowed.

Just then the sun lifted up over the coconut palms in a line along the beach and
sent long slanting rays over the silvery sand to touch her on the back of her head.
Enjoying their warmth, she stayed bowed for a little while, her feet still in the cold,
whispering waves. The sun lit up the pink and mauve waves with sparkles. Far out,
stretched along the horizon, was the fishing fleet that had been out all night, the sails
like white wings, or fins, lifting out of the sea. They were anchored and still: they
would not return before sundown.

2

The morning light was still soft as it filtered through the web of palm leaves, and
swirls of blue wood-smoke rose from fires in hidden huts and mingled with it. Dew
still lay on the rough grass and made the spider webs glitter. These webs were small
and thickly matted and stretched across the grass, each with a hole in the centre to
trap passing insects. Butterflies flew up out of the tussocks and bushes of wild
flowers – large zebra-striped ones with a faint tinge of blue to their wings, showy
black ones with scarlet-tipped wings, and little sulphur-yellow ones that fluttered
about in twos and threes.

Then there were all the birds flying out of the shadowy, soft-needled casuarina
trees and the thick jungle of pandanus, singing and calling and whistling louder than
at any other time of the day. Flute-voiced drongoes swooped and cut through the
air like dazzling knives that reflected the sun and glinted blue-black, and pert little

28

magpie robins frisked and flirted their tails as they hopped on the dewy grass, snatching at insects before they tumbled into the spider's traps. Pairs of crested bul-buls sang from the branches. A single crow-pheasant, invisible, called out 'coop-coop-coop' in its deep, bogey-man voice from under a bush, and a pigeon's voice cooed and gurgled on and on. It was the voice of the village Thul as much as the roar of the waves and the wind in the palms. It seemed to tell Lila to be calm and happy and all would be well and all would be just as it was before.

ANITA DESAI

Death

Not only fiction and poetry use figurative language, of course. It can be equally suitable for some kinds of factual writing. We will conclude this discussion of style by looking at a piece by the American novelist, essayist and journalist, Norman Mailer, which describes an actual event. It is a description of a world championship boxing match which took place in the early 1960s, between Emile Griffith, the challenger, and Benny Paret, who was the current world champion, a fight which had a tragic ending.

The rage in Emile Griffith was extreme. I was at the fight that night. I had never seen a fight like it. It was scheduled for fifteen rounds, but they fought without stopping from the bell which began the round to the bell which ended it, and then they fought after the bell, sometimes for as much as fifteen seconds before the referee could force them apart.

Paret was a Cuban, a proud club fighter who had become welterweight champion because of his unusual ability to take a punch. His style of fighting was to take three punches to the head in order to give back two. At the end of ten rounds, he would still be bouncing, his opponent would have a headache. But in the last two years, over the fifteen-round fights, he had started to take some bad maulings.

This fight had its turns. Griffith won most of the early rounds, but Paret knocked Griffith down in the sixth. Griffith had trouble getting up, but made it, came alive and was dominating Paret again before the round was over. Then Paret began to wilt. In the middle of the eighth round, after a clubbing punch had turned his back to Griffith, Paret walked three disgusted steps away, showing his hindquarters. For a champion he took much too long to turn back around. It was the first hint of weakness Paret had ever shown, and it must have inspired a particular shame, because he fought the rest of the fight as if he were seeking to demonstrate that he could take more punishment than any man alive. In the twelfth, Griffith caught him. Paret got trapped in a corner. Trying to duck away, his left arm and his head became tangled on the wrong side of the top rope. Griffith was in like a cat ready to rip the life out of a huge boxed rat. He hit him eighteen right hands in a row, an act which took perhaps three or four seconds, Griffith making a pent-up whimpering sound all the while he attacked, the right hand whipping like a piston rod which had broken through the crankcase, or like a baseball bat demolishing a pumpkin. I was sitting in the second row of that corner – they were not ten feet away from me, and like everybody else, I was hypnotised. I had never seen one man hit another so hard and so many times. Over the referee's face came a look of woe as if some spasm had passed its way through him, and then he leaped on Griffith to pull him away. It was the act of a brave man. Griffith was uncontrollable. His trainer leaped into the ring, his manager, his cut man, there were four people holding Griffith, but he was off on an orgy, he had left the Garden[1], he was back on a hoodlum's street. If he had been able to break loose from his handlers and the referee, he would have jumped Paret to the floor and whaled on him there.

And Paret? Paret died on his feet. As he took those eighteen punches something happened to everyone who was in psychic range of the event. Some part of his death reached out to us. One felt it hover in the air. He was still standing in the ropes, trapped as he had been before, he gave some little half-smile of regret, as if he were saying, 'I didn't know I was going to die just yet', and then, his head leaning back but still erect, his death came to breathe about him. He began to pass away. As he passed, so his limbs descended beneath him, and he sank slowly to the floor. He went down more slowly than any fighter had ever gone down, he went down like a large ship which turns on end and slides second by second into its grave. As he went down, the sound of Griffith's punches echoed in the mind like a heavy axe in the distance chopping into a wet log.

Paret lay on the ground, quivering gently, a small froth on his mouth. The house doctor jumped into the ring. He knelt. He pried Paret's eyelid open. He looked at the eyeball staring out. He let the lid snap shut. He reached into his satchel, took out a needle, jabbed Paret with a stimulant. Paret's back rose in a high arch. He writhed in real agony. They were calling him back from death. One wanted to cry out, 'Leave the man alone. Let him die'. But they saved Paret long enough to take him to a hospital where he lingered for days. He was in coma. He never came out of it. If he lived, he would have been a vegetable. His brain was smashed. But they held him in life for a week, they fed him chemicals, and made exploratory operations into his skull, and fed details of his condition to The Goat. And The Goat kicked clods of mud all over the place, and spoke harshly of prohibiting boxing. There was shock in the land. Children had seen the fight on television. There were editorials, gloomy forecasts that the Game was dead. The managers and the prize fighters got together. Gently in thick, depressed hypocrisies, they tried to defend their sport. They did not find it easy to explain that they shared an unstated view of life which was religious.

NORMAN MAILER

The immediate aftermath of the fight was that there was talk of charging Griffith with manslaughter, and Griffith vowed never to box again. A decade later he was still world champion.

Write a stylistic analysis of the passage. You should try to find three examples of each of the following: simile, metaphor, personification. You

1 Madison Square Garden in New York.

should discuss as fully as possible the effectiveness of each image. In addition, you should discuss at least one example of each of the four figures of sound analysed in this chapter, and make some comments on the syntax.

Bibliography

Brett, R.L.   *An Introduction to English Studies*, Edward Arnold, 1976
Desai, Anita   *The Village By The Sea*, Penguin, 1982
du Maurier, Daphne   *The Birds and Other Stories*, Longman, 1980
Mailer, Norman   *The Presidential Papers*, Penguin, 1968

SUMMARY SKILLS

Introduction

Summary work involves picking out the essense of a piece of writing, or a speech, or a meeting, or a broadcast, and re-expressing it in continuous sentences or notes. It is also called précis. It can take a variety of forms.

The traditional examination summary exercise, which involves rewriting a passage in about a third of its length, is the most detailed. Nowadays, examiners tend to set the exercise more in terms of journalistic practice, and it can take quite a wide variety of forms. The opposite extreme from the traditional one-third, full-sentence reduction would be the very highly condensed notes which a minuting secretary would take from a meeting. This would be difficult to set as an exercise in examination conditions, but condensed note-form exercises are becoming a feature of advanced exercises in summary skills. If continuous sentences are called for, and the whole passage is to be summarised, the required reduction could involve anything up to a tenth of the length of the original, or possibly even less.

In addition, the exercise may call for subtler forms of selection. It may require summary of some particular aspect of the set passage, whilst the rest is to be ignored. For example, the question may ask for only facts to be summarised, and the writer's opinions to be left out, or vice versa. Or it may require summary only of the essential arguments, and exclusion of all illustrative detail. Alternatively, summary may be required only of certain ideas or themes in the passage. Questions might also be set requiring comparative value judgements of the passage and your summary of it, in terms of style and effectiveness of communication.

Summary technique: general

Whatever form the summary exercise takes, certain basic techniques need to be applied, and we will consider these first, before looking in more detail at approaches to different types of summary question.

The first stage in any summary work is to achieve as full an understanding as possible of the passage to be summarised. This will probably mean reading it through two or three times before even picking up your pen. On your initial reading, the sense of much of the passage may well be obscured by the presence of difficult words. You should learn not to be thrown into a state of panic by this! It will be possible, after a couple more readings, to understand what the writer is saying, without necessarily knowing what is meant by every word he or she uses.

On the second reading you should be looking for the theme of the passage as a whole. Until you have worked this out, you cannot hope to begin your summary. Once you are sure of the theme, after your second or third reading, you should think of it constantly while you are working at the separate thoughts contained in the passage.

The next stage – that of working out a first draft – can be tackled in various ways. The simplest is to read through the passage once more, this time underlining sentences and phrases which you feel to be important to the argument or theme, and then begin writing a draft in continuous sentences, without making notes, and with the word limit in mind. Unless you are very lucky, of course, your first draft will require some pruning or expanding before you write it out again as a final draft. Some people advocate deliberately keeping your first draft short, and building it up to the word limit in the second, whilst others favour the inclusion of everything of major or minor relevance in the first draft, and cutting down in the second. It is purely a matter of personal preference. A more time-consuming general approach is to make full notes of the points to be included, before writing them out in sentences. You will discover soon enough whether you can manage to complete a set of notes and two drafts within the time limit, and which general technique suits you better. The second draft should be your perfected answer in the number of words stipulated (or as near as you can possibly manage).

One further general point needs to be made before analysing specific summary techniques. It is absolutely essential to tackle the passage in terms of ideas rather than sentences. If you attempt to summarise the passage sentence by sentence you are certain to end up with an incoherent and inaccurate answer. You must try to work out each idea and its relevance in terms of the overall line of argument of the passage, and only on that basis will you succeed.

Summaries of complete passages

Let us look at a short passage for summary, and consider approaches to two different kinds of questions set on it. The theme of the passage is the value of summary writing (!). It contains 373 words.

What price précis?

The art of writing a concise, well-balanced, comprehensive and accurate summary demands clarity both of thought and of written expression. It is not a question of reflecting on a writer's ideas in the light of one's own, nor of interpreting those ideas; it is, instead, a question of reproducing the ideas with precision, and in
5 summary form. It is an exercise in condensation. There can be little doubt, however, that many students, on undertaking a summary exercise, will wonder why they are expected to fritter away their time on a task which seems frustratingly tedious and futile; they will ask themselves, with a sigh, 'What is the point of slavishly rewriting what someone else has already said, when I could be producing
10 something original?' It must seem to many like sitting in front of a portrait by Rembrandt or Van Gogh, and being asked to copy it in outline form, without colour, light and shade, or atmosphere, when their artistic instinct demands that they be allowed to draw on the master's work as the inspiration for an original creation. They are apt to consider the whole business stultifying, the very antithesis
15 of creativity. And in one sense their criticism is valid: by summarising a writer's work one is taking away much of its essence, draining it of its colour, its tone, its subtlety, its imaginative vitality. It is rather like describing a 'cordon bleu' meal by mentioning only the ingredients.

Yet in another sense the criticism is profoundly unfair. There are many
20 aspects of the study of English language in addition to creative writing. And summary writing is by no means irrelevant to the demands of 'real life'. In business, in fact in all walks of professional life, it is frequently necessary to summarise factual information and the arguments presented by others: indeed, we are constantly engaged in verbal summary of television
25 programmes, film plots, conversations and comical incidents in the normal course of our daily lives. The conciseness and precision of expression which comes with summary practice is thus of no small value both as a necessary attribute of articulate men and women in its own right, and as a skill which is of practical value in work and in life.

These are the questions:

i Write a summary of the passage in continuous sentences, using no more than 125 words.

ii Summarise the main points of the passage in not more than 40 words of continuous prose.

Here is a specimen answer to question *i*:

Effective summary requires clear thinking and writing, involving accurate summary of another's ideas. Almost certainly, however, many students find the exercise monotonous, and question the value of mere reproduction rather than originality, comparing it to the sterile task of copying an old master's painting in outline. The criticism is partially valid, since a summary destroys much of the flavour and artistry of the original. In another way, however, it is unjust. English language involves more than merely creative writing, and summary has relevance to life. In all professions summary is often a necessary requirement, and in normal life we constantly summarise things seen and heard. Summary practice develops brevity and clarity of expression, and is therefore extremely useful in enhancing conversational and professional skills.

(124 words)

And now a specimen answer to question *ii*:

Summary writing is an exercise in condensation. Many students consider it pointless and uncreative, and summarising a passage certainly destroys its imaginative essence. Yet both professional and daily life necessitate summary; good technique is therefore of practical and personal value.

(40 words)

Now let us look at both of the questions and answers in terms of summary technique.

A couple of readings should establish the theme of the passage to be the drawbacks and virtues of learning summary skills. Having established that, we can begin working on the passage, selecting ideas which are essential to the argument, and discarding those which are unimportant.

Question *i*, however, allows us to use a third of the words in the original passage, whereas question *ii* necessitates discarding nearly nine-tenths. The technique involved is inevitably very different.

The difference, essentially, is that in the case of a roughly one-third summary, the argument needs to be presented in detail, whereas in a one-tenth summary only the bare bones can be presented.

If we take the passage and the answers section by section, we can observe the differences in technique.

The passage begins with an explanation of what summary writing involves (lines 1 to 5). The absolute essence of this section is the definition of summary in line 5: 'It is an exercise in condensation'. In the answer to question *ii*, this is all that is retained from the first five lines of the passage, and the word 'condensation' is kept. In a very abbreviated summary exercise, *selecting the right details* is what counts; it is less important to worry about choosing your own words. In the answer to question *i*, however, the opening sentence is also summarised, since this is an important statement about the precise nature of effective summary writing, a subtlety which is not allowed for in question *ii*. It should be noted that this opening sentence of the passage contains lists of adjectives and nouns. In detailed summary exercises, lists such as these pose problems. The best solution, in most cases, is to find a generalisation which covers all the items in the list, rather than selecting words or phrases from the list, which limits the meaning of the original. In the answer to question *i* the adjective 'effective' is used to cover the list of adjectives in line 1.

Even in the answer to question *i*, the first part of the second sentence is ignored: it is a negative statement, which is followed by a positive re-statement of the same idea. In any summary exercise, negative statements need to be turned into positive statements (or left out if they add nothing of significance to the meaning). In the passage, this idea is then restated in different words; mere repetition should also always be ignored in any summary exercise. Note that the opening three sentences in the passage have been summarised in the answer to question *i* in a single sentence, the ideas being linked together with a participle ('involving'). This is good technique, giving continuity and fluency to your writing, and avoiding sequences of short sentences. You will be marked partly for the style and coherence of your answer, so this is important.

The next section of the passage concerns students' responses to the task of summary writing (lines 5–15). In question *ii* we are looking only for the essence of the students' complaints, which boil down to futility and uncreativity. For question *i*, the word limit allows for more precision as to the nature of the complaints, and it will be noted that the specimen answer mentions the comparison with the copying of 'an old master's painting'. As a general rule, comparisons, illustrations and examples can be left out in any summary, but in this case the idea of copying a painting in outline, without colour etc., leads on directly to the idea which follows (in lines 15–18) of destroying the colour etc., of a piece of writing by summarising it. In an exercise in which you are allowed to use as many as a third of the words in the original passage, if an illustration or example actually forms a link in the argument, rather than being there merely to reinforce a point already made, then it is worth considering whether it should be included. It is worth noting that both specimen answers use the phrase 'many students'. This is a direct lift from the passage (line 6). Even when you have a comparatively generous word allowance, there is no need to worry about altering every word of the original: the copying of words and even short phrases will not be penalised if there is no obvious alternative which does not either distort the meaning of, or involve the use of more words than, the original, which is the case here. It would be tempting, especially in answering question *ii*, to abbreviate this phrase simply to 'students'. However, this would give the impression that *all* students dislike summary work, which gives a distorted impression of what the passage is saying. You must be on your guard constantly against *changing* the meaning of the passage, however slightly, for the sake of brevity. Lines 8–10 consist of an imaginary quoted question. In neither answer is quotation or question form used. If the idea contained in a quotation or question is important enough to be included in your answer, then it should be written in reported speech and statement form, as in the specimen answer to question *i*.

The third section (lines 15–18) considers the way in which students' criticisms of summary exercises are valid. In both answers, this time, the comparison (lines 17 and 18) is ignored, since it falls into the category of mere reinforcement. It should be noted that in the answers to question *ii* the essential point is made by quoting key words from the passage, whereas in the case of question *i* a slightly more precise generalisation is used.

In the final section (lines 19–29), which presents arguments in favour of the learning of summary technique, three sets of lists are to be found in a single sentence (in lines 21–6). These are all dealt with by varieties of generalisation in the answer to question *i*; broader generalisations are used in the answer to question *ii* to cover the whole paragraph in a single sentence.

A further point will have emerged from this analysis: the ideas should generally be summarised in the order in which they appear in the passage. It should be borne in mind also, however, that in writing a summary you, too, are presenting a coherent statement, and it is equally important to ensure that you connect your points together in a logical manner.

Selective and note–form summaries

Exercises in summary skills may also, as already stated, involve recognition and selection of details relevant to a particular theme or aspect of the passage, or the use of note-form. Let us look at an exercise which combines both of these question types.

Here is the passage:

Hypocrisy vividly laid bare

THEATRE

Mrs Warren's Profession
Citizens, Glasgow

Giles Havergal's new production of Shaw's *Mrs Warren's Profession* at the Citizens finally gives the lie to that old gibe at the theatre, that patrons come out whistling the sets. Instead of relying on sumptuous designs for effect, as the company did for its recent cycle of Wilde plays, Havergal turns the emphasis of Shaw's play on the acting.

There are only a few pieces of rehearsal furniture, battered tables, chairs and door frames, with the odd tatty couch or a garish parasol, registering all the more effectively in their drab surroundings. The actors wear modern clothes with minimal Edwardian touches. Apart from the women's dresses, the costumes could still be worn today. It gives the play a chilling relevance.

Quite why this should be is hard to determine. Most of the actors have worked at the Citizens before and Havergal is practised in the stripping down of plays, but seldom have the elements of a production welded themselves so effortlessly together. My guess is that it owes much to

37

the presence of Ann Mitchell. Mrs Warren could have been written for her.

From our first glimpse of her at the back of the stage looking slightly demure in a vaguely Edwardian hat dominated by a pair of bird's wings, she looks like the vulgarian she admits to being. She is slightly blowzy but motherly too, and this is the key to her power over men like Frank.

Mitchell's Mrs Warren reverts to her native Cockney accent with the subtlety and precise calculation which underlie everything she does. Her performance throws new light on the character and universalises the relation between mother and daughter. She is a mother, a bad and demanding one. Now that there is unlikely to be any frisson about her profession as the owner of the best little whore-house in Brussels, we can see clearly what Shaw actually wrote: a drama about the power politics between parents and children as much as any critique of the hypocrisy of society. As Vivie Warren says, we know all that. This interpretation is infinitely more provocative.

This Mrs Warren, however, is not a one-woman show, and the rest of the cast match Mitchell perfectly. Debra Gillett as Vivie, looking unsettlingly modern, is the prototype of the fanatical meritocrat denying all need for emotion. Despite her privilege she spouts cant about choices in life being available for all.

As Sir George Crofts, Michael MacKenzie is hideously recognisable as the baronet who would now be living in tax exile behind a number of offshore companies. Derwent Watson makes the silly-ass rector Samuel Gardner vicious as well as funny. Tristram Wymark, looking like a raddled cherub, works perfectly with Ann Mitchell to make the scene in which he attempts to seduce Mrs Warren alive with sexual tension.

The programme quoted Shaw on the exaggerated effect that scenery has on a play. Shaw was talking about the fondness of the Edwardians for stage decoration rather than a design which complements the play. But by going against tradition the Citizens has produced the most illuminating production of Shaw there has been for many years. A lady behind me told her friend rather indignantly that this was not the way they would have done it at Stratford. More fool Stratford.

ALASDAIR CAMERON, *The Times*, 4 September, 1990

This is the exercise:

List in note-form the *factual* information we are given about the production, ignoring the reviewer's comments and opinions. You should make between ten and twelve points.

Here is a specimen answer:

New production of Shaw's *Mrs Warren's Profession* is at Citizens Theatre, Glasgow.
Director: Giles Havergal.
Set: very basic, expressing drabness.
Emphasis of production on acting.
Costume: modern, with only slight Edwardian hints.
Using actors who have mostly played before at Citizens Theatre.

Ann Mitchell plays Mrs Warren:
   – wears a vaguely Edwardian hat with large birds' wings.
   – employs Cockney accent.
Debra Gillett plays Vivie.
Michael MacKenzie plays Sir George Crofts.
Derwent Watson plays rector, Samuel Gardner.

Let us now consider the techniques involved in approaching this kind of summary exercise.

The most immediately obvious feature of this answer is the way that it is set out. Generally speaking, unless the instructions are more specific, a note-form answer simply requires you to set down each new point on a separate line, perhaps with sub-points set out a little further to the right, with a dash before each. Writing in note-form implies that sentences are unnecessary. Your concern should be to get the point across as briefly as possible, which means that you can ignore, in particular, definite and indefinite articles, personal pronouns, (especially 'it') and past and present tenses of the verb 'to be'.

With regard to the distinction between fact and opinion, we will look at the first three paragraphs in detail. The opening sentence of the first paragraph repeats the information given immediately above as to the location of the production, and names the director. This is obviously factual. The second sentence is more problematic. Is the reviewer's statement about the production's non-reliance on 'sumptuous designs for effect' an incontestable fact or not? Might some other reviewer view it differently? This is the question you must always ask yourself when attempting to differentiate between facts and opinions. The opening sentence of the second paragraph provides the clue. The reviewer describes the set in some detail, establishing beyond doubt that the production does not rely on 'sumptuous designs'. There is no need to list the features of the set. A further difficulty arises with the final clause of the opening paragraph. Could the reviewer's statement that the director 'turns the emphasis of Shaw's play on the acting' be merely a comment, with which another reviewer might disagree? Since he establishes that there is no reliance or 'sumptuous designs', we are probably safe in assuming that the emphasis is, in fact, on the acting, and treat the statement as a fact. The statement in the second paragraph about the costumes is clearly factual, and the final observation, that the set and costumes provide a 'chilling relevance', is obviously an opinion. In the third paragraph, the only statement which is not open to question is the one about the actors having worked at the Citizens before. The reviewer's remark about the elements of the play welding themselves 'effortlessly together', and his 'guess about' the presence of 'Ann Mitchell' is clearly a personal opinion.

You might look at the rest of the passage and specimen answer, and attempt a similar analysis to the one above.

Style comparison questions

If you are asked to compare your answer with the set passage in terms of style and effectiveness of communication, there are certain points to make which will be of general application.

The most obvious one is that your piece of writing will inevitably be dry, and lacking in individuality, compared with the original. To create interest in what he or she has to say, a writer will almost always include examples, illustrations and comparisons, or historical and other details, or quotations or references. He or she will also shape the piece, and attempt to infuse it with vitality. When your sole concern is abbreviation, all of this has to go.

The way to answer a question calling for stylistic comparison, therefore, is to briefly *quote* examples of the features of the original which are missing in your summary, and attempt to explain what is lost by missing them out.

Summary of summary techniques

1 Use your own words as far as possible, but try to ensure that you retain the *exact meaning* of the original.

2 Keep, as far as possible, to the arrangement of ideas of the original passage.

3 Include only the points made in the passage; do not introduce any ideas of your own.

4 Leave out negative statements, or make them positive.

5 Do not write questions, but turn them into statements if they are relevant.

6 Do not include spoken words or quotations, but report the idea contained in them if it is relevant.

7 Do not include repetitions of ideas or phrases, and be as concise as possible in your wording.

8 Leave out examples, comparisons and details if they merely illustrate a point which is being made and do not contribute anything new to the main argument of the passage.

9 Try to find generalisations for the ideas contained in lists of words and phrases.

10 Use linking words and constructions, such as 'nevertheless', 'consequently', 'despite', 'because', 'although', 'however', 'therefore', 'thus', 'since', and participles ('-ing' verbs), to provide balance and continuity.

Additional points

There are a few more details which are worth mentioning:

1 You are quite likely to be asked to count the number of words you have used, and to record the total. Don't forget to do this, and try to be accurate. If your passage looks as if it might be longer than you have indicated, the examiner will certainly count the words him or herself. Using even a couple of words too many can seriously affect your mark. If you are many words under the limit, on the other hand, the chances are that you have missed some relevant points, and you should expand your summary.

2 If you are asked to supply a title for the passage, try to keep it short (no more than ten words at most) and think of a phrase which represents an encapsulation of the theme of the passage as a whole. You are not expected to include the title in your final word count.

3 There is no point in wasting words by using reported speech, with phrases like 'the writer said/says that . . .'. Simply summarise what is said without any kind of introduction.

4 It is generally considered appropriate for the summary to be written as a single paragraph, but if you split it into separate paragraphs at suitable points, it is extremely unlikely to be held against you. It is probably best not to follow the paragraphing of the original passage in your summary, since this is likely to result in some extremely short paragraphs.

5 It is best not to use abbreviations of any sort, except in a note-making exercise, since a summary is a piece of formal prose, and abbreviations are a rather unfair short-cut to word saving.

6 When your summary is complete, you should check carefully for spelling and punctuation errors, since marks will be allocated for technical accuracy.

Passages for summary

1 The passage which follows is an extract from *The Child, the Family, and the Outside World* by D. W. Winnicott. Your task is to summarise the main points of the passage in no more than 90 words. (The passage contains 533 words.)

What is the normal child like? Does he just eat and grow and smile sweetly? No, that is not what he is like. A normal child, if he has confidence in father and mother, pulls out all the stops. In the course of time he tries out his power to disrupt, to destroy, to frighten, to wear down, to waste, to wangle, to appropriate. Everything that takes people to the courts (or to the asylums, for that matter) has its normal equivalent in infancy and early childhood, in the relation of the child to his own home. If the home can stand up to all the child can do to disrupt it, he settles down to play, but business first, the tests must be made, and especially so if there is some doubt as to the stability of the parental set-up and the home (by which I mean so much more than house). At first the child needs to be conscious of a framework if he is to feel free, and if he is to be able to play, to draw his own pictures, to be an irresponsible child.

Why should this be? The fact is that the early stages of emotional development are full of potential conflict and disruption. The relation to external reality is not yet firmly rooted; the personality is not yet well integrated; primitive love has a destructive aim, and the small child has not yet learned to tolerate and cope with instincts. He can come to manage these things, and more, if his surroundings are stable and personal. At the start he absolutely needs to live in a circle of love and strength (with consequent tolerance) if he is not to be too fearful of his own thoughts and of his imaginings to make progress in his emotional development.

Now what happens if the home fails a child before he has got the idea of a framework as part of his own nature? The popular idea is that, finding himself 'free', he proceeds to enjoy himself. This is far from the truth. Finding the framework of his life broken, he no longer feels free. He becomes anxious, and if he has hope he proceeds to look for a framework elsewhere than at home. The child whose home fails to give a feeling of security looks outside his home for the four walls; he still has hope, and he looks to grandparents, uncles and aunts, friends of the family, school. He seeks an external stability without which he may go mad. Provided at the proper time, this stability might have grown into the child like the bones in his body, so that gradually in the course of the first months and years of his life he would have passed on to independence from dependence and a need to be managed. Often a child gets from relations and school what he missed in his actual home.

The antisocial child is merely looking a little further afield, looking to society instead of to his own family or school to provide the stability he needs if he is to pass through the early and quite essential stages of his emotional growth.

D. W. WINNICOTT

2 Write a summary of the following passage in not more than 115 words.
(The passage contains 342 words.)

Most of us will agree that previous training is desirable before we approach the arts. We mistrust untrained appreciation, believing that it often defeats its own ends. Appreciation ought to be enough. But unless we can learn by example and by failure and by comparison, appreciation will not bite. We shall tend to slip about on the surface of masterpieces, exclaiming with joy, but never penetrating. 'Oh, I do like Bach,' cries one appreciator, and the other cries, 'Do you? I don't. I like Chopin.' Exit in opposite directions chanting Bach and Chopin respectively, and hearing less the composers than their own voices. They resemble investors who proclaim the soundness of their financial assets. The Bach shares must not fall, the Chopin not fall further or one would have been proved a fool on the aesthetic stock exchange. The objection to untrained appreciation is not its naïveté but its tendency to lead to the appreciation of no one but oneself. Against such fatuity the critical spirit is a valuable corrective.

It is desirable to know why we like a work, and to be able to defend our preferences by argument. Our judgement has been strengthened and, if all goes well, the contacts will be intensified and increased and become more valuable.

I add the proviso 'if all goes well' because success lies on the knees of an unknown God. There is always the contrary danger; the danger that training may sterilise the sensitiveness that is being trained; that education may lead to knowledge instead of wisdom, and criticism to nothing but criticism; that spontaneous enjoyment, like the Progress of Poesy in Matthew Arnold's poem, may be checked because too much care has been taken to direct it into the right channel. Still, it is a risk to be faced, and if no care had been taken, the stream might have vanished even sooner. We hope criticism will help. We have faith in it as a respectable human activity, as an item in the larger heritage which differentiates us from the beasts.

E. M. FORSTER

3 The passage which follows was published in 1965, in a book called *The Popular Arts*. The television programmes and government reports referred to are now outdated, but the arguments presented are still considered to be valid. You have been asked to summarise the essential arguments, leaving out the illustrations, so that a version of the passage, with up-to-date illustrations, can subsequently be written. Your summary of the arguments should be made in no more than 150 words. (The passage contains 806 words.)

The question of violence looms large in any discussion of the mass media among educationalists. When the Pilkington Report set out to analyse the causes of public 'disquiet about television', it was obliged to begin with violence. Yet this question of violence in the media is more complex than appears at first sight. There may certainly be some point in the complaint that there is too much traffic in violent themes. But this complaint should be seen for what it is: a criticism of the balance of content in the media generally, and not a qualitative judgement on the particular kinds of violence treated, nor an informed opinion on their various effects. We must deal with the general question first. But since violence, death and human suffering have always been the subject matter of at least some great art, we must go on to draw the more complex distinctions between different kinds of violence: between, say, the violence of the BBC series of Shakespeare history plays on television, *Age of Kings*, and that of *Sunset Strip*, *Wagon Train*, *Whiplash* and *Gunsmoke*. Such distinctions are impossible without some attention to questions of style and treatment. We shall have to understand the different qualities expressed in these programmes, trying to decide how they work as dramatised experiences, and what their psychological impact is.

First, then, in general terms, so far as television is concerned, we are faced with problems of timing and volume. What is suitable for adults in the late evening may not be considered suitable for young children in the afternoon – always supposing that the television providers are alive to their educational responsibilities here, and that a time limit or boundary can be established. When, in a debate on the issue in Parliament in 1962, the Postmaster General said that the BBC assumed children were in bed by nine o'clock, a wise but unidentified backbench voice commented, 'They're wrong'. As for sheer volume, the Pilkington Report remarked simply that 'there was too much violence on television'. Few would disagree with this.

When an incorrect programme balance is combined with the general effects of repetition, the judgement is strengthened. Repetition is crucial. The steady networking of badly produced, low-level dramatised series – many of them American in origin or feeling – is one aspect of this saturation process. The 'competition' between the BBC and ITV for the peak viewing figures is probably another. Both the Nuffield Report (1958) and the Pilkington Report (1962) present disturbing evidence on this score.

Although it seems that only the child who is already emotionally disturbed will actually learn violence from a particular television programme (the evidence on this score seems fairly conclusive, in both *Television and the Child* and the comparable American study *Television in the Lives of our Children*), it is certainly true that we gradually become habituated to certain attitudes and situations if they are repeated often enough. The danger here is that we develop a permissive attitude towards the existence of violence in the world, come to regard it as a 'natural' solution to difficult social problems, or accept it as part of the background to life. This is what the Pilkington Report meant by the danger of a 'callous indifference'. The fear is strengthened when the whole balance is wrong, and when counter-images and attitudes, which enhance life or ennoble gentleness, kindness and love, are so difficult to evoke and often appear so trite and banal set beside the tension and vigour of the rougher scenes.

As the *Guardian* observed in an editorial: 'An isolated murder which strikes the viewer with horror is less corrupting than the incessant suggestion that murder is a bagatelle'. But the programmes in which this 'incessant suggestion' is made are those in which nothing seems to exist on the screen except the moment of violence – many of the television crime serials, for example, in which characters are, at most, two-dimensional stereotypes, the settings simply a procession of expensive penthouses, and the only visual moments of climax those when bodies slump to the floor. As the Pilkington Report commented:

> 'Many submissions recorded the view that it [violence] was often used gratuitously, that it often did little or nothing to develop plot or characterisation and that it was, presumably, thrown in "for kicks". Another common opinion was that it was often unnecessarily emphasised by being shown in close-up and by being lingered over. The damage was not necessarily repaired by ensuring that, in the end, the good were seen to win and the bad to lose, and that crime did not pay: conventional endings of this sort did not penetrate to the level at which the portrayal of violence had its emotional effect. What mattered was that violence provided the emotional energy, the dramatic content of the programme.'

STUART HALL and PADDY WHANNEL

4   Read the following review of the film, *A Room with a View*, and answer the questions which follow:

CINEMA

A Room with a View
('PG'. Curzon, Mayfair)

Pictures from Italy

The film has all the makings of a genteel elegance, from the carefully ironic credits at the beginning – 'Judi Dench: Eleanor Lavish, a novelist' – to the carefully modulated sense of loss at the close. It is a deliberate period piece, in other words, and with such attention lavished upon costumes and interiors that it acquires a slight museum-like air. One could almost feel the older members of the audience in Mayfair hugging themselves with pleasure at some of the wonderfully constructed Edwardian scenes.

The actors play up to their surroundings by putting on their best faces – in other words, by adopting the persona which has over the years best suited them. Denholm Elliott is once again the slightly eccentric, warm-hearted party with more than a suspicion of a cockney accent. Maggie Smith is sinewy and difficult, Simon Callow rubicund and ebullient. And then there are the assorted elderly actresses who are adept at playing English ladies in their lavender twilight years.

A Room with a View, then, verges on parody – not so much a parody of Forster or even of Edwardian society, but rather of the cinematic versions of that period. Of course this is not deliberate and the film-makers, Ismail Merchant and James Ivory, are well known for both their carefulness and their genius for cinematic adaptations of literary works. But carefulness can create a sense of artificiality, and adaptations often seem contrived. There are compensations, however: practically every scene shows such an elaborate orchestration of visual effects that, just as an exercise in composition, the film demands to be looked at.

The plot itself will be known to any one with the remotest knowledge of E. M. Forster – a dwindling minority, perhaps, but those who have not read this particular novel will still be able to follow the story of certain English people who 'come alive' at the impress of Florence on their inchoate souls. The film-makers are even more helpful than usual by interpolating Forster's arch chapter headings.

And the acting is excellent: leaving aside the slight tendency towards self-parody (which the director perhaps encouraged), the film contains a series of excellent performances. Judi Dench, as the female novelist, brought a certain majesty to the pseudo-romantic imagination; perhaps next time she should play E. M. Forster. And Helena Bonham-Carter, as the young heroine, looked absorbingly preoccupied and intelligent – she is one of those actresses whose thoughts the camera seems to photograph. All the way through, Maggie Smith quivers (there is no other word for it) with suppressed passion. And so, after a while, the elements of parody and artificiality no longer matter; A Room with a View may lack a certain continuity of rhythm (and this largely because the imposition of chapter headings tends to turn the narrative into a number of carefully modulated scenes) but it has the bravura which comes equally from creative conviction and from tight formal control.

It could be said, in fact, that this adaptation is almost too faithful. Merchant and Ivory (as well as Ruth Prawer Jhabvala, their screen-writer) have earned their large reputation principally by taking on the works of the more 'sophisticated' or elaborately humanistic Western novelists – subdued, complicated novels, the realism of which is finally touched by lyricism but is generally enmeshed in the obliquities of class or caste. It would be difficult to imagine them adapting Dickens, for example; he is too grotesque, too large. Henry James is their metier.

As a result they have definite vision, but it is one filtered through a certain kind of literature about a certain kind of life – it is admirable, but even as one responds to it, one cannot but feel and recognise the constrictions which press down upon it. But of course A Room with a View itself is concerned with those very constrictions, and on this occasion the film-makers have been able to use their carefully balanced scenarios precisely in order to render more vivid their images of violence or fragility. One of the most interesting aspects of this production is the way in which the elaborate tonalities of the English dialogue are placed against the soaring grandeur of the Florentine architecture – thus setting up a tension which the rest of the film explores. And so, when the scene returns to England, there are some wonderful moments largely concerned with the social embarrassment of everyone concerned. An episode of nude bathing is almost wilfully interrupted by two ladies, and there are various nerveless tea-parties at which Maggie Smith's manner is the star attraction.

PETER ACKROYD, *The Spectator*

a List in note form the *factual* information we are given about the film and its making.   (*10 marks*)

b In not more than 100 words of connected prose say what you understand the film to be about from what the critic writes.   (*10 marks*)

c What are the opinions of the critic about the film? Your answer should be no more than 150 words in length.   (*20 marks*)

Specimen answers to all the summary skills exercises in this chapter can be found in the Appendix on pages 290 and 291.

COMPREHENSION AND COMMENT

5

Varieties of question

The traditional comprehension exercise tests the student's understanding of a passage of prose, and the ability to express ideas and phrases contained in the passage in his or her own words. This is still an integral part of comprehension. However, modern comprehension exercises at an advanced level test more than this. They tend to focus on journalistic expertise, and test the student's skill in assessing the *presentation* of ideas and arguments, rather than merely explaining what the writer is saying.

The student may be expected to comment on the persuasiveness of the argument, and the means by which it is presented, on the style and tone of the piece, its use of bias, and how all these aspects of the writing offer clues as to the target audience. Newspaper articles are the most likely source for comprehension exercises, and most of the comprehension and comment passages in this book are taken from newspapers.

Initial approach to a comprehension exercise

Just as with summary skills exercises, the first essential in preparing to answer comprehension and comment questions on a passage is to read the passage through once or twice to gain some sense of what the passage is about. The questions can then be read, and the passage reread with the questions in mind.

When you begin answering the questions, you may find it useful to underline key phrases in the passage which are relevant to the question you are answering, as long as you either rub out your underlinings when you've finished your answer or write in the margin the number or letter of the question to which your underlining refers.

You should always be careful to check the number of marks allocated for each question, as this will give you a fairly clear idea of the amount of detail required in your answer. It is foolish to spent a lot of time on questions for which there are only two or three marks. In fact, since there is no requirement to answer the questions in order, it may be best to leave questions which carry few marks till the end, in case you run out of time.

Content questions

Traditional comprehension questions, requiring explanations of ideas or information contained in the passage, or of the writer's attitude to something which is described or analysed, test a student's ability to understand what a writer is saying, and to articulate this understanding.

In general, such questions will refer to a particular idea or ideas, frequently with line references, and the answer will normally be found in the lines surrounding this phrase or idea. This is not always the case, however, and some questions may refer to an idea which is developed in more than one paragraph. Care must be taken to check whether an idea is developed or information presented in more than one section of the passage, before attempting an answer. In either case, all the relevant details should be included in your answer.

On occasions, you will find that words or phrases are so specialised or precise as to be impossible to re-express without altering the sense, in which case it is acceptable to copy them.

Questions requiring explanation of phrases

In the case of questions which ask for explanations of vocabulary used in the passage, a brief answer is all that is required. There is no need to explain the context of the word or phrase, and your answer should not contain many more words than are contained in the phrase itself.

Style questions

Questions requiring evaluation of the style of a passage may take a variety of forms. You may simply be asked to 'comment on the style' of the passage, or the question may be more precise. You may, for instance, be asked to give your opinion as to whether the passage is 'well written', or exhibits 'good writing', in which case you are quite likely to be asked to explain your criteria for judging the writing style. Similarly, you may be asked to 'evaluate the effectiveness' of the style of writing.

You may also be instructed to consider particular aspects of the style, such as language/diction/vocabulary, syntax, register and imagery. A brief explanation of these essential elements of writing style may be useful.

49

Language (or diction or vocabulary)

A piece of writing may be consistent in the type of language it uses, or it may not. The first thing to look for is evidence of variations from the predominant language type; you should be prepared to quote and explain the purpose or effect of such variations.

A passage may be written in highly formal or highly informal language, or any variation in between. Formal language is likely to contain a fairly high proportion of complex or multisyllabic or abstract words. This does not, of course, necessarily make the style dull, and therefore ineffective. What you are essentially looking for, in terms of the effectiveness or otherwise of the language, is *freshness* of expression. Highly *in*formal language may contain clichéd expressions, which tend to destroy the sense of freshness in the writing.

Informal language will tend to be more simple and concrete, and its effectiveness can be gauged by its immediacy of appeal: it may be colloquial (employing the kind of phraseology normally associated with spoken rather than written language) and colourful (appealing to the imagination in the choice of words, particularly of adjectives and adverbs).

Syntax (or sentence structure)

The syntax of a piece may be essentially complex or simple. Generally speaking, the more intricately argued and formal the writing, the more complex its syntax is likely to be. You should look out in particular for sophistications of syntax, such as the proliferation of subordinate clauses within sentences, or the use of colons and semicolons.

Long and complex sentences, however, need not necessarily equate with good style, and can occasionally obscure the sense, though with skilled writers this is rare. It is perhaps a little risky to criticise a writer's syntax in terms of obscurity, since you may merely be revealing your inability to understand a carefully reasoned argument.

Less formal writing tends to use shorter sentences and simpler syntax. Again, this proves nothing about the comparative effectiveness of the writing. *Very* short sentences, however, are worth picking out from a passage and commenting on, since they inevitably stand out simply by the nature of their shortness, and tend to create a direct, 'punchy' or even dramatic effect.

In writing which employs largely complex syntax, you should look out for occasional examples of short, simple sentences, and be prepared to comment on the effect they produce. The same applies with occasional complex sentences in passages in which the syntax is generally simple.

Other features of syntax which you might look out for and comment on are the use of questions instead of statements, rhetorical repetition, balanced phrases in two separate parts of a sentence, and the deliberate use of ungrammatical or incomplete sentences.

Register

The register in which a piece is written reflects the social situation both of its writer and the audience for which it is intended. In the broadest sense, writing itself is a register, as distinct from speech. Again very broadly, we can differentiate between formal and informal registers in both speech and writing. More precisely, the immense number of dialects of English are all registers: for instance, we can talk of a Jamaican English register, or a black American English register, or a northern working-class English register.

These registers can, of course, be represented in writing as well as speech. The same person can and, in fact, inevitably does adopt different registers, depending on the audience. In a committee meeting a learned register might be adopted or else one reflecting the professional jargon of his or her peers, which would be quite different from the informal, colloquial register used with friends. In writing a report of the meeting he or she would employ a vocabulary, syntax and mode of punctuation designed to highlight his or her professional expertise and seriousness of intention; the style most probably would be formal, the vocabulary learned, the syntax complex and the punctuation strictly accurate. In a letter to a friend, however, the same person would be likely to eschew formalities, and write simple sentences, consciously ignoring the formal rules of punctuation by, for instance, using dashes, and adopting a style of writing more akin to speech.

Register, therefore, encompasses not only the type of language used, but also the sentence-structure and the mode or style of writing in general. A writer's intentions, and target audience, can normally be gauged from the register he or she chooses.

Imagery

Imagery is such a complex matter that it is dealt with in a separate chapter. You should familiarise yourself with a variety of figures of speech analysed in Chapter 3 as part of your preparation for comprehension and comment exercises.

As a broad generalisation, imagery can be divided into two classes: fresh and stale. Fresh, original images can greatly enhance writing, providing an extra dimension and imaginative focus on an idea. Stale imagery tends merely to reveal the writer's lack of originality. A constant feature of the popular press in Britain is the use of clichés, which are really overworked, 'dead' metaphors and similes.

Questions on tone

'Tone' and 'language' are difficult to separate, and questions which ask for analysis of tone are frequently posed in terms of 'language and tone'. One way of defining tone would be 'the emotional temperature of the language used'. A writer's feelings about a topic are revealed through the tone he or she adopts.

The tone of a passage, as well as its language, may vary. An expository passage, in an essentially neutral tone, may contain touches of humour, for instance, where the tone could be described as whimsical. Such variations should be illustrated, and the effects explained.

There is an immense range of tones in which a writer can express his or her feelings. These might be broadly categorised, and illustrated, as follows:

Neutral tones

Much formal writing is largely *neutral* in tone, conveying no impression of emotion. The tone of such writing might even be *detached*, where the writer creates no feeling of personal involvement whatsoever in the writing. When a writer is attempting to convey an impression of balance and reasonableness, the tone might be described as *measured*. It might, on the other hand, be *didactic*, making assertions which the reader is expected to accept as the truth.

Angry tones

When a writer is arguing against some perceived abuse or folly, emotions of anger are likely to be displayed in the choice of language. The tone is quite likely to be *bitter* or *disparaging*, *scornful*, *abusive*, or even, at the furthest extreme of anger, *vitriolic*.

A bitter tone is also likely to be exhibited when the writer sees no likelihood of the unsatisfactory situation which he or she is analysing being rectified; in these circumstances a *heavily ironic*, *sarcastic*, or *sardonic* tone is also likely. At the extreme, in this case, the tone may be *despairing*.

Humorous tones

Sarcasm, of course, is a form of humour, and can also be used in more light-hearted writing. Writers frequently resort to a *gently sarcastic* tone to poke fun at their targets. More light-hearted pieces of writing frequently exhibit a more lightly humorous tone: for instance, a *whimsical*, *wry*, or *lightly ironic* tone.

Tones reflecting strong conviction

If a writer is pursuing a crusade, and is determined to persuade the reader of the correctness of his or her views, the tone employed may be *hectoring*, in which he seems to be attempting to enforce acceptance of the views expressed. Subtler appeals to the reader may be made through a *familiar* tone, in which the reader is addressed as a like-minded individual who is certain to share the writer's attitudes; such an approach may, as its worst, employ a *patronising* tone, in which the writer talks down to the reader.

Enthusiastic tones

If the writer wishes to show his or her enthusiasm for something, the tone used may be *laudatory*, employing language ringing with praise, or *passionate*, *jubilant*, or even *triumphant*.

Whatever you perceive the tone of the passage you are analysing to be, you must make sure that you quote illustrations from the passage of the language displaying the tone.

To test your recognition of differences of tone, you might now attempt a simple exercise. Write down ten different sentences, each containing the phrase 'shut the door.' Then read some of them out loud, conveying the tone intended with your voice. The class can then define the tone of each.

Questions on effectiveness of argument

To answer questions on methods of argumentation and the persuasiveness or otherwise of arguments, you will need to look both at the way the argument itself is presented and at the manner in which it is written.

Perhaps the most important consideration in assessing argumentation is the presence or absence of *adequate supportive evidence*. Factual evidence, possibly including *figures and/or statistics*, is essential to provide a basis on which to judge the validity of the argument. Precise evidence, with up-to-date information, gives the necessary substance to an argument; without it, the case rests on unsubstantiated assertion. You should check to see if the evidence is *overly selective*, ignoring evidence which might invalidate the case. You should bear in mind that statistics are notoriously easy to misuse. If the writer uses statistics to back up an assertion, you should attempt to assess whether or not they are put to valid use.

Personal, inside knowledge is a useful way of adding an air of conviction to an argument and giving the impression that the writer 'knows what he or she is talking about'. A *personal anecdote* can also make the argument seem more 'real', but here you should think carefully about the use made of the anecdote; *arguing from the particular to the general* is one of the classic logical flaws. *Comparisons* are another useful tool in argument, where the writer presents a parallel or comparable case to back up his or her position. The comparisons must, of course, be relevant; *irrelevant analogies* are another basic error of logic.

As for the actual mode of writing, several factors should be looked for in terms of the effective presentation of an argument. A sense of a *personal, individual 'voice'* tends to predispose the reader towards acceptance of a viewpoint in contrast to a bland, abstract, impersonal series of propositions. *Emotive language*, as long as it is not overdone, helps to create a sense of personal conviction, especially a tone of scorn, anger or sarcasm, and *colloquial language* personalises the case. The use of *humour* can also be a useful way of giving credence to a viewpoint: the reader is more likely to accept the attacks on the writer's target by being made to laugh at them.

Syntax can also play a part: *short, punchy, statements* tend to create a particularly strong impact as long as they are not overused; *rhetorical questions* encourage the reader to share the writer's conviction in what he is saying. The *use of questions*, generally, is an effective tool of argumentation, forcing the reader to think for himself about the issues being raised.

Questions on bias

Much of what has been said in the above discussion of methods of argumentation is relevant to bias. These are the essential features to look for:

- lack of adequate supportive evidence;
- presenting only evidence which supports the writer's case, and ignoring valid counter-evidence;
- providing only a single piece of evidence, and falsely basing a general contention on it;
- irrelevant personal anecdotes;
- suggestions by the writer that he or she knows best, and those who disagree are either ignorant or wilfully misleading;
- attempts to cajole the reader into agreement, by suggesting, for instance, that any sensible person would view the issue the way the writer does;
- appeals to naked prejudice, such as racial or sexual chauvinism.

Questions on target audience

If you are asked to identify the kind of audience for which a piece of writing might have been intended, you should offer evidence both from the style and the content of the piece.

Vocabulary, syntax, register and tone all offer clues as to the readership at which it might have been targeted. You should consider the subject matter and the attitude which the writer takes towards it, the political stance (if any), the degree of sophistication of the arguments, and the level of cultural, historical and general awareness that a full understanding of the article requires. These factors will provide convincing evidence as to the age range, social class, political viewpoint, degree of education and sophistication, special interests, etc., of the target audience.

Answering comprehension and comment questions

The exercise and specimen answers which follow are designed to show you how to tackle questions of the analytical type which we have been considering above.

Comprehension and comment

Read the following passage which appeared in *The Independent* and answer the questions:

Curse of the day-glo dazzlers

St Thomas Aquinas was fond of saying that the man who was free only in his leisure time was a
5 slave. Aquinas lived a long time ago in Italy, however, and what he said is clearly anathema to the British in 1990.
10 The British believe in leisure. Leisure (along with shopping) is the new religion and its devotees work hard to
15 take it easy.

Among other things, they have caused the building of vast new temples of a type never
20 seen before: the shopping mall, the theme park and the leisure centre. These buildings are the cathedrals, mon-
25 asteries and hospices of our day.

If you find the leisure creed repugnant, you can escape the theme park
30 and the leisure centre. It is more difficult, however, to avoid the vast shopping mall and its mesmerising air-
35 conditioned nave, aisles, chapels and clerestories with their expensive offerings of luxury goods.
40 But it is impossible to escape from the habits – the clothes as well as the gum-chewing, burger-stuffing and soft-drink
45 suckling – of the leisure era. In dignified city streets, in country lanes, in shopping arcades up and down the country,
50 in churches, airports and country houses, leisure-wear is all intrusive.

A whole nation seems to be dressed, notably at
55 weekends, in man-made fabric representations of the contents of a packet of liquorice allsorts. The strident acid colours of
60 leisurewear dominate every view of every British street, lane and public building.

Architects trying to
65 build even the most sensitive modern building are given a hard time by interfering local planning committees. Anyone,

55

70 however, can don a garish polyester-nylon tracksuit and waddle shamelessly along a much-loved street lined 75 with beautiful buildings, without fear of censure. Yet leisurewear is visual pollution of the highest order.

80 It is also damning evidence of a slob culture that seeks to undermine urbane and civilised values. For leisurewear 85 means never having to think about appearances. Leisurewear means never having to straighten a tie or polish a pair of shoes. 90 Leisurewear means never having to step out of your pyjamas. Leisurewear means free advertising for manufacturers: 95 shoes, jeans and T-shirts decked with tags, labels and transfers celebrating company names.

Why do people pay 100 for these clothes? Surely they should be paid for their role as animated billboards? Traditionally, a good English suit hides 105 its label – if it has one – in the lining of an inside pocket.

Today's tracksuits, bomber jackets, trainers 110 and hooded 'mugger' tops are emblazoned with their makers' names, like crests on medieval soldiers' tunics. 115 Many carry crude or insulting messages.

How are you meant to respond to a fat, ill-shaven slob strolling 120 around a National Trust house in the Cotswolds wearing a garish and

Leisurewear dominates every British street

very sweaty sweat-shirt that reads: 'If I 125 wanted to listen to someone talking out of his arse, I would have farted'?

If, however, a Cots-130 wold resident wants to build a very small addition to the back of their house – one that cannot be seen from the road – it 135 will be refused planning permission unless it is designed in a style and materials that ape what went before. 140 But what is more offensive? A dignified new building that cannot be seen or a T-shirt that will pollute a hundred 145 streets, malls and railway stations?

Leisurewear is meant to be noisy. Its supposedly relaxed nature 150 cannot conceal a strident heart. If you go skiing today, you need dark glasses or goggles, not just to shield your eyes 155 from the sunlight, but to protect them from the kaleidoscopic glare dazzling off polychrome ski outfits. These outfits 160 are designed to draw attention to the individual skier, to say 'Hey! Look at me!'.

Traditional ski outfits 165 were designed in colours that blended with winter mountain scenery. The skier appeared a small part of a much bigger 170 creation. Today, the leisure skier has no such modesty.

The joy of traditional clothing – which can range from the most fogeyish city suit to an innovative couture dress – is that it enhances wearer, onlooker and surroundings.

If you stroll along a street in the City of London, you will still find clothes, taxis, buses, police and buildings working together to animate a scene harmoniously. On a country walk, it is still possible to find parts of Britain in which walker, country clothes, dog, horse, farmyard and scenery work together.

As soon as you see someone dressed in day-glo leisurewear in a city street, however, that civic harmony is upset. As soon as you clap eyes on an acolyte of leisure on a country walk, natural harmony is luridly sabotaged. Because it demands very little of people, leisurewear is infectious. Increasingly, people in uniformed jobs adapt their costume to accommodate the dictates of Leisure.

British Rail workers and bus staff have become famous for their scruffy appearance. They have done away with the tie, jettisoned the cap and replaced polished shoes with 'Levis for Feet'.

The point about a uniform is that it identifies public servants. It singles out the person who can be turned to for information or when something goes wrong. When the driver of a train, or the conductor of a bus is dressed Blade Runner-style – a cross between a shopped-out Saturday shopper and a jogger with a beer gut – are you sure you want to turn to him for help? His clothes suggest he doesn't really care about his job.

Perhaps the saddest thing about leisurewear is that it denies great chunks of British society the right to walk with dignity when they lose their youthful looks. Old men confined to leisurewear (through habit or because, at the price most can afford, the market offers little else) look particularly undignified.

Dressed in jacket, tie and hat, the most creaky old man looks good. That can be tested out by ambling through any Italian town. Perhaps old people are accorded greater dignity in Italy than they are in Britain, not because Italians are, on the whole, a more sociable lot than the British, but because they *look* dignified.

Leisurewear is unlikely to go away just yet. Anything easy is preferable to anything that requires effort, and that goes for dressing as much as it does for most British architecture and design of today.

Grandfather is unlikely ever again to don ironed shirt, tie and cap to prune the rose bushes. His dignity gone, he really doesn't mind looking like a liquorice allsort well past its sell-by date.

JONATHAN GLANCEY, *The Independent*

a Give an evaluation of the style of the passage, concentrating especially on language, register, syntax and imagery. (*12 marks*)

b Show how the writer's attitude to his subject is revealed through his tone. (*10 marks*)

c By what means does the writer attempt to convince you of the validity of his viewpoint? (*12 marks*)

d What kind of audience would you consider this piece to have been directed at? (*8 marks*)

e To what extent do you accept the writer's attack on contemporary fashion? *(8 marks)*
(Total of 50 marks)

Now study these specimen answers.

a Give an evaluation of the style of the passage, concentrating especially on language, register, syntax and imagery.

The passage is written in a lively and entertaining style. The tenor of the piece is personal, creating the impression that the writer is addressing the reader directly. An educated vocabulary, with words like 'clerestories', 'strident', 'urbane' and 'luridly sabotaged' is mixed with colloquial language, with the occasional use of slang words like 'slob', 'scruffy' and 'beer gut', to create a register which gives the impression of an infuriated academic deliberately slipping into the style of the mass culture which he derides. A particularly good example of this mixing of registers is in the phrase 'clap eyes on an acolyte of leisure'. The language of the passage as a whole is essentially concrete, and full of precise illustrations.

The syntax also reflects the mixing of registers. It is frequently used to help create the accents of speech, as in the sentence beginning in line 103, with its informal use of dashes. Few of the sentences are complex in construction, though it is rare to find sequences of short sentences. The paragraph beginning in line 164 is an exception in this respect. The paragraphs are mostly short. Rhetorical repetition is a device used to add forcefulness to the writing, as in the sequence of sentences beginning in line 84.

The imagery used in the passage creates a humorous effect. The comparison of people dressed in 'strident acid colours' with 'the contents of a packet of liquorice allsorts' is amusingly apt, as is the simile of 'crests on medieval uniforms' to mock the wearing of 'makers' names' on leisurewear. The style can be extremely expressive at times, as in the phrase in lines 42–5 ('the gum . . . suckling'), making effective use of assonance in 'gum', 'stuffing' and 'suckling', creating an overall onomatopoeic effect. At its best, the writing can capture a vivid sense-impression through its mixture of styles, notably in the phrase beginning in line 157: 'kaleidoscopic . . . outfits'.

b Show how the writer's attitude to his subject is revealed through his tone.

The writer's attitude to 'day-glo' fashion is one of anger and resentment; he feels that this particular aspect of the 'leisure creed' is a crude and frequently offensive intrusion into everyday contemporary life. This attitude is expressed through the tone, which is consistently angry, and becomes bitterly vituperative at times, as in the paragraph beginning in line 117, with its 'fat, ill-shaven slob . . . wearing a garish and very sweaty sweatshirt' with its obscene motto. Phrases like 'pollute a hundred

58

streets' and 'luridly sabotaged' display a tone of intense anger, and this is frequently mixed with a savagely contemptuous tone in descriptions such as 'gum-chewing, burger-stuffing and soft-drink suckling' and 'slob culture'. Even when the tone is humorous, it is a sardonic humour, as in the sentence beginning in line 53 with its comic comparison with 'liquorice allsorts'.

c   By what means does the writer attempt to convince you of the validity of his viewpoint?

This is a polemical article, in which the writer expresses his disgust at an aspect of modern life which he finds repugnant. His intention is therefore to encourage the reader to view the situation through his eyes, and share his repugnance.

He does this partly by direct, powerfully emotive assertions, as in lines 77–9 ('Yet leisurewear . . . order'). He uses language deliberately to attempt to create a sense of reciprocal repugnance in the reader, as in the compellingly sensuous description of 'the gum-chewing . . . suckling' in lines 42–5. The sense of outrage he conveys is allied to a sense of humour, by which the reader is invited, for instance, to laugh at the idea of the grandfather 'looking like a liquorice allsort well past its sell-by date'. He uses rhetorical questions to encourage acceptance of his viewpoint, as in lines 99–103 ('Why do . . . billboards'), and in the paragraph beginning in line 140.

He offers a wide variety of illustrative evidence of the fashions which he is deriding, and quotes a particularly offensive example of sweatshirt emblems: 'If I wanted . . . farted' (lines 124–8). He uses extended illustrations of his points at times, as in the section on 'British Rail workers and bus staff' (line 213 onwards), and is not afraid to employ exaggeration for comic effect, as in the description of the British Rail official 'dressed Bladerunner-style . . . beer gut' (lines 231–5). He also employs comparisons to add substance to his argument, as in the contrasting picture of the appearance of old people in Italy compared with Britain, and offers a parallel situation to create a feeling of injustice, in the section on the 'Cotswold resident' beginning in line 129. He offers an ideal against which to measure the situation which he is attacking, in the passage about 'a country walk' (lines 188–94).

d   What kind of audience would you consider the piece to have been directed at?

The passage is clearly directed at a relatively educated audience, who would be expected to understand words like 'anathema' and 'acolyte'. However, he gives the impression that he suspects some of his readers to be barely above the level of the 'slob culture' he derides, as is evidenced by his patronising explanation of the reference to Saint Thomas Aquinas in lines 5 and 6. The target audience is likely to be traditional in their values, people who favour 'traditional clothing' and who could be assumed to share the writer's revulsion at 'fat, ill-shaven slobs' wearing sweatshirts with 'crude or insulting messages'. The passage seems to be principally aimed at those who 'find the leisure creed repugnant'. Socially and politically the target audience could be assumed to be conservative, middle-class, and probably middle-aged people who would be likely to nod in agreement when the writer presents value judgements masquerading as facts, like 'British Rail workers and bus staff have become famous for their scruffy appearance'.

e To what extent do you accept the writer's attack on contemporary fashion?

I feel that the writer overstates his case in his attack on contemporary fashion. It is perfectly true that 'leisurewear' is ubiquitous in Britain: T-shirts and especially trainers have become the normal clothing outside working hours for large numbers of British people. However, it is not true to suggest, as the writer does, that a high proportion of old men are 'confined to leisurewear' and have therefore lost their 'dignity'. The great majority of old men dress relatively formally, and although jeans have been the norm amongst young people for decades, the 'day-glo' fashions which he derides are not as all-pervasive as he suggests. I personally find 'leisurewear' comfortable and relaxing, whilst ties in particular are uncomfortable and restricting. I find it hard to feel completely relaxed in a suit, and hard not to in a T-shirt and shorts. As for emblems on T-shirts, these are more often amusing than offensive, and the example he gives, though admittedly gross, is very much the exception rather than the rule.

Comprehension and comment practice exercises

The exercises which follow are designed to provide practice in the full range of comprehension and comment skills analysed in this chapter.

You are advised to spend about one and a half hours on each exercise.

1   The first extract which follows is an article which appeared in *The Sunday Times* in October 1990, and the second is an abridgement of a letter which appeared in the magazine *English* in November, 1990. Read both extracts carefully, and answer the following questions:

   a   Do you consider Norman Stone's article a 'good' piece of journalism, in which he presents his case convincingly?   (*10 marks*)

   b   Comment in some detail on the tone of Norman Stone's article.
                                                                   (*8 marks*)

   c   Give a precise explanation of the relevance of the picture which accompanies Bob Bibby's letter to the contents of the letter, and consider whether the wolf-child story adds to the persuasiveness of his argument.   (*6 marks*)

   d   Each writer refers to the idea that standards in English are declining;

the one treats it as a fact whilst the other describes it as a 'myth'. Do you find the one more convincing than the other and for what reasons? *(9 marks)*

e In paragraph 7 of his letter, Bibby makes an implicit defence of GCSE against the old O levels, and paragraph 11 of Stone's article explicitly attacks GCSE. Basing your answer on the arguments presented and on your own educational experience, say with which writer you are more inclined to agree. *(8 marks)*

f Comment on Stone's remarks about A levels in the light of your experience so far as an A-level student. *(9 marks)*

(50 marks total)

Pulling out A levels will not cure education's toothache

The team that produced a preposterous national curriculum is out to cause more havoc, warns Norman Stone

A cruel and not inaccurate description of the British monarchy is 'a gold filling in a mouthful of rotting teeth' – a remark made, I recall, by Lindsay Anderson. There are other institutions to which you can apply it: and one of them is under fire at the moment. We all, by and large, agree that our educational system is the worst in Europe. Its crowning element is the A level, in theory a rather testing examination for 18-year-olds, who are supposed to show a high degree of knowledge in two or three specialist subjects.

In the old days it certainly was a testing business: if you did French, for instance, you had to work through a stack of Racine, and the vocabulary was hard work. (To this day, thanks to a brilliant teacher at Glasgow Academy, I can still defeat my colleagues in French when it comes to words such as 'itinerant scissors-grinder' or 'maidenhair fern'.) Pressures are now mounting for the abolition of the A level. The team that snowed our teachers under with a preposterous national curriculum is now working out ways to wreck the rest.

Now, it is true that there is something wrong with the A level. It is, in many ways, a glossy, antiquated flagship galleon in a flotilla of bumboats. Nowadays, people with A levels in, say, English, history and economics will not have more than primitive French, and no other languages, let alone decent maths. No other country of my acquaintance encourages such narrow specialisation at an early age: on the Continent, the higher school leaving certificate requires knowledge of half a dozen subjects, which is no doubt healthy.

Again, the origins of the A level are strange. We never really had public systems of examination: in the 19th century, they came from private initiatives, usually from churchmen. The done

61

thing in those days was to specialise in classics, and you bashed away to a high degree. The argument for this now looks strange, but there is in my opinion much to be said for it: that the classics, properly taught, gave you a highly adaptable mind, capable of absorbing anything else.

In any event, modernisers, by 1900, muttered that we were falling behind the Americans because our education was not practical – in today's jargon, giving 'skills'. The higher certificate (the nomenclature of A levels did not come until later) therefore catered for other specialisations: history, modern languages, etc., to begin with, then economics and, in our own day, modish things such as sociology or political science (we have only just been spared 'peace studies', though no doubt women's history will come along some day).

The old system had much to commend it. In the first place, it relieved the universities of the burden of teaching elementary things, so that the English (as distinct from the Scottish) universities could in-and-out their students in three years. Then again, the specialisation did not really inhibit people from learning other things: this was done informally, and it was quite usual for boys of 17 at a good public or grammar school just to sit about reading.

Of late, the system has declined, rather. In some subjects, standards are still high, demonstrably so with the 'quantifiable' ones, such as maths or physics. In others, they are obviously not what they once were. I doubt if an A level in English nowadays amounts to much; instead of the great stacks of classics which once you had to know, many of the boards supply modish pap; spelling has badly declined; and in any case there is a very modern-English problem with examiners, in that they are swamped in scripts, marking which is demanding on the nerves, and are paid comical money per script (£1.83 and the like).

An examiner in these circumstances cannot be blamed if, with his 500 or 600 three-hour scripts containing mis-spelt effusions on, say, the plays of Edward Bond, he dishes out the beta-alphas with a pepperpot. These marks are now known, all too frequently, to be unreliable.

Voices are now raised for the abolition of this system. The Higginson Report spoke for something like the Scottish Highers, a multi-subject leaving certificate, not so highly specialised. One consequence of this could be that the university course would have to be lengthened to the Scots' usual four years and maybe even to most continentals' five and more. Another consequence, which deterred the Prime Minister herself from endorsing the report's suggestions, would be to weaken the flagship qualification. But more voices are now raised, not to abolish the A level, but to build into it some 'vocational' element – 'skills', in other words. Most school pupils after 16 will stay on in some form of education and get some A level or equivalent at the end, to include something that employers allegedly want.

That is tripe. Employers are not interested in grades: they just know if someone can read, write, count and be honest. Then again, a great part of our working-class culture does not fit with schooling beyond a certain age: if at 16 you can get a job earning £200 a week, schooling is not going to be attractive.

In any case, the new proposals suffer from that crippling English guilt about 'class'. In order to avoid class-discrimination and supposed hurt-feelings on the part of the non-academic, we have to devise an examination to fit everyone. This was done, in effect, when the old O levels were replaced by GCSE, an examination regarded with ribaldry and contempt by almost every

teacher whom I have consulted. Most of them
240 say that it could be, and has been, passed even by
a bright 10-year-old. If A levels are diluted in the
same way we shall end
245 up, as was rightly said the other day, in a country which produces neither brain surgeons nor plumbers.
250 There are many things wrong with A levels, and they are not what they were. But they still represent a standard of
255 some seriousness, at a time when standards elsewhere have slipped. They are also part of a culture, which is not
260 going to be altered simply by tinkering

away at its manifestations.
265 If you abolish or water down the A level, then you would also have
290 to extend university courses, rope trade unions into apprentice-
270 ship schemes, and make it compulsory for Sharon
295 and Tracey to stay on at school instead of heading for a job in a boutique or
275 a hairdressers.
In other words, you
300 would have to be a German. There, the unions, in enlightened fashion,
280 have just agreed that wage rates in East
305 Germany can be flexible; they will help out with extending apprentice-
285 ships, too. The German

school-teachers' union (and the lecturers' union) appealed to the voters in the recent local elec-
290 tions to vote only for parties that agree to 'pluralism' in education, i.e. without compulsory comprehensives.
295 None of these things, sadly, apply in England. Therefore, we cannot get a sensible system of vocational training for
300 the non-academically-inclined. The problem would only be worsened if we now try and use the battered old A level for a
305 purpose remote from it. You do not cure the rotten teeth by pulling out the gold filling.

NORMAN STONE, *The Sunday Times*, 21 October, 1990

Crying Wolf

Bob Bibby *urges the new Secretary of State not to fall prey to the myths of declining standards*

When I was a young teacher, there was a story current in the neighbourhood where I worked of a
5 young woman who had given birth to a child with a wolf's head. No one had ever actually seen this child but the story was widely
10 believed. I have since encountered this story, and variations of it, in other neighbourhoods in other times and have heard from
15 colleagues that it crops up in other parts of the coun-

try too. The story is, of course, a myth, no doubt arising from subconscious
20 fears within the human pscyhe, but nevertheless it is a powerful myth and all the more so because it will not go away.
25 There exists an equally powerful myth about English in our schools which says that standards are falling. The myth has
30 been propounded regularly throughout the quarter of a century I have been

a teacher (and, of course, for at least 100 years
35 before that). It has given rise to two major government inquiries into the state of English teaching which resulted in the 1975
40 Bullock Report, *A Language for Life*, and the 1988 Kingman Report, not to mention the Cox Report which has subsequently been
45 translated into the National Curriculum for English. Each of those two inquiries was in response to panic

63

about supposed falling standards. The myth's current manifestation will be telling you that standards of reading and spelling are falling. My worry is that you will fall prey to those myths rather than seek proper evidence.

For the evidence tells a very different story – a story of considerable success. It is there in the published reports of your Inspectorate, who state quite unequivocally in *The Teaching and Learning of Language and Literacy* , their survey of inspections carried out in primary schools between 1983 and 1988:

'The basic skills of reading and writing continue to receive a great deal of time and attention. The standards achieved are generally good and continue to improve.'

It is there in the published reports of the Assessment of Performance Unit (APU) which was set up in response to a previous panic and which summarised its sampling operations in schools by stating in 1988:

'Very few children appeared to have problems decoding the printed word. The initial stages of literacy have been passed by all but a tiny minority of 11-year-olds.'

It is there in the statistics which demonstrate a dramatic improvement in the achievements of 16-year-olds in English at GCSE and of 18-year-olds at A level.

I also have to tell you that the myth does not match with the reality I experience daily in my work as an English adviser, visiting classrooms and witnessing dedicated teachers at work, and as Chair of NATE, talking with and listening to teachers discussing their practice. From them I rediscover the excitements of learning, such as when a five-year-old finds for the first time that he can read a whole story to his teacher, or a non-reading eight-year-old discovers she can hold a group of secondary pupils enthralled with a story she has made up, or a 12-year-old can recognise the difficulty of explaining a playground game to a group of infants, or a 16-year-old can feel the confidence to write a letter to the Prince of Wales, following the latter's criticisms of the state of English teaching, which concludes:

'May I respectfully point out to your Highness that some people are 'cursed' with poor spelling. I am one of these disadvantaged few, but I have found that rechecking my work irons out these small discrepancies. If your staff

have the same problem, 160 led language users whose   So let me end this letter
why not tell them to   making of meaning will   where I began with a plea
check spellings with a   contribute massively to 180   to you in your new role as
145 dictionary?'   their present and future   Secretary of State for Edu-
   Sadly, I also find that identities as members of   cation. The plea is twofold:
many of these committed, 165 our society. They know   first, that you eschew the
conscientious and caring   that what they do, at their   myths about English
teachers feel bewildered   best, is more likely to pro- 185 teaching that inevitably you
150 by the constant media duce youngsters who will   will be exposed to and
attacks on them. They   'be able to participate   instead seek evidence of
know that what they are 170 effectively in a democracy' what is really happening;
helping their pupils to   (to quote the Kingman   and second, that you
achieve is way beyond   Report) than prodding 190   refuse the easy option of
155 what you or I were   them through the sorts of   blaming teachers of English
expected to achieve at a   decontextualised exercises   for the failings of the nation
similar age. They know that 175 in grammar and spelling and instead find words of
they are helping their   and reading that you and I   praise for what they are
pupils to become truly skil- passed through and forgot. 195 enabling their pupils to
achieve.

BOB BIBBY, *English*, November, 1990

2   Read the following article carefully and answer the questions on it.

   a   Briefly explain the 'two incidents' referred to in paragraph 5, and
       show why the writer considers them to be of 'the utmost relevance'.
       (8 marks)

   b   Examine the writer's claim that 'in modern society, paintings
       investigate, as nothing else but literature and religion can, the great
       questions of suffering, hope, love, death and redemption' (lines
       134–40). Show the ways in which you personally feel that literature
       can 'investigate' the 'great questions' mentioned.   *(12 marks)*

   c   Explain, in your own words, the arguments which the writer puts
       forward for asserting that 'Individuals, like nations, need to
       contemplate Piero and Rubens' (lines 141–3).   *(6 marks)*

   d   To what extent do you find the writer's arguments against
       introducing admission charges for public art galleries in Britain
       convincing? You should consider the methods by which he attempts
       to convince you.   *(10 marks)*

   e   Give a brief evaluation of the style of the article, concentrating on the
       use of language.   *(8 marks)*

   f   Explain what you understand by the quotation from Lord Clark in
       the final paragraph, and say why you feel that the author concluded
       his article with this quotation.   *(6 marks)*
       (50 marks total)

Charge that would be self-defeating

Neil MacGregor, director of the National Gallery, opposes any financial barriers between the public and its treasury of pictures

In the spring of of 1918, at one of the bleaker moments of the First World War, the government
5 resolved to make a special grant for the British nation. This allocation of extraordinary funds was voted not for
10 munitions or food, which were indisputably in short supply, but for paintings, to enable the Trustees of the National
15 Gallery to bid in Paris at the great sale held in March of that year of the pictures owned by Degas. With these
20 funds, the Trustees acquired for the nation Delacroix's portrait of Baron Schwiter, three works by Ingres, a
25 Gauguin still-life and the monumental fragments of Manet's *Execution of the Emperor Maximilian.*

Twenty-three years
30 later, in March 1941, when the United States was preparing to intervene in the Second World War, President
35 Roosevelt accepted, on behalf of the American people, the National Gallery of Art in Washington, given by Mr
40 Andrew Mellon, enriched by the gifts of Messrs Kress and Widener, and modelled in every material respect on the
45 National Gallery in London.

Like its sister institution in Trafalgar Square, the Washington Nation-
50 al Gallery was to be maintained at public expense, to present the highest achievements of Western art and to be
55 open to all free of charge: access to great art was one of the defining characteristics of a free nation.

60 In a striking phrase, President Roosevelt argued that 'great works of art have a way of breaking out of private
65 ownership into public use'. And that use, he went on, was to stand as 'symbols of the human spirit and of the
70 work the freedom of the human spirit made'.

These two incidents are, I believe, of the utmost relevance today.
75 Anglo-Saxons are not, as is often alleged, Philistines, nor have we ever been. On the contrary, the peoples of Northern
80 Europe and North America have set the standards in public access to art.

The great achievement
85 of the British Museum, the National Gallery and our other national collections has been envied and emulated abroad:
90 the complex of Smithsonian museums and art collections in the Mall in Washington is, like our public collections, a
95 tangible result of the Enlightenment ideal that every citizen should have the right of access to the highest. And that ideal is
100 today a reality not only in London and Washington, but in Glasgow and Leeds; Fort Worth, St Louis, Cleveland and
105 Malibu; Copenhagen and Berlin.

In recent years there have been critics of this achievement. They argue
110 that the cost of free galleries is too high, or that things not paid for are never fully appreciated. They would have
115 us follow the example of Paris or New York. They argue that financial conditions in the United Kingdom are now such
120 that we should abandon the tradition of two centuries, remove from the public the right of easy familiarity with their
125 paintings, and charge for entrance. The suggestions are seriously made and must be seriously considered.

130 Wartime insistence on the central place of art is of course inspiring, but it is in no sense surprising. In modern society, paint-
135 ings investigate, as

nothing else but literature and religion can, the great questions of suffering, hope, love, death and redemption. Individuals, like nations, need to contemplate Piero and Rubens for exactly the reasons they need to read Dante and Shakespeare: in joy or in distress, the unconsidered life is no life at all. Our art galleries have the crucial task of allowing people to take themselves seriously. They exist that we may not only have life, but have it abundantly.

And not just on one free day a week. Anyone who has used a gallery for respite knows the importance of even a brief visit – indeed, especially of a brief visit when the opportunity occurs. From the very foundation of the National Gallery, the significance of free entry and easy access for all was stressed. The gallery was to be situated not in a pleasant, leafy suburb (although that might have been better for the pictures than the sulphurous centre), but 'in the very gangway of London', so that all might reach it with ease. And the prime minister responsible for its foundation, that arch-Tory Lord Liverpool, was from the beginning insistent that even babes in arms should be allowed in; for if babes were excluded, so would

be all parents without servants to tend them.

I find it hard to believe that the need for access to beauty in daily life is less now than it was 170 years ago. During that time, around 1,300 of the National Gallery's paintings have been given to the nation, while the other 700 or so have been bought for it. They were given or purchased (like those bought in 1918) on the understanding that they would be available to all, and in normal circumstances all are on view.

Galleries exist, as Roosevelt said, for public use. Each person uses them in his or her own way, but to use a gallery, you must visit it. If we reduce the number of visitors by 40 per cent (and the evidence from art museums suggests that this would be the minimum effect of introducing a charge of any sort), then we reduce by the same proportion the use the public makes of its collections.

The value of a visit to a museum or gallery is, of course, unquantifiable. We cannot know how many lives have been affected, or in what degree, by contact with great paintings. What we can quantify is the number of people who use the gallery, and that has now climbed to well over three million a year: to accommodate and serve them better, we are

opening the Sainsbury Wing in 1991. What they gain from their visit only they know, but the numbers, and the numbers of those who return, suggest it is something of great value.

We should be proud to have led the world in the tradition of free museums and galleries.

The economic aspects of this question are peripheral. Since 1824, the National Gallery has been outstandingly fortunate in its friends, and never more so than in the last five years. Charging for admission is, nonetheless, always an option to be considered, given the huge sums required to put the building to rights or to buy paintings worthy of the collection.

At best the National Gallery might raise a net £500,000 a year from entrance charges. We already earn nearly twice that much each year from our shop (the proceeds of which recently bought the Caspar David Friedrich 'Winter Landscape'), and gifts to the gallery in cash and in kind exceeded £5 million last year. Customers in the shop are visitors to the gallery, and their numbers would dwindle if they were made to pay for entrance.

There can be no doubt that benefactors want their pictures to be seen and enjoyed by as many people as possible. In the same way, our sponsors would like as many as possible to enjoy the fruits of their sponsorship. If shop receipts, gifts and sponsorship are jeopardized, the net gain – £500,000 at the outside – is likely to be considerably less than we shall lose.

Even so £500,000 represents less than 5 per cent of our annual expenditure. Of course, the National Gallery must do what it can to raise money, but all our experience suggests that the money can be raised in ways that do not keep the public from their pictures.

Disraeli once remarked that it is private life that governs the world. This argument concerns free access to one of the most important things in private life. One of my predecessors at the National Gallery, Lord Clark, memorably observed: 'You ask me what is the purpose of art? I can only reply, what is the purpose of love?'

NEIL MACGREGOR, *The Times*, December 1989

3 The following passage is part of a review, published in the *Times Literary Supplement* in 1965, of Edith Sitwell's autobiography. Read it carefully and answer the questions below, as far as possible in your own words.

a What evidence can you find of Dame Edith's having been 'vicious'? *(6 marks)*

b What other different aspects of Dame Edith's personality does the reviewer reveal? *(10 marks)*

c Providing evidence from the tone of the passage, show what the reviewer's evaluation is of:

(i) *Taken Care Of;*
(ii) Dame Edith herself. *(12 marks)*

d Say in your own words what, according to the passage, are the 'two characteristics of an aristocrat'. (line 53) *(4 marks)*

e Comment on and evaluate the effectiveness of the reviewer's prose style, looking carefully at the use of language, register and syntax of the review. *(10 marks)*

f To what extent do you agree that a good critic need not be 'fair and balanced' (line 48)? Give reasons for your opinion. *(8 marks)*

Edith Sitwell

Taken Care Of

Dame Edith Sitwell's posthumous short autobiography, brisk, digressive, written very much in a speaking style, might be considered as a kind of last rally against a certain kind of critic she had long been at war with. There is nothing in the tone of this scrappy and lively and gossipy book, written though it was with a swollen hand and in conditions of physical pain, that suggests the slightly forced solemnities and the formal and not wholly sincere reconciliations of a death-bed. There is rather eldritch laughter, cackles of wild gaiety. There is no reconsideration of claims, recantation of attacks, or, indeed, failure of loyalties. There is a fine rashness and simplicity about the book; one thinks of some grand ship of the line going down in flames, but with its flags still flying, and its deck-guns firing to the last. Even the ranks of *Scrutiny*, perhaps, could scarce forbear to cheer. To use a distinction Miss Pamela Hansford Johnson has made about her, the paying off of old scores here is perhaps vicious (like a cat that scratches when its fur is stroked the wrong way) but not spiteful. Dame Edith could not hate people. Those who attacked her or bored her also made her laugh; and she conveys her helpless amusement, her sense of funniness, even where she cannot convey where exactly, for her, the joke lies.

A writer in these columns, for instance, said about another very distinguished woman poet, one at the opposite pole from Dame Edith in that this other woman poet is noted not for her ornateness but for her transparency of diction: 'The frailty of these poems is their distinction. At their very best, they seem to be just on the verge of being not there at all.' One could perhaps think of happier ways of phrasing a sound critical perception. Dame Edith pins this unfortunate reviewer to her page and then relates how she remembers the poet in question (with a tactfulness towards her own sex she does not name her, but it was in fact Miss Kathleen Raine) saying to her: 'The mind is a vortex.' So, to be sure, the mind is. But Dame Edith then quoted a wonderful piece from Dickens:

'Mind and matter,' said the lady with the wig, 'glide swift into the vortex of immensity. Howls the sublime and softly sleeps the calm ideal in the whispering chambers of imagination. To hear it, sweet it is. But then, out laughs the stern philosopher, and saith to the Grotesque "What ho! Arrest for me that agency. Go bring it here!" And so the vision fadeth.'

This is shockingly unfair but both Miss Raine and her reviewer would have to admit that it is extremely funny.

Dame Edith was not good at abstract argument; but she was wonderfully good at detecting possible false notes and at bringing out the ludicrous side of persons or attitudes of which she disapproved. A passage about Dr Leavis, similarly, is introduced with surprising effectiveness by a quotation from Plato; and the passage ends with some quotations from Dr Leavis's famous chapter on Milton, and with some lines from *Paradise Lost* analysed by him. Dame Edith's comment is, 'It is sad to see Milton's great lines bobbing up and down in the sandy desert of Dr Leavis's mind with the grace of a fleet of weary camels.' Again, this is strikingly unfair; but for visual aptness and grotesque humour, for

45   the quality which in poetry Dr Leavis himself calls 'enactment', it could hardly be
bettered . . .

    The house of criticism has many mansions and, in heaven, Dame Edith will
perhaps share one with Swinburne and Landor. None of these three critics is
fair and balanced, each has a taste which is in some degree narrow and

50   eccentric. Each can praise memorably, and attack with humorous fury. Each also
is a performer, what Wyndham Lewis, one of Dame Edith's other targets here,
called a 'personal-appearance artist'.

    Dame Edith combined two characteristics of the aristocrat, a frank delight in
personal display, and a certain fundamental reticence. She does not go in detail

55   in this book, for instance, into the unhappiness of her childhood or into her
conversion to full Christian belief. She says little about her deep personal
affection for her brothers. She disliked the middle-class habit of what may,
perhaps, most aptly be called 'unbosoming'. Thus, having described the
appearance and manners of D. H. Lawrence vividly and with sympathy, she

60   adds tartly:

> Though courteous and amiable, he was determined to impress us that he was a
> son of toil (that was the great romance, apart from his marriage with Mrs
> Lawrence, in his life) and he seemed to be trying to make us uncomfortable by
> references to the contrast between our childhood and his. But this was not our
65   > fault. Our childhood was hell, and we refused to be discomfited.

    Taken Care Of is not an elaborate, ornate, subtly composed tapestry like Sir
Osbert's autobiographies. It is abrupt, informal, tangential. Yet the very slightness of
structure and directness of attack means a lack of disguise. Here is a very strange
and rich personality, to be taken or left. The humour, the sharpness, the good heart

70   come out in this little anecdote about Dylan Thomas: 'On another occasion he
came to luncheon with me, and, as he arrived, said to me, "I am sorry to smell so
awful, Edith. It's Margate". I said, "Yes, of course, my dear boy, it's Margate".'

from the *Times Literary Supplement*, 1965

THE THIRD WORLD

6

More than half the people in the world are living in serious poverty, under-nourished, or at best malnourished, and hence prevented from having any hope of achieving their full potential. One in every three is living in absolute, abject poverty[1]: underfed and, as a consequence, lacking in vitality and highly prone to disease; ill-housed; most probably underemployed and illiterate. Many millions of people in Latin America, Asia and Africa are destitute. It is to the majority of countries in these areas that the term 'Third World' applies. Every day, on average, 15,000 people there starve to death.

The purpose of this chapter is to explore the crisis of world hunger, and perhaps provoke some discussion of tentative solutions. The passage for comprehension is a 'utopian' solution to the world crisis in general. Then follows a glimpse of individual lives of some of the world's poor. The remainder of the chapter presents the two main schools of thought on the crisis of world hunger: first, that the root of the problem is the 'population explosion', and secondly, that it lies in the unequal distribution of the world's food and resources. Each of these views will be explored largely through selections from works by two influential writers.[2]

Comprehension and comment

The passage which follows was written by the English novelist and social critic, H. G. Wells, in 1931. Entitled 'Our world in 50 years' time', it was reprinted in *The Observer* 50 years later on 28 December, 1980. Read it carefully, and answer the questions below. You are advised to spend about one and a half hours on this exercise.

1 According to the International Labour Office, quoted in Paul Harrison, *Inside the Third World*, pp. 405–6.
2 It is perhaps worth mentioning that this chapter is closely related to the one which follows, on the environmental crisis. The two chapters can be taken together, and treated at length, over two or three sessions, as a single topic: 'The World in Crisis'. Some of the essay questions and the debate suggestion at the end of Chapter 7 invite this treatment.

a Explain what Wells means when he says 'the abolition of distance . . . has made all the governments in the world misfits'. (lines 5–6)   (*4 marks*)

b Why are 'peoples' (line 17) and 'modern democracy' (line 32) in inverted commas?   (*3 marks*)

c Explain in your own words Wells' view of politicians and the nature of international politics.   (*6 marks*)

d What, according to Wells, would be needed to reverse the drift towards 'catastrophe'?   (*5 marks*)

e Explain briefly, in your own words, Wells' vision of the future of the world, if his ideas were accepted and put into practice.   (*7 marks*)

f Write an evaluation of Wells' style of writing in this passage, with particular reference to his uses of language, syntax and imagery.
     (*10 marks*)

g How persuasive have you found this piece of writing?   (*8 marks*)

h In your opinion, have recent world events tended to indicate that Wells' pessimism was justified or not?   (*7 marks*)

     (*50 marks total*)

Instead of progress there is crisis everywhere. There is no government, not even the American, which has now the manifest fixity of the 'Great Powers' of the 1880s. There is a growing scepticism whether any existing government is as necessary as it ought to be. All contemporary governments have been outgrown – physically and
5 mentally – by the needs of mankind. The abolition of distance, foretold fifty years ago, is achieved. That has made all the governments in the world misfits. Seventy odd sovereign governments, all acting independently and competitively, all jammed together by that abolition of distance, are trying to carry on the affairs of our race, which now, under the new conditions, would be far more conveniently and
10 successfully dealt with as one world business. Human life has become a world-wide thing, but governments remain cramped and partial things.
     More and more people are coming to realise this. Yet none of us knows clearly how to change over to a more comprehensive and securer way of running the world.
15   While we puzzle over the riddle, armaments go on, and the old – and now utterly stupid – tradition of malevolence between sovereign governments and their 'peoples' is maintained. International politics still consist largely of idiotic attempts on the part of these seventy-odd governments, amid which our affairs are entangled, to get the better of their rivals, to maintain a flaming prosperity within their borders
20 while restricting and injuring the welfare of all other peoples.
     The old game goes on because the world lacks the mental energy to call it off. So we are all drifting through needless and wasteful economic war towards actual

military war. Some years ago I wrote that the salvaging of civilisation was a race between education and catastrophe. Nowadays I am forced to add a qualification.

25 Catastrophe indeed travels briskly; tariffs strangle trade; gold – the life blood of trade – is being hoarded against some fresh day of reckoning; armaments increase; the friction between states intensifies. The new air war is being prepared. The new gas war is being prepared. But education has not even started yet. There is no race. It looks like a walk-over for catastrophe.

30   In the schools of Britain, America, France, Germany, Italy, Japan today the school-teachers are still doing the fundamental work of mental armament. There are few exceptions. And the hundreds of millions of 'modern democracy' show as much ability to protect their minds from subjugation and arrest the advancing disaster, which will enslave, torture, mutilate, and destroy the greater proportion of them, as

35 a trainload of hogs bound for Chicago.

Gladly would the prophet prophesy pleasant things. But his duty is to tell what he sees. He sees a world still firmly controlled by soldiers, patriots, usurers, and financial adventurers; a world surrendered to suspicion and hatred, losing what is left of its private liberties very rapidly, blundering toward bitter class conflicts, and

40 preparing for new wars.

The economic machine is stalling in every country in the world. The decline is going on under our eye. Production is diminishing, trade is declining; presently we shall find even our present educational and hygiene services too costly for our existing methods of payment. Few people realise yet how flimsy are the liberties

45 and securities, the plenty and the leisure, we still enjoy.

The prophet must say what he sees. It is as if I was watching a dark curtain fall steadily, fold after fold, across the bright spectacle of hope with which the century dawned. The way toward a great world state of power, freedom, and general happiness is still plainly open to mankind. We have been brought to the very

50 borders of the Promised Land of Progress. And the amount of visible human determination to cross those borders and escape from the age-long sequences of quarrelling, futile insufficiency, wars, and wasted generations that fill the blood-stained pages of history is contemptible.

There is no inevitability in the approaching catastrophe. I confess I see no signs

55 whatever of any such awakening as might save us, but who can tell what may be happening among the young, among the intelligent and wilful, outside one's range. It would need nothing superhuman to avert the decline. We are not being beaten in an honourable struggle; we are loitering and rotting down to disaster. A few thousand resolute spirits, the tithe of a tithe of the misdirected heroism that went

60 to waste in the Great War, a few hundred million dollars for a world campaign for the new order, might still turn the destinies of mankind right round toward a new life for our race.

It needs only that the governments of the United States, Britain, France, Germany, and Russia should get together in order to set up an effective control of

65 currency, credit, production, and distribution; that is to say, an effective 'dictatorship of prosperity' for the whole world.

The other sixty-odd states would have to join in or accommodate themselves to the overruling decisions of these major powers. It is as simple a business as that, which our presidents, potentates, statesmen, kings of finance, and so forth, do not
70 even realise they could carry through, with human decay and disaster plain before them!

They just fumble along. The bands play and we 'troop the colours'. The party men twaddle about debts and security. They cant patriotism. They love their countries so that they would rather see them starve than let them cooperate with
75 nasty foreigners. They do their best to reassure the world – and do, it seems, succeed in reassuring the world – that this skimped, anxious, dangerous life we lead is the best that can be done for us. These rulers and leaders and statesmen of ours get in front of the cameras at every possible opportunity to put their fatuous selves on record, while Death, the Ultimate Creditor, and Collapse, the Final Stabiliser,
80 add up their inexorable accounts.

But given that wave of sanity, that sudden miraculous resolve to stop this foolery, and what sort of world might we not have before another half century has passed?

Everyone alive might be by then a citizen of the whole world. All of us would then be free to go where we would about this fascinating and sometimes so lovely
85 planet, which would have become our own. For most of our lives we should be released from toil. All the necessities of the human population – food, abundant transport, clean, fresh, and beautiful housing and furniture, adequate health services, education, social security – could be supplied now under modern conditions by something between twelve and twenty years of not too arduous
90 work on the part of everyone. The town, the countryside would be undergoing constant revision and improvement: the world city would be constantly more gracious and pleasant; the world garden constantly more beautiful. The layout of industry could be as exciting as a game.

These are not the assertions of an 'imaginative writer'; they are possibilities
95 proved up to the hilt by economists and by the scientific examination of these matters. Some fifteen or twenty years of growth, education, and preparation there would have to be for everyone, and the rest of life would be free for creative work, for graceful living, for movement and experience.

There is no need why any human being now should be underfed or ill-clad, badly
100 housed or sickly. The whole world could be run as one concern and yield a universal well-being.

And it is no good mincing matters when it comes to saying why we have not this universal well-being at the present time. Most of our rulers and directors are, to put it plainly, narrow-minded, self-centred, mentally indolent, pompous, and
105 pretentious creatures of the past; and we others are fools enough to tolerate their mismanagement. These ruling and controlling people have got enough for themselves, they stick to the controls like barnacles, they live in relative comfort and immense dignity, chiefly engaged in the defence of their own conceit, and the mass of us lacks the spirit, will, and understanding to call them to account.
110 A thousand million human beings are leading lives of want, limitation, humiliation,

and toil, scores of millions are in immediate danger of the futile tortures of war, and these dull, self-protective folk in control of things do nothing of what they might do and pose for our respect and admiration with infinite self-complacency.

But in another 50 years after that renascence – if, after all, it should occur – things
115 will be different. For an ignorant world we shall have a soundly educated world, aware of its origins, capable of measuring and realising its possibilities, and controlling its destinies.

Every human being born into that world of plenty will learn from the beginning of the varied loveliness of the life before it, and of the expanding drama of human
120 achievement in which it has to play its part. Its distinctive gifts will be developed. It will be taught another history than that of kings and conquerors and armies. It will do its fair and definite share in the productive or other necessary service of mankind, and for the rest it will be released to accomplish whatever possibilities it has of innovation, happiness, and interesting living.
125 That wide fine life is within reach of mankind; it is there for the taking. But mankind is not taking it. The curtain is falling. When the Promised Land is cut off forever, 'Homo sapiens' will be readily convinced there never was a Promised Land. The last thing we human beings will produce is concerted effort; only under the spur of greed or panic do we produce that. We shake our heads sagely at the
130 'dreamers'. As long as possible we will go on living the close, ignoble lives of thieves, bullies, and drudges to which we are accustomed. We will snuffle our satisfaction that we are not in any 'fantastic Utopia'.

And when presently the rifles are put into our hands again, we shall kill. The whips will be behind us and the 'enemy' in front. The Old History will go on
135 because we had not the vigour to accept the new.

H. G. WELLS

Themes for discussion

Some of the issues raised by H. G. Wells in this passage are perhaps of sufficient importance to warrant fuller discussion and analysis. Three of these issues are selected here. The first is of particular relevance to the world of the late 20th century, the second has been relevant since the dawn of mankind, and the third is of at least academic relevance to you, as a student.

1 The world economy
Is Wells' idea of a world government, or a 'dictatorship of prosperity', possible, or desirable? What factors continue to prevent it from happening?

Which countries are currently most in debt to the west? What are they, and the creditor nations, doing about it?

What is the IMF, and what does it do to help bring about world prosperity?

75

2 War

Wells talks about the 'now utterly stupid tradition of malevolence' between nations. Is war always 'utterly stupid', or are some wars essential?

Are there any circumstances in which it is right to be a conscientious objector?

What international wars are being fought at the moment? What civil wars are being fought in which other nations have significant military or economic involvement?

For what reasons were wars generally fought in the past? Are the motives of warring nations today fundamentally different, on the whole?

3 Worldwide education

In which sense can it be argued that only 'education' can save the world from 'catastrophe', as Wells says?

How many people in the world are still illiterate? How might their lives be improved if they became literate? Is literacy always desirable?

Does it make any real difference to you if you read essays and works of fiction by creative writers such as H. G. Wells, or is literature simply 'art for art's sake'?

Preparing for discussion

Discussion, if it is to be more than a matter of 'sounding off' ideas, or 'letting off steam', needs to be informed. A fully effective discussion of some of the issues raised above will probably require at least some of the students in the class to do more than merely read the H. G. Wells passage. Here are some suggestions for preparing for such a discussion:

1 Read through the discussion questions and think about them before the class.

2 Look out for and collect items from newspapers and magazines on the discussion topics.

3 Be prepared to introduce this material into the class discussion.

4 In the case of very specific questions, such as the role of the IMF, and the situation of debtor and creditor nations, interested students, with advance warning of the discussion, should be prepared to undertake private research, and to report their findings to the class when the discussion takes place. It should be possible to find passages from books, magazines and newspapers, or to jot down details from television and radio programmes, which are relevant to the issue which they are researching. Students who specialise in or have studied other disciplines

than English – economics, history and sociology in the case of the three themes suggested above – should be in a particularly strong position to provide factual information to help with the discussions.

Creative essay

Write an essay of about 450 words on one of the following titles:

a   What do you imagine the world will be like 50 years from now?

b   Write the essay on 'the condition of humanity' which H. G. Wells might have written if he had been alive today.

Life in the Third World

For millions of Third World families, even when the husband has a regular income, life can be a perpetual struggle to preserve a degree of dignity and the semblance of a decent, happy life. In the following extract, Domitila Barrios de Chungara, the wife of a tin miner in Bolivia, describes her family's circumstances:

Our houses are very small, that is, we have a little room measuring four by five or six metres. That little room has to be living room, dining room, pantry, and bedroom. In some houses there are two little rooms, and one of them is the kitchen; they also have a little corridor. This is what the company housing is like, only the four walls, without any water or sanitary installations. And that's how we have to live, with our children, all crowded together. In my case, we set up three beds in the room; that's all that will fit. That's where my seven children sleep, that's where they do their homework, that's where we eat, that's where the kids play. In the little back room I have a table and a bed where I sleep with my husband. The few things we have just have to be piled one on top of the other, or hung from the ceiling, in the corridor. And the babies, well, some of them have to sleep in the beds and some of them under the beds. Wherever . . .

For some hours during the day and all through the night we have electric light in the camp which the company gives us.

We also have drinking water. But not in the houses. In the neighbourhoods there are public water pumps. You have to line up to get water.

So you see, we don't have too many comforts. For example, we don't have a bath in the house. Of course, there are public baths, but there are ten to 12 showers for everyone, for so many people, and these showers are for the whole camp. So the showers are open on alternate days; one day for the women and one day for the men. The showers only work when there's oil. Because the water is heated by oil.

Not only that, but there are only sanitary facilities, latrines, in the houses of the company's technical personnel. There aren't in the workers' houses. There are public latrines but only about ten of them, for a whole neighbourhood. For a whole neighbourhood! They get dirty very fast and there's no running water. In the mornings the company workers assigned to the job clean them; but afterward, all day long they're very dirty. And if there's no water, they're dirty for several days. Even so, we have to use them. Just like they are.

There are plenty of problems with water, especially in the non-company villages. They suffer there more than we do. They have to stand in long lines. They have to come from very far away to get their water. And in these villages they don't have electric light like us. Their life is really hard.

DOMITILA BARRIOS DE CHUNGARA

For the landless peasant's family the struggle is often a hopeless one. Here the English journalist and writer Paul Harrison illustrates the cycles of despair through which such people travel. The passage describes a family he met in Brazil:

Francisco's mother Fatima is small for her age. She is visibly weak, distant, yet easily irritated by the children. Years of pregnancy and menstruation, along with an iron-poor diet of maize, have made her chronically anaemic. Her husband Jaime is a landless labourer, with a low, erratic income barely enough to keep them all alive and clothed. No one eats enough, and when there's not enough to go round Fatima goes without, even when she's pregnant. And that is frequently, as the couple use no form of contraception. They have had ten children, six of whom survived to adulthood.

Fatima went through several periods of undernourishment while Francisco was in her womb. There were times when Jaime could not get regular work and everyone went hungry. Fatima also had several attacks of stress and anxiety when Jaime beat her. Francisco probably suffered his first bout of growth retardation, both mental and physical, before he even saw the light of day.

He was born underweight, and his brain was already smaller than normal size. For the first few months he was breast-fed and suffered few infections, as he was partly protected by the antibodies in his mother's milk. Then he was weaned onto thin gruels and soups, taken off the breast and put onto tinned evaporated milk, thinned down with polluted water from the well. His diet, in itself, was inadequate. Then he started to get more and more infections, fever, bronchitis, measles and regular bouts of gastro-enteritis. With well-fed children these pass within a few days, but in his case they went on for weeks and sometimes a month or more. In these periods he could tolerate no milk and few solids, and so was given weak broths, tea or sugar water. By now he was 25 per cent underweight. Because of poor nutrition, he was even more susceptible to infection, and each time he was ill, he lost his appetite and ate even less. Then he got bronchitis which developed into pneumonia.

But Fatima borrowed money off a relative, went to town and got antibiotics for him.

So he survived. But malnutrition made him withdrawn and apathetic. His mother got no reward for playing with him, so he received little of the stimulation his brain needed to develop properly. As he grew older, infections grew less frequent, but by the time he went to school, aged eight, he was already a year behind normal physical development and two years behind mentally. The school, in any case, was a poor one, with only three classes, no equipment, and a poorly qualified teacher. As Francisco was continually worried about whether and what he was going to eat that day, he was distracted, unable to concentrate, and seemed to show little interest in schoolwork. The teacher confirmed that he was a slow learner, and could not seem to get the hang of maths or reading and writing. As the family was poor, they did not want to keep him on at school. He was doing so badly anyway that there seemed no point. He did a year, then was away for three years helping an uncle who had a farm, then did another year, then left for good, barely able to read or write more than a few letters. He soon forgot what little he had learned. So, like his father, he began tramping round the local ranches asking for work. Without any educational qualifications or skills, that was all he could ever hope for. And because so many were in the same boat, pay was low. When he was twenty-two he married a local girl, Graciela, aged only fifteen. She too had been undernourished and was illiterate. She soon became pregnant and had to feed another organism inside her before she herself had fully developed. Graciela had heard about family planning from a friend, but Francisco would not let her use it and anyway she was not sure she wanted to. So by the age of only twenty-five, Graciela already had five children and had lost two. The children had every prospect of growing up much as Francisco and Graciela did, overpopulating, underfed, in poor health and illiterate.

PAUL HARRISON

At the very bottom of the pile are the destitute. Paul Harrison met many people without work or hope in the Indian city of Calcutta. He describes some of them:

And there are the street dwellers . . .

The street dwellers are variously estimated to number anything from 40,000 to 200,000. You see them curled up on a straw mat or a piece of cardboard by the odd aluminium pot, along the staid colonial shopping arcades, under the subways, camped on a roundabout by the gigantic pylons of Howra bridge. A random line of them under a high wall by the riverside warehouses of Strand Road: a family of three living in a tiny shelter of torn khaki canvas slung over bamboo poles, not more than four feet square. A woman dreaming on her charpoy string bed, baby at her side with a tattered shirt over its face, pots, pans and boxes stuffed under the bed. A large family of eight under an awning, their tea cups neatly hanging from a string tacked to the wall. All this in full gaze of passers-by and a noisy flow of traffic. Street life is, by definition, a life lived in public.

Each of these faces hides a personal disaster: a fifteen-year-old boy whose parents died of cholera four years earlier. His uncles neglected him so he left his home village for Calcutta, and he earns two rupees a day collecting rags and scrap paper. A twenty-five-year-old woman whose husband deserted her, so she had to move out of their bustee room. Now she lives on the pavement near the railway station, working as a domestic servant in the daytime and at night as a prostitute. A widow of forty with five children: when her husband died she couldn't work the family smallholding and bring up the children, so she fell into debt and had to pay it off by selling house and land. Now she lives on a platform at Ballygunge railway station where she has to pay protection money to thugs to stop them driving her away. She supplements her meagre servant's pay by begging.   PAUL HARRISON

Suggestion for writing

Write a story, or a brief biography, about the life of either the 15-year-old boy or the 25-year-old woman in Calcutta referred to above.

The population explosion

Two writers who argue that the population explosion is the fundamental problem to be tackled, before world hunger and want can be eased, are the American environmentalists, Paul Erhlich and Gordon Rattray Taylor. These extracts are taken from Ehrlich's *The Population Bomb*, published in 1968, and Taylor's *The Doomsday Book*, published in 1972. Despite the passage of two decades, the situation these writers describe has remained fundamentally the same.

What the 'population explosion' means in simple terms is that the world's population is expanding at a rate vastly greater than at any previous period in human history and at a faster rate than resources and living space are likely to expand.

Recent projections of world population growth are contained in *Our Common Future: The World Commission on Environment and Development*, published in 1987:

Our human world of five billion must make room in a finite environment for another human world. The population could stabilize at between eight billion and 14 billion sometime next century, according to UN projections. More than 90 per cent of the increase will occur in the poorest countries, and 90 per cent of that growth in already bursting cities.

What this means in human terms is graphically suggested by Ehrlich on the front cover of the paperback edition of *The Population Bomb*:

'While you are reading these words four people will have died of starvation. Most of them children.'

Rich and poor in Latin America.

The principal reason for the explosion in world population is the vast increase in the proportion of people surviving infancy:

Around 1800, when the standard of living in what are today the DCs (Developed Countries) was dramatically increasing due to industrialisation, population growth really began to accelerate. The development of medical science was the straw that broke the camel's back. While lowering death rates in the DCs were due in part to other factors, there is no question that 'instant death control', exported by the DCs, has been responsible for the drastic lowering of death rates in the UDCs.[3] Medical science, with its efficient public health programmes, has been able to depress the death rate with astonishing rapidity and at the same time drastically increase the birth rate.

PAUL EHRLICH

The fact that so many more people are surviving infancy results in an increasing proportion being at or near child-rearing age, which in itself accelerates the 'population explosion'.
  It is already the case that in the under-developed world, about half the population is under 15 years of age.

GORDON RATTRAY TAYLOR

A rapidly expanding population in the 'Third World' has many repercussions in addition to malnourishment and starvation amongst the poor:

More people with more technology spells more pollution, more environmental distortion and less privacy. Much of the damage will come from attempts which will necessarily be made to feed the ever-increasing number of mouths, and to house their owners. The crash of falling timber, as forests are felled, will be echoed by the thunder of explosives, as canals and harbours are blasted into existence.
  It is obvious that this process cannot continue for ever: when will the poison-point come? Some maintain the world could support 15,000 million people, one or two have put the figure as high as 30,000 million. The earlier figure could come in the lifetime of those now living, so the question is not an academic one.

GORDON RATTRAY TAYLOR

Think what it means for the population of a country to double in 25 years. In order just to keep living standards at the present inadequate level, the food available for the people must be doubled. Every structure and road must be duplicated. The amount of power must be doubled. The capacity of the transport system must be doubled. The number of trained doctors, nurses, teachers and administrators must be doubled. This would be a fantastically difficult job, say, even in the United States – a rich country with a fine agricultural system, immense industries, and rich natural resources. Think of what it means to a country with none of these.   PAUL EHRLICH

3 Under Developed Countries, referred to later in this chapter as 'developing countries.'

The problems of providing schools and teachers become immense . . . In some African countries, already, despite unprecedented programmes of school-building, the percentage of children receiving education is falling: children are born faster than schools can be put up to receive them.   GORDON RATTRAY TAYLOR

In developing countries, cities are growing at a terrifying rate . . . The extreme instance of city growth is expected to be Calcutta.[4] . . . Already it is in a state of social disorganisation. The Metropolitan Planning Commission says that it sees 'no prospect' of housing the population over the next 25 years. At the moment, open-sided sheds are being built to provide some sort of shelter. Twenty or thirty people share a single cold tap. Sewage runs in open gutters in the streets, and at times of river-flood may be washed anywhere. People wash their clothes and themselves in the polluted water. Other parts of the city, of course, are highly civilised – but the disorganised sector is growing. . . .

New York, with a much longer experience, finds it hard enough to function at 12 million. Cities like Calcutta can hardly avoid becoming jungles, in which crime cannot be controlled, in which health standards cannot be maintained and in which people die on the pavement without the fact even being remarked . . .[5]

In short, it seems certain that the mushrooming cities of the immediate future will be plagued by crime and mental disturbance of various kinds.

GORDON RATTRAY TAYLOR

Whilst population growth in developed countries like Britain has slowed to zero with the help of easily available birth control methods, the same methods in countries like India have had negligible effects, despite the fact that India has had an official birth control programme since 1952. The main reason is poverty:

Large families are a response to high death-rates in infancy and childhood. In many oriental countries the figure is 10 or 12 children born, of whom formerly only 2 or 3 would survive. Now that death rates have been cut dramatically, people begin to attempt to limit their families, but not by the full amount required. Custom is important, and a family of 2 seems ridiculous in a culture geared to 12. Experience shows that it takes several generations for people to make a full response. The first generation cuts back from 10 to 7 or 8; the next to 5 or 6 and so on. But the period we are looking at is little more than one generation . . .

Unfortunately, it is not the case that, when people are poor, they try to restrict the family to a size they can afford. Sometimes they hope their position will improve; sometimes they see their children as an asset, able to work in the fields or

4 At the beginning of the 1990s the city with the fastest growth was Mexico City: in 1950 its population was 3.05 million; by 1982 it was at 16.0 million, and the UN projection for 2000 is 26.3 million. (Figures taken from *Our Common Future: The World Commission on Environment and Development*, 1987.)

5 The work of Mother Teresa of Calcutta has alerted the world to the extent of the breakdown of normal human life in this city at the beginning of the 1990s.

support them when they are old. There is thus little hope that the provision of contraception will, of itself, make much impact. The prime need is to convince people that *two* is the best family size. GORDON RATTRAY TAYLOR

Writers such as Ehrlich and Taylor see hope only in controlling the world's birth-rate.

Basically, then, there are only two kinds of solution to the population problem. One is a 'birth-rate solution', in which we find ways to lower the birth-rate. The other is a 'death-rate solution', in which ways to raise the death-rate – war, famine, pestilence – *find us* . . .

Men do not seem to be able to focus emotionally on distant or long-term events. Immediacy seems to be necessary to elicit 'selfless' responses. Few Americans could sit in the same room with a child and watch it starve to death. But the death of several million children this year from starvation is a distant, impersonal, hard-to-grasp event. You will note that I put quotes around 'selfish' and 'selfless'. The words describe the behaviour only out of context. The 'selfless' actions necessary to aid the rest of the world and stabilise the population are the only hope for survival. The 'selfish' ones work only towards destruction . . .

Remember, above all, that more than half of the world is in misery now. That alone should be enough to galvanise us into action, regardless of the exact dimensions of the future disaster now staring 'Homo Sapiens' in the face.

PAUL EHRLICH

The situation described in these extracts has shown little sign of improvement over the past quarter of a century.

In 1990, Paul Ehrlich, together with his wife Anne, published a follow-up to *The Population Bomb* called *The Population Explosion*. This book analyses the ways in which the picture presented in 1968 has changed. Here are some extracts.

When *The Population Bomb* was written, we and our colleagues were enormously worried about the course that humanity was on. Yet it is sobering to recall that the book appeared *before* depletion of the ozone layer had been discovered, *before* acid precipitation had been recognized as a major problem, *before* the current rate of tropical-forest destruction had been achieved, let alone recognized, *before* the true dimensions of the extinction crisis had been perceived, *before* most of the scientific community had recognized the possibility of a nuclear winter, and *before* the AIDS epidemic.

The size of the human population is now 5.3 billion, and still climbing. In the six seconds it takes you to read this sentence, 18 more people will be added. Each hour there are 11,000 more mouths to feed: each year, more than 95 million. Yet the world has hundreds of billions *fewer* tons of topsoil and hundreds of trillions *fewer* gallons of groundwater with which to grow food crops than it had in 1968.

India suffered greatly from hunger in the early 1970s. In 1987, environmental analyst R. N. Roy of the Catalyst Group in Madras described the outlook succinctly: 'With two-thirds of India's land threatened by erosion, water shortages and salinity, and with the added threat of pollution and increasing urban industrial demand, the country appears to be facing a catastrophic problem in the 1990s, if not earlier.' And don't forget: with an annual population growth rate of 2.2 per cent, India must somehow feed an additional 16 million people each year.

Since 1968, food production per person in Africa south of the Sahara has declined by some 20 per cent. Tropical African nations are too poor and debt-burdened to make up for all of the deficit with imports, and far too little food has been made available for donation. The result has been a continuous erosion of the nutritional status of Africans. Remarkably little has been accomplished in population control in the 20 years since *The Population Bomb* appeared. Global population growth has slowed a little, but nearly all of that slowdown is due to fertility reductions in two principal regions: China and the industrialized nations, especially the West. A few other developing nations have achieved significant fertility declines, but most are growing as rapidly as before.

Discussion suggestion

Assuming that the 'population explosion' *is* a serious world problem, you might discuss how the 'birth-rate solution' could be made more effective. You could consider such options as:

- wider early education about birth control and family limitation;
- free distribution of the pill or other birth-control devices, and education in their use;
- free abortion on demand;
- financial or other penalties for families which have more than, say, two, children;
- government encouragement or enforcement of late marriage;
- compulsory sterilisation.

Some of these suggestions may seem grotesque, but all have been tried out somewhere in the world. Whether you find them acceptable or offensive, you should be able to explain why. Wide reading by one or more selected students will, of course, assist the discussion.

Note-taking

As well as jotting down interesting points brought up in class discussion, it can be a useful exercise to make summary notes of relevant articles and extracts which you have read. It is much easier to remember information and ideas if you have made notes on them.

As a preliminary exercise in note-taking, you could try listing, in note-form, the main general points covered in the preceeding section (**The Population Explosion**) under the following five headings:

Meaning   Causes   Effects
Reasons for failure of policies   Future prospects

Distribution of resources

Over the past decade, a shift of emphasis in the analysis of world poverty has been noticeable. Many writers on population and global politics tend now to stress the unequal distribution of wealth as much as overpopulation as the principal cause of starvation and malnourishment.

This alternative analysis of world poverty is again represented by extracts from two books by influential writers: *How the Other Half Dies*, by the American writer, Susan George, published in 1976, and *The Creation of World Poverty*, by the British writer, Teresa Hayter, published in 1981.

Rich and poor: the global situation

The extent of world poverty and destitution today, and the contrast between rich and poor countries, is suggested by Teresa Hayter:

Wage rates in underdeveloped countries are often one-twentieth to one-thirtieth of those in the richer countries, for the same type of work . . .

Today the World Bank says that, 'excluding the centrally planned economies', there are about 800 million people, or almost 40 per cent of the population of the so-called developing countries, who live in 'absolute poverty': 'a condition of life so characterised by malnutrition, illiteracy and disease as to be beneath any reasonable definition of human decency'. In some countries one child in four dies before the age of five. Millions of people live in houses or huts made of corrugated tin, cardboard boxes and other 'impermanent' materials. They have no running water and no toilets. Electricity is a luxury. Health services are rarely within walking distance, and have to be paid for. Primary education may be available and free, but often children are needed to work. There is generally no social security or unemployment pay, and many people, some 300 million, according to the ILO (International Labour Organisation), are without any kind of employment.

TERESA HAYTER

Susan George also quotes from a statement by a representative of the World Bank (the major lending organisation):

World Bank figures show that 'on average the one billion people in the countries with per capita incomes below $200 consume only about 1 per cent as much energy per capita as the citizens of the United States'. The Bank's Mr McNamara

also hopes that 'once the people of the United States understand that they, with 6 per cent of the world's population, consume about 35 per cent of the world's total resources, and yet in terms of economic assistance as a percentage of GNP rank 14th among the 16 developed nations . . . [they will not] turn away in cynicism and indifference'.
SUSAN GEORGE

The moral implications of this are starkly suggested by Rene Dumont, quoted by George:

'The rich white man, with his overconsumption of meat and his lack of generosity for poor people, behaves like a veritable cannibal – an indirect cannibal. By consuming meat, which wastes the grain that could have saved them, last year we ate the children of the Sahel, Ethiopia and Bangladesh. And we continue to eat them this year with undiminished appetite.'[6]

Hayter sees low income, more than overpopulation, as the principal cause of destitution in the countryside, in the Third World:

The most likely explanation for probably increasing impoverishment in rural areas is not to be found in population increases, but rather in an increasingly unequal distribution of income.
TERESA HAYTER

Division between developed and developing countries

It is easy, and consoling, to assume that the developed Western nations have no responsibility for the plight of the other half of humanity, that 'charity begins at home', and that it is somehow their own fault that the world's poor and destitute have to wage a bitter struggle simply to survive; that they should sort out their problems for themselves.

Writers such as George and Hayter point out, however, that the imbalance between rich and poor nations owes a great deal to the process of colonisation which began five centuries ago:

One of the results of colonial policy in dependent territories seems to have been, in many cases, actually to produce hunger where it did not exist before, as self-sufficient farming gave way to cash crop production for export to the colonial nation, and local industries were deliberately held back and destroyed in the interests of the export of raw materials to and of finished products from the controlling power.
SUSAN GEORGE

As early as the 17th century, when the British began enacting the protective Navigation Acts, colonies were prohibited by law from turning to any industry which might compete with the industry of the mother country. For example, the

6 Rene Dumont, *Population and Cannibalism* (UN Development Forum).

North American colonists were forbidden to manufacture caps, hats, woollen or iron goods. They were expected to send the raw materials for these products to England to be manufactured and then to buy them back from England.

TERESA HAYTER

Hayter quotes from a report by Lord Cromer, governor of Egypt from 1883 to 1907, which provides a startling illustration of the way in which colonialism benefited the ruling country to the detriment of the ruled. Explaining Britain's policy of running down Egyptian industry and forcing Egyptian industrial workers back into agriculture, Lord Cromer stated proudly, looking back on his career:

'The difference is apparent to any man whose recollections go back some ten or fifteen years. Some quarters (of Cairo) that formerly used to be veritable centres of varied industries – spinning, weaving, ribbonmaking, dyeing, tentmaking, embroidery, shoemaking, jewellery making, spice grinding, copper work, the manufacture of bottles out of animal skins, saddlery, sieve making, locksmithing in wood and metal, etc. – have shrunk considerably or vanished. Now there are coffee houses and European novelty shops where once there were prosperous workshops'.

The destructive effects of cash crop plantation are vividly illustrated by a quotation from the Latin America writer, Eduardo Galeano:

'Early chroniclers told of travelling across all of Cuba in the shade of giant palms and through forests abounding in mahogany, cedar and ebony. Cuba's precious woods may still be admired in . . . Madrid, but in Cuba the sugarcane invasion sent the best virgin forests up in smoke. In the same years it was destroying its own timberlands, Cuba became the chief purchaser of United States timber. The extensive plunder-culture of sugarcane meant not only the death of the forest but also, in the long run, the death of the island's famous fertility. With forests surrendered to the flames, erosion soon did its work on the defenceless soil and thousands of streams dried up.'[7]

Why mass poverty continues in the post-colonial era

For most of the nations of Latin America, colonial exploitation ended in the early 19th century, whilst most countries of Africa and Asia were ruled by European governments until the 1950s and 1960s. Though almost all of them are now independent, however, desperate poverty on a mass scale persists, as we have seen.

This can partly be explained by the positions in which the developing countries were left after independence. The general pattern in Third-World ex-colonies is that local élites and landowners, left behind (and often

7   Eduardo Galeano, *The Open Veins of Latin America: Five Centuries of the Pillage of a Continent.*

originally created) by the colonial country, are still in control and still largely dependent on cash crop and raw material export for their income, instead of concentrating on producing food for consumption by their own people.

Third World governments and people are thus still at the mercy of fluctuations in the worldwide market for their commodities:

The fluctuations in commodity prices can be dramatic. They are accentuated by speculation on commodity markets, many of them in London, which are of course outside the control of the underdeveloped countries. In the mid-1970s, the price paid for sugar dropped from 64 cents a pound to 6 cents a pound in 18 months.

TERESA HAYTER

The system by which the great majority of the land is owned by a small number of rich landowners makes the life of the rural poor precarious in the extreme:

In India, peasants have become deeply indebted to landowners and traders who are able to force them to sell their crops cheaply in order to obtain further credit. Such traders hoard food and sell it in times of scarcity at prices that peasants cannot afford.

A. K. Sen gives evidence to show that the famines in Ethiopia in 1973 and 1974, which were responsible for the deaths of between 50,000 and 200,000 people, were not the result of overall food shortages in Ethiopia as a whole, but of a terrible decline in the purchasing power of people in the areas affected by the famines . . .[8]

Massive unemployment and migration from impoverished rural areas into cities have become the most obvious features of current forms of underdevelopment.

TERESA HAYTER

This migration from the countryside into the cities accounts, in part, for the situation in cities like Calcutta, described earlier.

Recent changes in relations between developed and developing countries

Since the mid-1970s, the World Bank, and groups of Western politicians such as those who produced the 'Brandt Report', and the 'Bruntland Commission on the Environment', have become conscious of some of the factors outlined above, and called for a more responsible attitude from the governments of developed countries towards developing countries.

Susan George quotes Robert McNamara, former president of the World Bank, who argued that the governments of the developed countries must not only increase their aid, but also link it to land reform and redistribution in the recipient countries if it is genuinely to help the poor.

8   A. K. Sen, *Ingredients of Famine Analysis.*

'The average citizen of a developed country enjoys wealth beyond the wildest dreams of the one billion people in countries with per capita incomes under $200 . . . We must . . . give as much attention to promoting the inherent potential and productivity of the poor as is generally given to protecting the power of the privileged . . . Land reform is not exclusively about land. It is about the uses and abuses of power and the social structure through which it is exercised.'

Yet as Hayter points out, loans continue to be given regardless of whether they benefit the poor or not. She quotes the example of Brazil:

Brazil is one of the biggest recipients of World Bank loans, but its record on income distribution is one of the most notoriously bad. Between 1960 and 1977, according to Brazilian official sources, the share of national income of the poorest half of the population fell from 17 per cent to 13 per cent, while the share of the richest one per cent rose from 12 per cent to 18 per cent, or more than the poorest half receive.

TERESA HAYTER

In fact, aid is rarely given to underdeveloped countries with the aim simply of helping the poor, and with no strings attached. Hayter quotes a statement by Hubert Humphrey, who was later to become Vice-President of America, made in 1957, which puts the issue of aid with unusual frankness:

'I have heard . . . that people may become dependent on us for food. I know that was not supposed to be good news. To me, that was good news, because before people can do anything they have got to eat. And if you are looking for a way to get people to lean on you and be dependent on you, in terms of their cooperation with you, it seems to me that food dependence would be terrific.'

The developed world has recently begun to affect the economies of the underdeveloped countries in another significant way, through the operations of multinational companies which, according to Hayter, 'today control between a quarter and a third of all world production'. Increasingly, 'labour-intensive' manufacture is being located in underdeveloped countries, 'in order to take advantage of the extreme cheapness of the labour there'. Once again the benefits generally are not experienced by the poor; the profits go to the shareholders of the companies and the élites in the countries where they are operating.

A partial, short-term solution to the problems of Third-World poverty put forward by writers like George and Hayter is that of 'intermediate technology', a term invented by Ernst Schumacher, meaning small-scale, low-cost technologies which can be developed independently of Western expertise and financing, producing goods of immediate use to the local community. George feels that the governments of underdeveloped countries should make it *public policy* to seek out and produce intermediate, low-cost solutions to their problems involving maximum participation on the part of the rural poor themselves.

Conclusion

The argument of writers who consider that the redistribution of resources is a more pressing need than population control is summed up by Susan George:

So long as thoroughgoing land reform, regrouping and distribution of resources to the poorest, bottom half of the population does not take place, Third World countries can go on increasing their production till hell freezes and hunger will remain, for the production will go to those who already have plenty – to the developed world or to the wealthy in the Third World itself. Poverty and hunger walk hand in hand.

SUSAN GEORGE

The final word on the whole situation in the Third World is left to Paul Ehrlich, in *The Population Explosion*:

In short, the 'does population growth cause poverty or vice versa' argument is counterproductive if the goal is to provide everyone with a decent life. If that is the goal, then all of us should be working very hard to end both poverty and population growth, not wasting our efforts trying to determine which causes which.

PAUL EHRLICH

Written or oral comprehension

A good way to check whether you've fully understood and assimilated material you have read is to test yourself on it. You could try *briefly* answering the following questions, *without* looking at the book, either in the form of a written test, or as a series of oral questions round the class. Try to explain the ideas in your own words rather than learning parrot-fashion 'definitions'.

1   What is 'absolute poverty'?

2   List six ways in which 'absolute poverty' is revealed in practice.

3   What is the explanation given for 'increasing impoverishment in rural areas'?

4   How did 'cash crop production' help to widen the gap between rich and poor nations?

5   What generally happened to the raw materials and the industries of colonised countries?

6   How do 'fluctuations in the worldwide market' affect the economies of Third World countries?

7   What are the two main results of 'the system by which the great majority of the land is owned by small numbers of landowners'?

8   Explain the term 'strings' as applied to aid to developing countries.

9   What is the normal policy of multinational companies towards developing countries?

10   What is the meaning of the term 'intermediate technology'?

Themes for discussion

What do you imagine happens to Third World families in which the breadwinner has no regular paid employment?

Do you think that Robert McNamara was being over-optimistic when he expressed the hope that 'the people of the United States . . . will not turn away in cynicism and indifference' when they realise the problems of the Third World? Do you think the people of the USA or Britain are generally aware of these problems *yet*? If not, why not? Does it matter?

Do you think that developed countries such as Britain and the USA are still, in any respects, to blame for Third World poverty?

Why do you think so little progress has been made towards land reform and income redistribution in most Third World countries since independence?

Is there anything that Western governments and aid agencies can, or should, do to encourage reforms?

Do you think that major worldwide fundraising efforts like the Live Aid, Sport Aid and Comic Relief campaigns have any significant effect? What happened to the money they raised?

Are there any signs that Third World governments are attempting to diversify their economies to counter the effects of market fluctuations in their dominant export commodity?

Do you think that the general situation of the poorer half of the world's population has improved or worsened in the last 25 years? Will it have changed for better or worse by the end of the century?

Suggestions for debate

If the issues in this chapter are to be tackled by means of formal debate rather than informal discussion, here are two debate motions:[9]

a   'Charity begins at home.'
    We should solve the problems in our own country before we start worrying about the problems of others.

9 A further debate topic, taking in the issues of Chapters 6 and 7 as a whole, is suggested on page 110.

b Enforced sterilisation is the only answer to the problems of countries like India.

Essay titles

Essays on global problems are frequently fairly general, so that an answer might well be concerned equally with the material contained in the next chapter, on environmental issues, as with population and poverty. You may wish, therefore, to write an essay only after dealing with *both* chapters.

Here are three titles which relate specifically to this chapter:

a 'We must share the world's resources more fairly than we have done in the past, even if we reduce the standard of living in the Western World.'

b The arguments for and against the United Kingdom making money available to the underdeveloped and developing countries.

c What suggestions do you have to offer the world community in tackling famine?

Bibliography

Books

Barrios de Chungara, Domitila, with Moema Viezzer, *Let Me Speak!: Testimony of Domitila, a woman of the Bolivian mines*, Stage 1, 1979

Clark, John, *For Richer, For Poorer*, Oxford, 1986

Ehrlich, Paul R., *The Population Bomb*, Ballantine, Friends of the Earth, 1968

Ehrlich, Paul R. and Anne H., *The Population Explosion*, Simon and Schuster, 1990

Galeano, Eduardo, *The Open Veins of Latin America: Five Centuries of the Pillage of the Continent*, Monthly Review Press, 1971

George, Susan, *How the Other Half Dies: the real reasons for world hunger*, Penguin, 1976

Harrison, Paul, *Inside the Third World: the anatomy of poverty*, Penguin, 1979

Harrison, Paul and Rowley, John, *Human Numbers, Human Need*, International Planned Parenthood Federation, 1984

Hayter, Teresa, *The Creation of World Poverty*, Pluto Press in association with Third World First, 1981

Lappé, Frances Moore and Collins, Joseph, *Food First*, Abacus, 1982

Schumacher, E. F., *Small is Beautiful: a study of economics as if people mattered*, Abacus, 1978

Taylor, Gordon Rattray, *The Doomsday Book*, Panther, 1972

World Commission on Environment and Development, *Our Common Future*, Oxford, 1987

Periodicals

New Internationalist

Additional materials

Various resources, ranging from free pamphlets to photopacks, slides, videos and films, are available from the major organisations concerned with alleviating hunger and poverty in the Third World.

   Catalogues, resources and suggestions can be obtained from the following:

CAFOD (Catholic Fund for Overseas Development)
2 Garden Close
Stockwell Road
London SW9 9TY

CWDE (Centre for World Development Education)
1 Catton Street
Holborn
London WC1R 4AB

Christian Aid
PO Box No 1
London SW9 8BH

Oxfam
274 Banbury Road
Oxford OX2 7DZ

Speakers can often be booked to visit schools and colleges to show videos and films, and discuss the issues.

Advice on writing: varieties of essay question

If you are given seven or eight titles to choose from for a lengthy piece of continuous writing in exam conditions, making the right choice can be a problem in itself. You need to feel confident that you can write for the full recommended time on a subject, without long pauses before you start. It is advisable, therefore, when you have chosen a title, to spend a few minutes jotting down ideas. This is an essential aspect of essay planning in any case, as is made clear in Chapter 1, and it is the only way that you can discover whether, in fact, you *have* enough ideas to produce an adequate essay. If you cannot think of much to say, it is probably best to try another title.

   There are five types of question which might feature on your exam paper: discussion, narrative, personal, discursive and descriptive. The first two are dealt with in detail in Chapters 1 and 2. The third, the personal essay, is obviously one in which you focus your writing on personal experience, analysing your feelings about the topic, based on that experience. A discursive essay is factual or informative in content; the subject is considered from various angles, and information and reflections on each are offered. A descriptive essay is simply a long physical description or series of descriptions.

Most titles are likely to offer no alternative to the formal discussion essay. Titles which ask you to 'discuss', or 'consider', or 'argue/present a case for or against' something, or are posed in the form of a question on some issue, require arguments. It is with this type of quetion that this book is primarily concerned.

On the other hand, you may find that the title is more open, and allows for more than one type of approach. Titles such as 'The right to strike' or 'In defence of discipline and order' or 'The problems posed by hunger strikes', whilst most obviously encouraging discussion essays, could also be treated as titles for stories. Titles which consist simply of a word or short phrase, like 'Hope', 'Paradise', 'Silence', 'Swimming against the current' or 'The river', could be treated in a variety of ways. Each of them could be used as the title of a short story. 'Hope', 'Paradise', 'Silence' and 'Swimming against the current' could also be treated as personal essays, either focusing on one particular episode in your life, or offering a more general analysis of your experiences in relation to the topic. They could also be treated as discursive essays, in which you explain different people's or cultures' visions of 'Paradise', for instance, or the importance of 'Hope' or 'Silence' or the dangers of 'Swimming against the current', in different human situations. 'The river' could be treated as a discursive or descriptive as well as a narrative title. One particular river, or several, could be dealt with discursively.

The main danger with the personal essay is triviality. If the most vivid experiences of 'Hope' that you can think of, for instance, are on the level of hoping to pass an examination or win a prize, you are unlikely to produce a very interesting or thoughtful personal essay. You must be able to convey a sense of genuine personal involvement in the experiences you are relating for a personal essay to be successful. Personal and narrative essays, of course, are often indistinguishable, and a story about a single personal experience which is relevant to the title can make a very effective answer.

The danger with discursive essays is dullness. Essays which begin: 'There are many types of . . .' and which go on to explain laboriously how 'the river' can be used for leisure, sport, transportation, and so on, are almost invariably turgid. Extended descriptive essays tend to ramble and run out of steam, and are probably best avoided unless you have a real flair for this kind of writing.

THE ENVIRONMENTAL CRISIS

7

Poverty and overpopulation have an immediate effect on the day-to-day lives of hundreds of millions of people in the developing world. The destruction of the world environment, by contrast, has a less obvious impact on human life; yet in the long run it may prove to be the greatest threat of all to humanity.

The subject of environmental decay is vast and complex, requiring, for an adequate understanding, a study of ecology, which is a far more ambitious task than can be undertaken here. All that can be attempted in a brief survey is to indicate some of the problems which are considered by experts to pose the greatest threat to our environment and the future of the human race.

The chapter begins with a summary exercise on the rainforests.

Summary skills

The article and accompanying 'Fact File' which follow appeared in *The Guardian* newspaper on 8 December, 1989.

After reading the material carefully, answer the following questions:

a   Write a set of notes, with sub-headings, under the general title: 'The Value of the Rainforest'. You should use no more than 40 words in total, including the sub-headings. You may wish to use the following as a guide:

The Value of the Rainforest
    Use values
        Source of timber   (*8 marks*)

b   In no more than 130 words, summarise the arguments for conserving the tropical rainforests, based on 'existence value'.   (*20 marks*) c Taking any eight of the ten points in the 'Rainforest Fact File', write eight brief newspaper headlines (no more than ten words per headline), capturing the essence of the information in headline style. (*12 marks*)

You are advised to spend about one hour on this question.

Options for the forest

Governments and conservationists are split on how to save the world's rainforests. Should there be a total ban on logging or is the problem one of underdevelopment? **David Pearce**, the economics adviser to Christopher Patten and author of the Pearce Report, outlines his views.

Despite the popular attention given to big dams as agents of environmental destruction, they are in fact very minor causes of deforestation. Something like 7.3 million hectares of tropical forest were being destroyed annually in the early 1980s. Updated estimates are expected soon, and may well be larger. Almost all of this clearance is for agriculture. Perhaps another 4.4 million hectares are selectively felled every year for timber, all of it, bar a trivial amount, unsustainably. At these rates, all tropical forests would be cleared in about 170 years. But for some countries, such as Ivory Coast, Sri Lanka, and Costa Rica, virtual extinction of tropical forests will come in 20–

30 years. Is it all necessary? Must development be at the expense of these unique, beautiful ecosystems?

There is a strong moral case for calling a halt to most deforestation. But appeals to moral principles are not always very persuasive among the powers-that-be who have to balance what they see as immediate needs for food, land, energy, minerals and foreign exchange against the concerns of much richer people in far-off lands, many of whom hardly offer an example in terms of their own environmental record.

Economic arguments can be marshalled to defend the tropical forests. Environmental economists speak of the 'total economic value' of a natural resource. This

is made up of use and non-use values. Use values include the worth of the forest as timber resource; as the source of many other forest products; as a food source for indigenous peoples; as a repository of germ-plasm for medicinal and crop-breeding uses; as a facility for 'ecotourists'.

Indirect use values include the watershed protection functions of tropical forests – the role they play in containing erosion and sedimentation, and in the cycling of nutrients which would otherwise be released as pollutants to aquatic systems. Perhaps the most widely discussed indirect use function is carbon fixation, the role of forests as a 'carbon sink' to contain the greenhouse effect.

Beyond the use value

lies what economists call 'existence values'. These are the values many people have for conserving tropical forests regardless of any direct use they make of them now or in the future. Existence value is what is being expressed when money floods into environmental charities aiming to save the whale, protect the panda and conserve the elephant.

But it is an issue of getting the 'signals' right. That means the true worth of conservation must be demonstrated. It also means that there has to be fairer treatment of the less powerful who, all too often, have no secure land and resource rights to enable them to combat the forest colonists.

Existence value provides one of the other major arguments for tropical forest conservation. Environmental economists have researched what people are willing to pay for unique species of animal or habitat. By adopting sophisticated questionnaire techniques, it is possible to get sensible individual valuations. No-one has yet, to my knowledge, done this for a tropical forest. But, interestingly, values for blue whales, California sea otters and other species can be shown to cluster around $8 per adult. Values for the bald eagle and the grizzly bear are higher still, as one would expect of American respondents. Values for the visibility of the Grand Canyon were $22 per adult. It hardly seems feasible that existence values for say Amazonia will be less.

Even at $8 per adult for the richest countries in the world, we would have an hypothetical conservation fund of $3.2 billion. To get a feel for the significance of this sum, the entire contribution by the Amazon area to Brazil's Gross National Product (GNP) is around $6 billion. Since many of the uses of the area are wholly consistent with conservation, existence value alone could be used to compensate Brazil for not engaging in destructive developments.

Of course the numbers are speculative. It is not the exact size that matters. Rather it is the principle that conservation values, in economic terms, can be very large indeed.

But big existence values won't mean much to Brazil, Malaysia or Indonesia if they cannot be converted into cash or kind. Yet this is exactly what must now happen if the forests are to be saved. No small part of their conservation value accrues to us in the rich world, in the form of appreciation of the wonder of a tropical forest, in plant-based drugs that we use, as educational and scientific resources, as carbon sinks. Their value to the people of the nations that own the forest is also increasingly appreciated, something we may not always recognise. If we all gain from tropical forest conservation we have to retreat rapidly from the stance that it is somehow all their fault and that we should not have to pay. A little less of a moralistic stance and more of an economic approach will work wonders.

David Pearce is Professor of Economics at University College and Director of the IIED Environmental Economics Centre.

DAVID PEARCE, *The Guardian*, 8 December 1989

RAINFOREST FACT FILE

- Tropical rainforests play a critical role in regulating the climate and what is called the greenhouse effect. They act as the earth's lungs by producing vast quantities of oxygen and using up carbon dioxide during photosynthesis.
- Burning the forests sends at least two billion tonnes of carbon dioxide per year into the air. This increases global warming. The practice of burning fossil fuels currently adds around 5.6 billion tonnes to this per year.
- Forest cover is disappearing at a rate of more than 200,000 acres a year in Brazil, Colombia, Indonesia, Mexico, Thailand, Ivory Coast, Ecuador, Nigeria, Peru and Malaysia. All these countries lie wholly or mainly in the tropics.
- Constant media references to tropical rainforests suggests that all forests in the tropics are rainforests and consist of an extremely complex and fragile web of flora and fauna. This is not true. Not all moist tropical forests are evergreen, nor are all tropical forests moist.
- Commercial logging is directly responsible for only 20 per cent of the deforestation in tropical rainforests. But related activities, including road building and damage to other trees as logs are pulled clear, increase the toll.
- More critically, road construction in logging areas opens up huge tracts of forest to the landless poor who then move in to practise a version of the traditional method of cultivation that has been carried on for years. However, these 'shifting cultivators' do not leave the forest soil long enough for it to recover its fertility before returning to clear the trees and farm again.
- Radical environmentalists say that commercial development of the forests is the root of the destruction. The World Bank says that lack of commercial development, by creating armies of landless poor, is to blame.
- Drier and more open tropical forest formations, together with the shrubland into which they merge (and which falls under the definition of forest) are even more acutely threatened and their shrinkage should give cause for concern.
- Since 1945 40 per cent of the world's rainforests have been destroyed. As a result, over 50 species of plants and animals become extinct every day.
- Rainforests cover only 6 per cent of the total land surface but contain at least 50 per cent of all species of life on earth.

From *The Guardian*, 8 December, 1989

How to save the world

One of the most thorough analyses of the environmental crisis is contained in *World Conservation Strategy*, published by the three major international conservation agencies.[1] This vast document is summarised for the general

---

1 International Union for Conservation of Nature and Natural Resources (IUCN); United Nations Environment Programme (UNEP); Worldwide Fund for Nature (WWF).

reader in a book called *How to Save the World* by Robert Allen, published in 1980. During the decade which followed the publication of this book, the problems which it analyses have become more pressing, and are at last beginning to be taken seriously by world leaders. Each of the problems has been addressed by various international bodies at the highest level. At the beginning of the 1990s, however, no drastic steps had been taken internationally to solve them.

The extracts which follow are taken from Robert Allen's book:

How pollution is related to poverty and overpopulation

Much habitat destruction and over-exploitation of living resources by individuals, communities and nations in the developing world[2] is a response to relative poverty, caused or exacerbated by a combination of rising human numbers and inequities within and among nations. Peasant communities, for example, may be forced to cultivate steep, unstable slopes because their growing numbers exceed the capacity of the land and because the fertile, easily managed valley bottoms have been taken over by large landowners. Similarly, many developing countries have so few natural resources and operate under such unfavourable conditions of international trade that often they have very little choice but to exploit forests, fisheries and other living resources unsustainably . . . Every country should have a conscious and deliberate population policy to achieve a balance between numbers and environment. At the same time it is essential that the affluent constrain their demands on resources, and ideally reduce them, shifting some of their wealth to assisting the deprived. To a significant extent the survival and future of the poor depends on conservation and sharing by the rich.

The worst environmental problems

Loss of soil

The bottom is dropping out of the world's breadbasket. Prime farmland is being obliterated by roads and buildings. Croplands and grazing land are being mutilated on a huge scale by farming methods that more resemble mining than good husbandry. Wild and traditional crop varieties, the main weapons against pests and diseases that could wipe out harvest after harvest, are vanishing . . .

Not only is farmland disappearing at an alarming rate, but much that remains is being heavily degraded by bad farming practices. As much as one-third of the world's cropland will be destroyed in the next 20 years if current rates of land degradation continue.

---

2 Referred to earlier as the 'underdeveloped countries' or the 'Third World'.

Spreading deserts

The creation of new desert areas is happening on a colossal scale. All over the world people are busy making life more difficult than it already is. They are turning semi-desert into desert and desert in extreme desert, transforming the barely productive into the unproductively bare . . .

The vulnerable areas are the drylands. Drylands, where rainfall is low and evaporation and transpiration are high, cover about a third of the earth's land surface. They are extremely prone to desertification (the process by which land becomes desert) unless used with care and skill, and they represent the most extensive ecological problem area on this planet.

It is estimated that almost 80 million people are immediately threatened by a desertification-induced drop in productivity of the land on which (directly or indirectly) they depend. Regions already in the grip of desertification or at very high risk cover 20 million square kilometres (nine million square miles), or an area twice the size of Canada . . . Most of it is in Africa and Asia.

Deforestation

Forests are the prime example of natural areas that contribute heavily to human welfare by acting as environmental buffers . . . Removal or degradation of watershed forests and pastures can cause great human suffering. Without the sponge-like effect of their vegetation, which retains moisture and releases it slowly, the flow of water becomes erratic, leading to both floods and water shortages. The increased rate of water run-off causes additional damage by stripping the soil away, depriving agriculture of nutrients while clogging reservoirs, irrigation systems, canals and docks with silt, and smothering coral reefs . . .

Badly organised timber operations are degrading the forests as effectively as expansionist agricultural and settlement schemes. In a given forest section, only a few species . . . may be considered of commercial value. Yet to reach them, 75 per cent of the surrounding canopy is destroyed. The *apparently* endless supply discourages caution . . .

In many parts of South America . . . large tracts of forest are being burned down and converted into ranchland. The beef is raised cheaply enough to satisfy demand in the United States, Canada and Europe, but it is a destructive business; the pasture is invaded by scrub so rapidly that after a few years it becomes uneconomic to maintain and is abandoned.

We are at the point now where what goes now is gone forever. Once destruction is widespread, tropical rainforests can no longer be reconstructed . . .

Destruction of tropical rainforests may have serious climatic effects well beyond the tropics. Tropical forests contain in their wood, leaves, litter and humus, an enormous store (estimated to be 340 thousand million tonnes) of carbon. Carbon is burned when fossil fuels are destroyed and it accumulates in the atmosphere . . . The likely consequence of the accumulation of carbon dioxide in the atmosphere is that the global climate will become warmer, and that the warming will be greater at the poles than between them. Nobody knows the effects of this uneven warming, but it is quite possible that one of the effects would be a general drying of the wheat areas of North America. Another possible effect is an increase in sea level if the western ice sheet in Antarctica were to melt, as it did in earlier geological times during a similar warm period.

Overfishing and sea pollution
The world's most valuable wild animals are almost certainly shrimps. Their closest rivals are cod and herring. The total annual value of exports of fresh and frozen shrimps from developing to developed countries is already close to $1000 million . . . Unfortunately use of fisheries is often not sustainable and their contribution to national diets and incomes is likely to diminish . . . At least 25 of the world's most valuable fisheries are seriously depleted. Many more are now so fully exploited that they can expect to become depleted within a decade or so, because of the effects of exploitation either alone or in combination with those of pollution and habitat destruction . . .

Over-exploitation is waste: the substitution of relatively small short-term gains for much bigger medium or long-term losses. A sobering measure of this wastage is the conversion over the years of poor people's food into rich people's food. There was a time in the UK, before over-exploitation and pollution did their work, when oysters and fresh salmon were a monotonously common feature of the poor person's diet. This is no longer the case and both are now beyond the pocket of the average family. Now the cod . . . seems to be going in the same direction.

Why immediate action is necessary

Current attempts by a quarter of the world's people to carry on consuming two-thirds of the world's resources and by half of the people simply to stay alive are destroying the means by which all people can survive and prosper. Everywhere fertile soil is either built on or flushed into the sea; otherwise renewable resources are exploited beyond recovery, and pollutants are thrown like wrenches into the machinery of climate. As a result, the planet's capacity to support people is being irreversibly reduced at the very time when rising human numbers and consumption are making increasingly heavy demands on it . . .

Unless concerted action is taken immediately, there will be a further decline in the planet's capacity to support its population. Subsequent generations will be left a sorry heritage. The decision is not one we can postpone or ignore. Doing nothing is itself a decision to allow the world to be a much less fruitful and promising place than that in which we were born.

ROBERT ALLEN

The *World Conservation Strategy* contains a wide range of suggestions for international action to 'save the world', far too diverse to attempt to summarise. Here is an illustration of the type of action which it proposes, taken, again, from Robert Allen's book:

Proposals for action

Governments should first of all make a decision to give precedence to agriculture and other uses for high quality land. They can enforce that decision by prohibiting the sale of farmland, dropping government assistance for projects that would encourage conversion of farmland, and promoting the use of lower quality land as sites for urban development . . . People need incentives to conserve. The best possible incentive for the farmer is demonstration that soil conservation brings big enough benefits, such as higher average yields for lower overall costs, quickly enough to make it worth the effort and expense. Every country, therefore, should have a soil conservation service with sufficient technical staff to help with as many demonstration projects as may be needed and professional staff to provide the technical workers with expert back-up.

If, however, it is clear that the benefits from conservation will be too gradual for the farmer alone to support the costs of conservation, other incentives, such as low-cost credit or tax concessions for installing and maintaining drains, retaining tree cover and recycling farm wastes, should be given. Land reform is often another indispensable incentive. People cannot be expected to look after land they do not own and from which they may be expelled without notice. 'Land to the tiller' is a cardinal maxim, and it must not be just the land the wealthy do not want.

ROBERT ALLEN

Discussion points

What are the effects of the destruction of cropland and the spread of deserts worldwide?

What would be likely to happen if the wheat areas of North America dried?

Why are the world's rainforests being burnt, sawn and bulldozed down?

What are the effects of rainforest destruction?

Why are overfishing and pollution of the sea such serious problems?

Is the world still 'doing nothing' to solve the problems analysed by Allen?

Is there anything Britain and the Western world can do to encourage the 'land reform' which Allen talks about?

Global warming

Scientists are now virtually unanimous in declaring that global warming is the principal threat to mankind's continued existence. In the extracts which follow from the book *It's a Matter of Survival* by the Canadian environmentalists, Anita Gordon and David Suzuki, published in 1990, this threat is explored.

The danger

The 'Big Warming' we expect is the result of human activity. We release heat-trapping molecules of such gases as carbon dioxide and methane as the byproducts of our civilization; carbon dioxide from burning coal and oil, driving our cars, and heating our homes, and from the destruction of forests; methane from cattle herds, and from rice paddies. . . .

We also add heat-trapping gases like CFCs from the consumer products we have made part of our lives: spray cans, air conditioners, and refrigerators. Like a pane of glass in a greenhouse, all these molecules let lots of sunlight in but prevent a large amount of heat from escaping the Earth's atmosphere into outer space. . . . With global warming will come a rise in sea level of as much as 1.5 metres (5 ft). . . .

Something in the order of a third of the world's population and more than a third of the world's economic infrastructure are concentrated in coastal regions with altitudes below 1.5 metres (5 ft). 'All that is at risk over the next 40 to 60 years,' says McNeil.[3] Whole nations are at risk. . . . The temperature of the planet is higher than it's been since record keeping began, . . . The six hottest years of the past 110 years all occurred in the 1980s. . . .

Food scarcity is emerging as the most profound and immediate consequence of global environmental degradation. It is already affecting the welfare of hundreds of millions of people, and will begin to affect North Americans directly in this decade. . . . Every day around the world 40,000 people die of hunger. That's 28 human beings every minute, and three out of four of them are children under the age of five. And that is the toll in times of relative plenty. . . .

Perhaps a billion or more of the world's people already spend 70 per cent of their income on food. For many in this group, a dramatic rise in the cost of grain is life-threatening. . . .

The specter of Ethiopia is abroad. The television images are haunting: an 18-year-old Eritrean, driven out of her homeland because of starvation, stands and gives birth to an emaciated infant. Do we want that quality of human life?

The principal causes

The disappearance of the rainforest would be nothing less than an incalculable disaster for the whole planet. The rainforests are, in effect, 'the lungs of the planet,'

3 Jim McNeil, secretary general of the 1987 Brundtland Commission on the Environment.

Malaysian rainforest
destroyed to make
way for agricultural
development.

helping to regulate the exchange of oxygen and carbon dioxide, just as our own lungs do. In the Amazon region alone, 75 billion tons of carbon are filtered out of the air by trees. . . . As those trees are cut or burned, they release their carbon into the air as carbon dioxide, exacerbating the greenhouse effect.

Perhaps the hardest question of all that we must face is whether, given the state of the world, there can be a future for the automobile. . . . The automobile is proving itself to be incompatible with human survival and the well-being of the planet. It destroys our quality of life, the air we breathe, our crops and our trees with toxic emissions. It destroys the ozone layer. It is responsible for the paving over of our cropland and wilderness. Every time we climb into a car and put our foot on the gas, we're jeopardizing our family's future. . . .

More than 400 million vehicles clog the world's streets today, and the production and use of fuels for automobiles accounts for an estimated 17 per cent of all carbon dioxide released from fossil fuels. . . .

China and India together account for 38 per cent of the world's population, and at this point, they own scarcely 0.5 per cent of its automobiles. . . . Imagine one billion Chinese deciding they all want to have a car. It could happen. . . .

The heart of the dilemma is energy, the world's reliance on fossil fuel. . . . The industrial countries' fossil-fuel emissions are going to heat the atmosphere for the whole world. . . . And the route the Third World takes to industrialization could determine the future for the whole planet. . . .

One North American does 20 to 100 times more damage to the planet than one person in the Third World, and one rich North American causes 1,000 times more destruction.

The profligacy of the United States has already put us in grave peril; if the Third World follows our example, it will finish us off.

What needs to be done

Twenty per cent of the world is living an orgy of mindless consumption, and the rest struggle to survive by destroying the life-support systems of the planet. Each one of us is responsible for the carnage of the rainforests as surely as if we were to take an axe or a match to the forests ourselves. . . . The goal of development, for rich and for poor, must be to create conserver societies; that basically means the rich must live more simply so the poor may simply live. . . . There is no quick fix for the environmental crisis; however, each of us has the power to make a crucial difference to the mounting odds against survival. . . . In the world of garbage management, recycling is one of the three Rs – recycle, reuse, and reduce. Glass bottles, aluminium beverage cans and newspapers can be ground up and reprocessed and then recycled, at a real energy saving. . . .

If recycling glass bottles to be ground up and remade uses 25 per cent less energy than creating a bottle from virgin material, imagine the energy saving, not to mention the pollution that isn't being created or the resources that aren't being used up, if those same glass bottles are simply washed out and reused for pop or milk. Standardizing glass containers for food would go a long way toward creating that kind of saving. . . .

Reuse is heading in the right direction, but the journey is futile without restraint: the most efficient way to avert the looming garbage crisis is to avoid producing garbage at all. . . .

Starting with Berkeley, California, in 1987, a number of municipalities have joined the rush to ban plastics and packaging. . . . [However], for survival's sake, we must add a fourth R to the garbage-management primer – *rethink* – and that, in the end, is what will save us. . . . What we've got to rethink is our consumer society.

As the car overruns us, more and more people are becoming convinced that the true solution is much more brutal than fuel efficiency and alternative funds. We must restrict our driving. . . .

Stockholm may become the first European capital to charge for road use, with the money collected devoted to improving public transport. . . . The major policy of the Western world has to be 'to virtually eliminate dependence on fossil fuels overall, as fast as is humanly possible to achieve.'[4] . . . Not only are we going to have to cut carbon emissions by as much as 80 per cent, we're going to have to do it in this decade if we want to avoid a hothouse future; yet, as of this writing, not a single national government has implemented a plan to reduce CO_2 emissions. . . .

Now that we are faced with this greenhouse apocalypse, it is extraordinary to discover that there are – researched, developed and ready to go – technologies that could clean up the First World's mess and provide the Third World with an

---

4 The author is quoting Stephen Lewis, former Canadian ambassador to the United Nations.

alternative route to development. We must tell our legislators at every level that they must lead us into this new world, with hope and with vision, and we must speak with one voice:

  – If our leaders must legislate us into a new era of renewable energy, then do it.
  – If they must redistribute the pie to help Third World countries so we all survive, then do it.
  – If we must be legislated out of our cars, then do it.
  – If industry must be legislated in order to become environmentally responsible, then do it. . . .

Our own cheap road to prosperity is leading to the end of global civilization; there is no future via that route. Even if a fraction of the remaining 80 per cent of the planet headed down the same highway, the ecological chaos could bring all our civilizations tumbling down. . . . In June 1990, faced with new research that showed the ozone layer was deteriorating much more rapidly than previously predicted, the 56 nations that had signed the original Montreal protocol[5] voted to establish a world fund. They pledged US $240 million to help the developing world to stop producing and using chemicals that damage the Earth's ozone layer. . . . 'Why is it that our generation in the 1980s and 1990s has the right to reach back through millions of years of geologic time to get deposits that fuel our civilization, and then quickly transform them into pollution that will be here for thousands and hundreds of thouands of years into the future?' asks US Senator Al Gore. 'Don't we need to think about those who come after us? That's really the bottom line, isn't it? How do we get up in the morning and look our children in the eye and tell them that we spent their future?' . . .

This is the test for humanity. Will we degenerate into territorial creatures struggling for power, land, and survival, or will we emerge with a new collective image of ourselves as a species integrated into the natural world?

In times of crisis, people have pulled together and forgotten their mistrust and petty rivalries. They've sacrificed and worked to change their lives. There has never been a bigger crisis than the one we now face. And we are the last generation that can pull us out of it. We must act because this is the only home we have. It is a matter of survival.   ANITA GORDON AND DAVID SUZUKI

Questions for discussion and analysis

What do you imagine will happen if the sea level rises to the extent predicted in these extracts?

What is the relationship between global warming and food scarcity? What other factors cause severe famine and malnutrition?

What is meant by describing the rainforests as the 'lungs of the planet'?

5 An international agreement, signed in 1987, aimed at halving most CFC emissions by 1998.

In what ways can the automobile be regarded as the single most significant contributor to global warming?

In what ways can it be said that people in North America do between 20 and 1,000 times more damage to the planet than the Third World's poor?

How practical do you consider the ideas for recycling and reusing throw-away containers to be?

Do you think plastics and packaging should be banned by law?

What is your reaction to the suggestions for courses of action that 'we must tell our legislators' to take?

How can the Western world persuade the developing world not to follow the environmentally disastrous 'road to prosperity' which the industrialised world has taken?

Is it still possible for the world to 'pull together to save the planet'? Are there any signs of it happening before it becomes too late?

Pollution in the Third World

Millions of the Third World's poor live their lives amidst pollution on a scale unimaginable to most people in Britain. A glimpse of the impact of atmospheric pollution at its worst is provided in the following article by Sue Branford, which appeared in a 1985 edition of *The Times*:

Sirens, similar to those used in Britain during the Second World War, are being installed in the town of Cubatao on the coast of Brazil to warn the population, not of an imminent air raid, but of a more insidious enemy – toxic chemicals and inflammable oil derivates.

Cubatao is a town of 100,000 about 35 miles from the industrial metropolis of Sao Paulo. Conveniently situated about eight miles from the port of Santos, Cubatao has taken on dirty servicing tasks for Brazil's industrial sector. Using largely imported crude oil, it produces fertilizers, petrochemicals and oil derivatives, as well as steel products.

This concentration has turned Cubatao into probably the most polluted city in the world.

Cubatao achieved temporary international notoriety in February 1984, when petrol leaked from one of the huge pipes taking oil derivatives over the mountain to Sao Paulo. The petrol went up in flames in the middle of the night, setting fire to a large shanty town. An unknown number of people, possibly as many as 1,000, were killed.

Since the fire, there have been other leaks of toxic or inflammable products. The most serious, of ammonia, led to the evacuation in the middle of the night of another shanty town, perched outside the gates of one of the factories. It is hoped that the system of sirens, to be used with loudspeakers, will reduce the level of panic.

SUE BRANFORD

Discussion points

Do you know of any other cities where pollution is particularly severe?

Why do countries like Brazil allow pollution to reach the level of cities like Cubatao?

Have we in the Western world any responsibility for such environmental horrors?

Research and discussion

One way of organising a discussion of such a wide-ranging issue as pollution is for individual students or small groups to choose an aspect of the subject on which to research, and report briefly to the rest of the group. Students who have studied geography and biology might well take a lead in this research.

Research might be useful on:

1   river pollution
2   lead pollution
3   noise pollution
4   insecticides and the ecological balance
5   nuclear waste and radiation

A research 'pot-pourri'

As a way of developing conciseness and confidence in public speaking, students might be asked to deliver a five-minute prepared speech on one of the following topics:

acid rain; bilharzia (or schistosomiasis); Brundtland Report; cesium; CFCs; eutrophication; food chains; 'Green Revolution'; kwashiorkor; ozone layer; PCBs; World Wide Fund for Nature.

Attacking Pollution

Finally, to show that environmentalists have been offering plans of action for tackling the problems outlined in this chapter for at least two decades, here is an extract from *The Doomsday Book* by Gordon Rattray Taylor, published at the beginning of the 1970s.

First, [pollution] must be recognised as a world problem. Not just a world-wide problem, in the sense that every country should tackle its own pollution, but an international problem in the sense that the wastes of each country affect, or may affect, the climate and health of other countries or even the whole world . . . An international organisation is needed . . .

Second, it is essential to increase by many orders of magnitude the scale and scope of research into these problems . . .

Thirdly, we need a decisive educational effort . . . This does not mean a few vague lessons on ecology, but a planned attempt to give the student a sense of man's place in the scheme of things . . .

Fourthly, there is the attack on pollution activities . . . A much tauter structure for pollution control is needed.

Fifthly and finally, though one could lengthen the list, I put the need to reconsider far more thoroughly the setting of acceptable standards of purity, including freedom from radioactivity, for water, air and soil.

A glimpse of what might be possible was afforded when, in July 1968, the *New York Times* published a paper by Andrei D. Sakharov, the father of the Russian H-Bomb, entitled: 'Progress, Co-existence and Intellectual Freedom'. Departing entirely from the conventional attitude expected, he argued that civilisation is emperilled by the threat of nuclear war, famine, degenerating mass culture and 'bureaucratic dogmatism' . . . In such circumstances, he said, 'Only universal co-operation . . . will preserve civilisation'. He pinpointed the problem of hunger and over-population, proposing a 15-year tax equal to 20 per cent of national income on developed nations to help in stabilising the situation. The silence which greeted this suggestion could be heard round the world.

GORDON RATTRAY TAYLOR

Suggestion for debate

The following debate motion assumes that Chapters 6 and 7 are treated as a single topic:

For the next decade, the rich nations should devote 20 per cent of their Gross National Product to solving the problems of poverty and pollution in the Third World which they have helped to create.

Essay titles

a 'I have often heard it said that posterity must look after itself. I can think of no more callous viewpoint.'

b 'It is lack of confidence, more than anything else, that kills a civilisation. We can destroy ourselves by cynicism and disillusion just as effectively as by bombs.'

c The importance of international co-operation.

110

d 'Science solves problems and occasionally creates them.' What do you consider is the major scientific problem today and how do you think it can be solved?

e The river.

f How can we avoid an energy crisis?

g How far do you agree that despite man's attempts to control Nature, Nature has found very successful ways of controlling man?

h Many people are concerned to protect our environment. Do you support the conservationists or do you think they overstate their case?

Bibliography

Books

Allen, Robert, *How to Save the World: Strategy for World Conservation*, Kogan Page, 1980

Caulfield, Catherine, *In the Rainforest*, Alfred A. Knopf, 1985

Durrell, Lee, *State of the Ark: An Atlas of Conservation in Action*, Bodley Head, 1986

Gordon, Anita and Suzuki, David, *It's a Matter of Survival*, Allen and Unwin, 1990

Gribbin, John, *Hothouse Earth*, Black Swan/Bantam Press, 1990

Lovelock, J.E., *Gaia: A New Look at Life on Earth*, Oxford University Press, 1987

McKibben, Bill, *The End of Nature*, Viking, 1989

Myers, Norman, *The Gaia Atlas of Future Worlds: Challenge and Opportunity in an Age of Change*, Penguin, 1990

Porritt, Jonathan, *Seeing Green*, Basil Blackwell, 1984

Taylor, Gordon Rattray, *The Doomsday Book*, Panther, 1972

World Commission on Environment and Development *Our Common Future*, Oxford University Press, 1987

World Resources 1990–91 *A Report by the World Resources Institute, in Collaboration with The United Nations Environment Programme and the United Nations Development Programme*, Oxford University Press, 1990

Periodicals

The Ecologist
New Internationalist

Audio-visual materials

Several commercial companies produce good videos, film-strips and tape-slide material on the environmental crisis. Here are some companies from which catalogues can be obtained:

Audio-visual Productions
Hocker Hill House
Chepstow
Gwent NP6 5ER

Concord Films Council
201 Felixstowe Road
Ipswich
Suffolk

Diana Wyllie Ltd
1 Park Road
Baker Street
London NW1 6XP

Visual Publications
The Green
Northleach
Cheltenham GL54 3EX

Friends of the Earth
(UK)
Education Section
26–28 Underwood Street
London N1 7JQ

Advice on writing: essay writing – use and misuse of information

Many students fare badly in the discussion essay through lack of ideas and information. The possession of an encyclopaedic knowledge of facts and factors relevant to a question, on the other hand, is no guarantee of success. You have still got to know how to use that information effectively to produce a well-structured, coherent and relevant essay.

One of the most ruinous pitfalls in language essay writing is, in fact, irrelevance. Though it is uncommon for post GCSE-level students of English to miss the point of a question completely, there are nevertheless many snares into which you can fall – with possibly fatal consequences – while *seeming* to be answering the question.

Let us look at a question for which the material contained in Chapters 6 and 7 would be ideally suited, and see what can go wrong! Read through the following essay plan, and try to work out its failings as an embryonic answer to the question:

'The world will not live in harmony so long as two-thirds of its inhabitants find difficulty in living at all.'

Paragraph 1 – Introduction
living conditions in developed countries compared with those in Third-World countries

Paragraph 2 – Poverty
'absolute poverty' in Third World
unequal distribution of resources in Third-World countries, e.g. Brazil
imbalance in affluence between developed and developing countries

112

Paragraph 3 – Population explosion
causes: developments in medicine and lack of birth control
effects: doubling of populations requiring doubling of resources
description of situation in Calcutta to illustrate horrors of poverty and
population explosion

Paragraph 4 – Effects of poverty and population explosion on environment
deforestation
spreading deserts and soil erosion
overfishing and sea pollution

Paragraph 5 – Conclusion
Gap between rich and poor nations is widening. Adequate birth control
policies and redistribution of resources in Third World countries
needed if starvation and malnutrition not to increase further

All of this is relevant, *potentially*. But an essay based on this plan would not
score very high marks. The points outlined are simply not related
sufficiently closely to the question. Had the question been more general, had
it been worded, for instance: 'While a third of the world's population lives in
comparative luxury, two thirds find difficulty in living at all', the plan would
have been perfectly adequate. The core of the question, however, lies in the
phrase about the world living 'in harmony', and unless the analysis of the
global imbalance of wealth is specifically related to this idea, the essay will
merely skirt around the central issue.

A useful exercise would be to try to relate this plan more closely to the
title, making any additions and alterations necessary, but retaining as many
of the points as possible. Alternatively, you could ignore the above plan
altogether, and write one of your own.

A still more damaging failing in language essay writing can spring from
the attempt to twist a question to fit material which you have learnt. An
ingenious student can often manage this successfully, but skill and
confidence are needed for such adaptation to be convincing.

A case in point might be the question about 'the major scientific problem
today' in the list of essay titles. The 'scientific problem' treated could be
pollution, and the entire essay could be successfully based on it. A question
which reads: 'The successes and failures of technology', on the other hand,
would require broader treatment, and a too heavy concentration on the issue
of pollution would result in a seriously unbalanced essay. Similarly, if the
question was: 'Should the 'haves' support the 'have nots'?', it would be
valid to treat Britain and the Western World as the 'haves' and the Third
World as the 'have nots', but if you interpreted the title *only* in this way,
your essay would be too limited. You would also need to show some
awareness of poverty and deprivation *within* Britain and the Western World.

EDUCATION

8

What is education for? At the time when Forster's Education Act introduced universal education to Britain in 1870 the answer was simple. The act was a response to the requirements of an increasingly industrialised society for an educated workforce. No such certainty about the purposes of education exists today. The nurturing of interests and aptitudes for life and leisure, as well as for employment; the development of social and personal awareness; the goal of social cohesion: all these take their place beside the original concentration on literacy, numeracy and skill learning, in the thinking of modern educationalists.

The chapter begins with an exercise combining summary skills and comment, on the age-old issue of declining educational standards. A full comprehension exercise, specifically on the teaching of English, can be found in Chapter 5, on pages 60-65.

Summary skills, comprehension and comment

The following report appeared in *The Times* newspaper in June 1990. Read it carefully, and answer the following questions:

a Summary Skills: summarise the points made about the teaching of English and history in not more than 100 words. *(20 marks)*

b Comprehension and Comment: give a detailed personal response to the points made about A-level English, on the basis of your study of English language and literature. *(20 marks)*

You are advised to spend about one hour on this exercise.

Public school heads attack government over 'easy' A-level exams

Senior staff at top public schools are to challenge the government's claim that educational standards among 18-year-olds, and the quality of A-level candidates, are improving.

Heads of department from 25 leading schools, including Eton and Rugby, will next month hold an unusual joint meeting, with A-level standards top of the agenda.

The move is expected to be the first in a sustained campaign to persuade examination boards and the government to stop further changes to the exam, which the schools say is becoming less rigorous.

The decision follows last week's publication of A-level results for the first generation of teenagers to have moved on from the new-style GCSE. They appeared to show a small improvement in standards and were enthusiastically welcomed by the government.

Michael Fallon, the junior education minister, said he was delighted with an A-level pass rate that had gone up to 77 per cent in a year when a record number of pupils had entered for the examination.

But a comparison with A-level papers 30 years ago shows that in the 1990s pupils study more opinion and less fact.

In 1961, candidates in the Associated Examining Board's English paper were expected to write a fluent précis, in 250 words, of a 750-word essay on archaeology. This year, the exercise was replaced by a 'test of skills of summary writing' in which pupils were asked to list in a table the main points of a newspaper article.

Thirty years ago, English literature students were asked factual essay questions about poetry, such as: 'In what ways does Wordsworth utilise the themes of youth and old age?'. In 1990 the questions are much more likely to be subjective: 'Is Wordsworth, in your view, too much like a teacher? If he is not a teacher, then what is he?'

Instead of being asked historical facts, pupils today may be given an extract from a contemporary account and asked to assess the 'validity' of the writer's point of view.

Such changes, according to senior teachers such as Jonathan Smith, add up to a drop in stan-

dards in the past two years as A-level examiners fall into line with the more informal methods of GCSE.

Smith, head of English at Tonbridge School, Kent, said: 'There is far less emphasis on precise knowledge of the meaning of words, and more on interpretation. In the past they would ask you to explain the meaning of lines 17 to 22 of Hamlet's soliloquy; now they ask you how Hamlet felt about it.'

Smith believes it will soon be possible to pass A-level English literature without studying Chaucer, Wordsworth, Milton and Dickens. Next year the Oxford and Cambridge board, which Smith uses, will drop compulsory questions on Chaucer.

Fred Marsden, head of science at Tonbridge, said: 'There is no doubt that the content of the A-level syllabus has been substantially diluted since the advent of the GCSE. Every year A levels become a bit easier, despite the exam boards' denials. The goalposts are being moved.'

Marsden said that in recent years, 15–20 per cent of the factual content of Oxford and Cambridge chemistry papers had been removed, making the exams easier to pass. He has written a letter of protest to John MacGregor, the education secretary.

Critics say the changes are taking place in spite of government assurances that A levels will remain as they always have been – academically rigorous.

Vivian Anthony, secretary of the Head Masters Conference of top public schools, and an economics chief examiner, blames the School Examinations and Assessment Council, a quango that oversees exam syllabuses, for a 'behind the scenes' alteration.

The Centre for Policy Studies is so concerned about standards that it will call this autumn for an exam for high-flyers to supplement A levels. Dr Sheila Lawlor, deputy director, said: 'A-level papers are shrinking in content. An independent inquiry should be held to investigate the claim that the A-level results today are the equal to those in the past.'

MICHAEL DURHAM, *The Times*, June 1990

The views of students

The reflections of a large number of students in British schools on different aspects of their education were collected by Edward Blishen and published in 1969 in a book called *The School that I'd like*. Here are some extracts:

Three cheers for the GCE and this product of the examination system: a stuffed puppet, reeling off facts and dates and predigested ideas, at the pull of a string, wondering if it was worth it and if this really is intelligence.

Boredom. Twenty-eight pairs of vacant eyes regarding with a hollow stare the woman at the front of the room who does the churning. Twenty-eight minds too apathetic to think, and 28 bodies, too lethargic to do anything except scrawl over desks and carve names, with infinite care, on the lids.

This is education. This is the way in which a child's enthusiasm for learning is quelled to a point of non-existence. Is it surprising that so many escape after O level, the climax of the whole ludicrous system?

ELIZABETH, 16

Teachers and pupils are bogged down, from 13 and 14 onwards, in the heavy mire of accumulation of often undigested and unrelated knowledge which can be spewed out as a turgid mark-gaining mess during the examination. The whole school week becomes geared to the GCE and all extra-curricular activities are forced to prostrate themselves in front of this almighty God.

This, surely, is not our ideal British education?

KENNETH, 17

In secondary education today the emphasis is on passing O and A levels. Half-educated children emerge from school clutching their exam certificates, having been filled to capacity with information about T.S. Eliot and Plato. They believe themselves to be 'educated'. To some extent they are, I suppose. But are they equipped to understand and live with their fellow human beings? Moreover, has their education encouraged them to think creatively and originally? Isn't this what education should be about?

ANTHONY, 18

But what is the main purpose of schools – to educate young people so that when they go out into the world they will be prepared for it? But are they? We learn our mathematics, English, physics, etc., but what do we learn about sex, marriage and things like this? These are just as important, but we don't learn very much about them.

DAVID, 15

We ought to be taught the meaning of local government and how elections work. We should be told of the difference between the different parties, and the people they represent. We should also be taught about other countries' politics and have discussions on which is the best method used to govern the countries.

RUTH, 13

I hope that all the schools of tomorrow will primarily have much more freedom and variety than those of today. By freedom I mean much more time to work individually on subjects or aspects of subjects the people find interesting; and by variety I mean more flexibility in the weekly programme of lessons.

GILLIAN, 14

Themes for discussion

What is your view of the British public examination system? Do you think that A-level courses are an effective way of developing specialist knowledge and interest?

Do you think your education has encouraged you 'to think creatively and originally'? Which aspects of your education have been the most creative and stimulating?

Do you think your education has taught you to think sufficiently about adult life? Is it important 'to learn about sex, marriage and things like this' at school?

Do you feel that you should have learnt more about politics and current affairs at school. Is it right for teachers to deal with controversial political issues in the classroom?

What changes would you have liked to see in the curriculum of your secondary education?

Teaching and learning: purposes and methods

Guidelines for the future of secondary education in Britain were set out in *The Newsom Report: Half Our Future*, published in 1963. Here is a key passage from this seminal government report.

Skills, qualities of character, knowledge, physical well-being are all to be desired. Boys and girls need to be helped to develop certain skills of communication in speech and in writing, in reading with understanding, and in calculations involving numbers and measurement. These skills are basic, in that they are tools to other learning, and without some mastery of them the pupils will be cut off from whole areas of human thought and experience. But they do not by themselves represent an adequate minimum education at which to aim.

All boys and girls need to develop, as well as skills, capacities for thought, judgement, enjoyment, curiosity. They need to develop a sense of responsibility for their work and towards other people, and to begin to arrive at some code of moral and social behaviour which is self-imposed. It is important that they should have some understanding of the physical world and of the human society in which they are growing up.

Since Newsom, a bewildering variety of views have been expressed as to how these objectives can be attained, and even as to the possibility of attaining them within the limitations of the normal classroom. The four extracts which follow reflect the spectrum of opinion.

The first two passages can be said broadly to represent the more 'traditional' viewpoint. Both appeared in *The Black Papers on Education*, edited by C.B. Cox and A.E. Dyson. The latter two sets of extracts represent more 'progressive' educational thinking. They are taken from books by Americans: the psychologist, Dr Benjamin Spock, and the educationalist, John Holt.

I The importance of discipline

No one would wish to return to the days when junior school children were rigidly confined to their rows of desks and learnt long lists of largely unrelated facts. But what is happening now? The restrictions of the old 11+ have almost disappeared, but the resulting freedom has been used in a multiplicity of ways. The children moving on to secondary schools present a bewildering problem even among the brightest groups.

Some at 11 can write fluently and imaginatively, paying due attention to paragraphing, punctuation and spelling, with none of their enthusiasm dampened. Others, of comparable intelligence, write illegibly, have no idea of arrangement of work and are thoroughly frustrated.

According to some present day psychologists, all teaching of young children must be child-centred: the teaching must grow from the child's interests and not be limited by any time-table division. Freedom of expression is all important and the method of conveying it is relatively unimportant. So far so good, but at what point should the child learn that correctness and accuracy have their place? All may be well at the junior school stage, but the freedom of the look-and-say method of teaching, of the outpouring of ideas without arrangement or plan has disastrous results at a later stage. For instance, when learning a foreign language, one incorrect letter may well alter the whole meaning of a sentence.

Some of my friends in junior schools tell me that marking and correcting is a thing of the past as it may bring a sense of failure to a child. So one sees mistakes becoming firmly implanted in the child's mind. Many schools arrange projects for their children and some begin through this to learn the excitement of indepedent research and the joy of exploring in the library. Others undertake the work but do little more than copy passages from the encyclopaedia and stick cut-out pictures in their books.

It is interesting to find that the children who, by the age of 11, have mastered the skills of the three Rs have gained a freedom which enables them to extend their horizons without the frustrations felt by those who at this stage realise the limitations imposed on them by the lack of disciplined thought . . .

Attitudes and behaviour in the country as a whole, of course, exert great pressure on our young people, but the schools must take a share of the blame. At the very heart of the problem is the need for self-discipline, for freedom within certain defined limits, for the security resulting from a realisation of cause and effect, from having certain decisions imposed and being able to enjoy the peace and security that comes from an ordered life.

The world is a noisy, chaotic and restless place, yet in schools we see the same lack of quiet encouraged. It is putting a great strain on young children to leave them constantly to make decisions with rarely any time in the day when they are quiet and listening. This feeling was expressed in a delightfully naïve manner by a little 11-year-old, beginning life in an ordered secondary school, who said she liked her new school because discipline was allowed.

A child who has always followed his own inclination finds it hard to sit down and learn his French and Latin verbs or his tables and yet, this knowledge acquired, he has the freedom to make rapid progress towards the exciting discoveries awaiting him at a more advanced stage. How comforting it is to know that, whatever distress there may be among the nations, two and two still make four.

The child who has been free to wander in his junior school much as he pleases, fails to see at a later stage why he should not wander further afield. Many children who come before juvenile courts have committed their offences during school hours, although the truancy is rarely known at the school. The boy has been present for registration and then has disappeared . . .

Many of my colleagues who are working in secondary schools would agree that the children who are the most well-balanced and who make the steadiest progress are those who come from the junior schools where the children have had plenty of opportunity for independent, free study, but who have learnt the importance of listening and concentrating and who have found the satisfaction which comes from doing something, at whatever standard, really well.

It is generally accepted that the home is the strongest influence on a child's development, so the child from the inadequate home, more than any other, needs security, an ordered school life, sensible discipline and quiet. C.M. JOHNSON

2 Discovery methods

Children manifest wide differences in developmental sophistication; some barely ever emerge from the stage of concrete operations; others enter on the stage of formal operations (implying the ability to handle certain sorts of abstractions) at a remarkably early age. It is these very bright children who often show considerable boredom with the leisurely informal pace of discovery methods – who yearn in fact to be told the answers to the questions they are asking because the answers will enable them to rush on to the next step in their eager intellectual enquiry. If discovery methods are used with these, they should be of the much more tightly structured type that Socrates used with the slave boy, when he led him from stage to stage by carefully framed questions; and indeed, the Socratic question is one of the best techniques by which a teacher can enable a child to make a discovery on his own; but, of course, it needs to be a very precise question, put by a teacher who knows exactly where he is going.

Discovery methods constitute an important but limited addition to the vocabulary of teaching. They are probably particularly useful for arousing interest – their function as motivators should not be underestimated; and with a child population many of whom are uninterested in school, this is not a factor to be despised. Furthermore, they can introduce children to a range of possibilities well beyond that of the old formal methods – they can make the world seem a more interesting place. Again, they help children to learn how to learn, without always having a teacher standing over them demanding a set piece in a set time. Children learn to rely on their own initiative to find out things, look up in books, etc.

But this enthusiastic picture needs to be curbed by a careful and thorough understanding on the part of the teachers as to exactly what they are aiming to accomplish, otherwise all the children acquire are a set of bits and pieces, orts and greasy relics, soon forgotten if ever really appreciated. The essence of their successful usage lies in their taking their place in a definite pedagogic scheme designed to aid initiation into complex learning structures which the teacher should have at his full command. To put it bluntly, he must work out for himself where he is going. He may find that 'discovery' methods possibly work best in subjects the basis of which is empirical (like the sciences, in their early stages) or whose development is logical (like mathematics). He must know that 'discovery' can and should be made from books – but that their use needs careful practice and a trained ability to glean relevant material from their contents. He should realise that in some subjects – such as literature – the main emphasis will still remain on his own personal charisma – on his ability to read well and feelingly in a class situation, for instance; and indeed that his power to excite interest and attention will always be fundamental. He will need to remember that instruction and planned repetitive work will still have vital roles to play, so that processes can be thoroughly explained, grasped and internalised by practice. He will even on occasions find that rote learning has a part to play – in the learning of spellings and tables, for instance. The point is that 'discovery methods' need to be collated with carefully presented and meaningful but quite formal instructions; and that the effectiveness of the Socratic question depends on his pedagogic skill and not on some spontaneous inner ripening on the part of the child.

There is, in fact, no one way. Subject matter differs enormously in nature and demands quite different sorts of pedagogic devices for its efficient transmission. And effective learning is the most important function of the school – it is the only institution in our society explicitly set up for such a purpose, and if it is not accomplished there it will not be accomplished anywhere else. Used competently, with an awareness of their place in the general armoury of tools at the teachers' disposal, these new (not so new, as we have seen) methods have a great deal to offer. Used incompetently, as a gimmick or a fashion, they are probably more disastrous to learning than an exclusive reliance on the old formal methods.

G.M. BANTOCK

3   What a school is for

The main lesson in school is how to get along in the world. Different subjects are merely means to this end. In the olden days, it used to be thought that all a school had to do was make children learn to read, write, add up and memorise a certain number of facts about the world. You learn only when things mean something to you. One job of a school is to make subjects so interesting and real that the children want to learn and remember.

You can go only so far with books and talk. You learn better from actually living the things you are studying. Children pick up more arithmetic in a week from running a school shop, giving change, and keeping the books than they learn in a month out of a book of cold figures.

It's no use knowing a lot if you can't be happy, can't get along with people, can't hold the kind of job you want. The good teacher tries to understand each child in order to help each pupil overcome weak points and develop into a well-rounded person. The child who lacks self-confidence needs chances to succeed. The trouble-making show-off has to learn how to gain the recognition he craves through doing good work. The child who doesn't know how to make friends needs help in becoming sociable and appealing. The child who seems to be lazy has to have her or his enthusiasm discovered.

A school can go only so far with a cut-and-dried programme in which everyone in the class reads from page 17 to page 23 in the reader at the same time and then does the examples on page 128 of the arithmetic book. It works well enough for the average child who is adjusted anyway. But it's too dull for the bright pupils, too speedy for the slow ones. It gives the boy who hates books a chance to stick paper clips in the pigtails of the girl in front. It does nothing to help the girl who is lonely or the boy who needs to learn cooperation.

How school work is made real and interesting

If you start with a topic that is real and interesting, you can use it to teach all manner of subjects. Take the case of a class in which the work of the year revolves around Indians.[1] The more the children find out about Indians, the more they want to know. The reader is a story of the Indians, and they really want to know what it says. For arithmetic they study how the Indians counted and what they used for money. Then arithmetic isn't a separate subject at all but a useful part of life. Geography isn't spots on a map, it's where the Indians lived and travelled and how life on the plains is different from forest life. In science study the children makes dyes from berries and dye cloth, or grow corn. They can make bows and arrows and Indian costumes.

The 'open classroom' means that several activities are going on at the same time in a classroom and that each child is free to participate in the one which appeals most at that time. This philosophy may seem much too permissive to be effective, to parents accustomed to the traditional classroom. But the method has been used extensively in Britain and the United States and it produces highly satisfactory results in the hands of competent teachers. Classroom order can be maintained. Each child gets round to all the necessary subjects in time and makes good progress. The great advantage is that the children, instead of developing the attitude we all developed – of waiting for the teacher to tell them what to do and how – take the initiative in learning, go at their own pace, keep a positive sense of discovery and joy about it, and seek individual help from the teacher as they need it.

The teachers in a good school know well that every child needs to develop self-discipline to be a useful adult. But they have learned that you can't snap discipline on to children from the outside, like handcuffs; it's something that children have to develop inside, like a backbone, by first understanding the purpose of their work and feeling a sense of responsibility to others in how they perform it.

How a school helps a difficult child

A flexible, interesting programme does more than just make school work appealing. It can be adjusted for the individual pupil. Take the case of a girl who had spent her first two years in a school where teaching was done by separate subjects. She was a girl who had great difficulty in learning to read and write. She had fallen behind the rest of the class. Inside, she felt ashamed about being a failure. Outwardly she wouldn't admit anything except that she hated school. She had never got on too easily with other children anyway, even before her school

1 North American Indians. The project outlined here is designed for American school pupils.

122

troubles began. Feeling that she was a duffer in the eyes of the others made matters worse. She had a chip on her shoulder. Once in a while she would show off to the class like a smart-alec. Her teacher used to think that she was just trying to be bad. Of course, she was really attempting, in this unfortunate way, to gain some kind of attention from the group. It was a healthy impulse to keep herself from being shut out.

She transferred to a school that was interested in helping her not only to read and write but to find her place in the group. The teacher learned in a conference with her mother that she used tools well and loved to paint and draw. He saw ways to use her strong points in the class. The children were all painting together a large picture of Indian life to hang on the wall. They were also working cooperatively on a model of an Indian village. The teacher arranged for the girl to have a part in both these jobs. Here were things she could do well without nervousness. As the days went by, she became more and more fascinated with Indians. In order to paint her part of the picture well, in order to make her part of the model correctly, she needed to find out more from the books about Indians. She wanted to learn to read. She tried harder. Her new classmates didn't think of her as a dope because she couldn't read. They thought more about what a help she was on the painting and the model. They occasionally commented on how good her work was and asked her to help them on their parts. She began to warm up. After all, she had been aching for recognition and friendliness for a long while. As she felt more accepted, she become more friendly and sociable.

Linking school with the world

A school wants its pupils to learn at first hand about the outside world, about the jobs of the local farmers and businessmen and workers, so that they will see the connection between their school work and real life. It arranges trips to near-by industries, asks people from the outside to come in and talk, encourages classroom discussion.

DR BENJAMIN SPOCK

4   The importance of active involvement

Sit still! Be quiet! These are the great watchwords of school. If an enemy spy from outer space were planning to take over the earth, and if his strategy were to prepare mankind for this takeover by making men's children as stupid as possible, he could find no better way to do it than to require them, for many hours a day, to be still and quiet. It is absolutely guaranteed to work. Children live all of a piece. Their bodies, their muscles, their voices and their brains are all hooked together. Turn off a part of them, and you turn them off altogether . . .

A child is most intelligent when the reality before him arouses in him a high degree of attention, interest, concentration, involvement – in short, when he cares most about what he is doing. This is why we should make schoolrooms and schoolwork as interesting and exciting as possible, not just so that school will be a pleasant place, but so that children in school will act intelligently and get into *the habit* of acting intelligently. The case against boredom in school is the same as the case against fear; it makes children behave stupidly, some on purpose, most because they cannot help it. If this goes on long enough, as it does in school, they forget what it is like to grasp at something, as they once grasped at everything, with all their minds and senses.

The child who wants to know something remembers it and uses it once he has it; the child who learns something to please or appease someone else forgets it when the need for pleasing or the danger of not appeasing is past. This is why children quickly forget all but a small part of what they learn in school. It is of no use or direct interest to them; they do not want, or expect, or even intend to remember it. The only difference between bad and good students in this respect is that the bad students forget right away, while the good students are careful to wait until after the exam. If for no other reason, we could well afford to throw out most of what we teach in school because the children throw out almost all of it anyway . . .

The alternative – I can see no other – is to have schools and classrooms in which each child in his own way can satisfy his curiosity, develop his abilities and talents, pursue his interests, and from the adults and other children around him get a glimpse of the great variety and richness of life. In short, the school should be a great smorgasbord of intellectual, artistic, creative, and athletic activities, from which each child could take whatever he wanted, and as much as he wanted, or as little.

About the future of work, two things seem clear. There is likely to be less and less of it; what there is, is likely to seem less and less like work . . . Men will tend more and more complicated machines; the proof that the job is going right will be that nothing is happening; only on the rare occasion when something goes wrong will they have something to do; usually it will be someone else's job to make sure that something doesn't go wrong again . . .

If so, more and more people will face two problems: how to justify, make meaningful their own lives, and how to fill up their time. The answer in both cases is to do something that seems very much worth doing. An important part of the business of education will be the finding of that something. Schools, therefore, will be places where children – and adults – may have time and opportunity to *do* a great many things, so as to find out which seem most worth doing. I emphasise the *do*. Very little of a child's time in school today is spent in *doing* anything; most of the time he is, or is supposed to be, either taking in information or, to prove that he has taken it in, spewing it back out. Sprinkled around here and there may be a tiny bit of art, or crafts, or sport, or drama, or music, or dance, but very few children are given enough time, *in school*, to work seriously on any of these things. If they do work seriously on them, it is outside of school, and their parents usually have to pay . . . Thus we have a huge vacuum in the minds and spirits of most children, and create a splendid market for mass entertainers and sensation peddlers of all kinds. The kinds of serious extracurricular interest that now occupy, and fill, and make worth living, the lives of a minority of people, will have to be found and enjoyed by all.
JOHN HOLT

124

Discovery or
discipline in the classroom;
two very different approaches.

Themes for discussion

Do you agree with Johnson that learning is best carried out in an
environment of order and strict discipline and comparative silence, or do
you agree with Holt that enforced silence is counter-productive, and that
children learn best when allowed to talk and move around the classroom?

What is meant by 'child-centred' education? What do you think is the most
common result of it: to promote selfishness and lack of self-discipline, as
Johnson claims, or to promote happiness, self-confidence and co-operation,
as Spock suggests?

Bantock claims that project-style 'discovery methods' of learning generally
result in students picking up 'bits and pieces' of knowledge which are 'soon
forgotten'; Holt claims that formal class teaching, in which the class spends a
good proportion of its time listening to and undertaking tasks imposed by
the teacher, results in children quickly forgetting all but 'a small part of what
they learn in school'. Which style of teaching have you found more
valuable?

Do you agree with Bantock that 'discovery methods' work best in
conjunction with structured learning such as 'the trained ability to glean
relevant material' from books?

Can you see any advantages in the kind of 'open classroom' approach
advocated by Spock, in which the teacher becomes an adviser, and where a
significant proportion of the time is spent outside the classroom itself?

Do you agree with Holt's scenario of the future of employment? How, and
to what extent, should schools concentrate on 'education for leisure'?

A 'progressive' school

The most famous 'progressive' school in Britain is Summerhill. The school was set up in the 1920s, on the principle of non-coercion, and the rules for the school are made and altered at weekly General School Meetings, at which all the staff and pupils have the right to vote, on a basis of complete equality.

Summerhill was founded by A. S. Neill, who was headmaster for half a century, and the extracts which follow are from his book *Summerhill: A Radical Approach to Education*.

The School

Summerhill was founded in 1921. The school is situated within the village of Leiston, in Suffolk, and is about a hundred miles from London.

Just a word about Summerhill pupils. Some children come to Summerhill at the age of five years, and others as late as 15. The children generally remain at the school until they are 16 years old. We generally have about 25 boys and 20 girls.

The Theory

Obviously, a school that makes active children sit at desks studying mostly useless subjects is a bad school. It is a good school only for those who believe in such a school, for those uncreative citizens who want docile, uncreative children who will fit into a civilisation whose standard of success is money . . .

When my wife and I began the school, we had one main idea: *to make the school fit the child* – instead of making the child fit the school . . .

Well, we set out to make a school in which we should allow children freedom to be themselves. In order to do this, we had to renounce all discipline, all direction, all suggestion, all moral training, all religious instruction. We have been called brave, but it did not require courage. All it required was what we had – a complete belief in the child as a good, not an evil, being. For almost 40 years, this belief in the goodness of the child has never wavered; it rather has become a final faith.

My view is that a child is innately wise and realistic. If left to himself without adult suggestion of any kind, he will develop as far as he is capable of developing. Logically, Summerhill is a place in which people who have the innate ability and wish to be scholars will be scholars; while those who are only fit to sweep the streets will sweep the streets. But we have not produced a street cleaner so far. Nor do I write this snobbishly, for I would rather see a school produce a happy street cleaner than a neurotic scholar.

The Practice

What is Summerhill like? Well, for one thing, lessons are optional. Children can go to them or stay away from them – for years if they want to. There *is* a timetable, but only for the teachers.

The children have classes usually according to their age, but sometimes according to their interests. We have no new methods of teaching, because we do not consider that teaching in itself matters very much. Whether a school has or has not a special method for teaching long division is of no significance, for long division is of no importance except to those who *want* to learn it. And the child who *wants* to learn long division *will* learn it no matter how it is taught.

Children who come to Summerhill as kindergarteners attend lessons from the beginning of their stay; but pupils from other schools vow that they will never attend any beastly lessons again at any time. They play and cycle and get in people's way, but they fight shy of lessons. This sometimes goes on for months. The recovery time is proportionate to the hatred their last school gave them. One record case was a girl from a convent. She loafed for three years. The average period of recovery from lesson aversion is three months . . .

In Summerhill, everyone has equal rights. No one is allowed to walk on my grand piano, and I am not allowed to borrow a boy's cycle without his permission. At a General School Meeting, the vote of a child of six counts for as much as my vote does.

But, says the knowing one, in practice the voices of grown-ups count. Doesn't the child of six wait to see how you vote before he raises his hand? I wish he sometimes would, for too many of my proposals are beaten. Free children are not easily influenced; the absence of fear accounts for this phenomenon. Indeed, the absence of fear is the finest thing that can happen to a child . . .

No pupil is compelled to attend lessons. But if Jimmy comes to English on Monday and does not make an appearance again until Friday of the following week, the others quite rightly object that he is holding back the work, and they may throw him out for impeding progress . . .

Afternoons are completely free for everyone. What they all do in the afternoon I do not know. I garden, and seldom see youngsters about. I see the juniors playing gangsters. Some of the seniors busy themselves with motors and radios and drawing and painting. In good weather, seniors play games. Some tinker about in the workshop, mending their bicycles or making boats or revolvers.

Tea is served at four. At five various activities begin. The juniors like to be read to. The middle group like to work in the Art room – painting, linoleum cuts, leather work, basket making. There is usually a busy group in the pottery; in fact, the pottery seems to be the favourite haunt morning and evening. The oldest group works from five onward. The wood and metal workshop is full every night . . .

Saturday night is our most important one, for it is General School Meeting night.

Some objections

Summerhill has always had a bit of a struggle to keep going. Few parents have the patience and faith to send their children to a school in which the youngsters can play as an alternative to learning . . .

Summerhill pupils are mostly children whose parents want them to be brought up without restrictive discipline . . . But we have never been able to take the children of the very poor. That is a pity, for we have had to confine our study to only the children of the middle class . . .

An American visitor, a professor of psychology, criticised our school on the grounds that it is an island, that it is not fitting into a community, and that it is not part of a larger social unit. My answer is this: if I were to found a school in a small town, attempting to make it a part of the community, what would happen? Out of a hundred parents, what percentage would approve of free choice in attending lessons?

From the word go, I should have to compromise with what I believe to be the truth.

A.S. NEILL

Discussion points

How do you think you would have coped with ten years at Summerhill?

Do you think that the extremes to which A.S. Neill took his ideas of non-coercion and democracy, and of the innate wisdom of children freed from adult pressure, would be likely to have helped your academic and personal development?

Do you think it is desirable or possible for a state school to concentrate, as Summerhill does, on the individual happiness and creativity of the pupils?

The Education Reform Act

In 1988, the British government introduced a new body of legislation for education in Britain, the first major reform of the entire education system since the 1944 Education Act.

In the following extracts from an article in the *Independent*, in July 1988, the main provisions of the Act are summarised, together with a cross-section of viewpoints on it.

A framework has been set for the future of education that could last for half a century. Kenneth Baker, Secretary of State for Education, sees it as an attempt to raise standards by freeing schools from professional and bureaucratic straitjackets, to create a service that responds to its consumers' needs. Many critics, pointing to Mr Baker's 415 new powers, see it as an irreversible shift of power to the centre, the biggest attack on local democracy made this century.

Others, pointing to the application of market forces, see it as a charter for the rich and powerful, reversing the 1944 principle that children should enjoy equality of opportunity, perhaps even paving the way for a privatised education service.

So what are the main points of the Bill?[2]

National Curriculum

Described by Mr Baker as the cornerstone of his reforms, the curriculum requires maths, English, science, history, geography, technology, music, art and physical education to be taught to children of all ages, a modern foreign language to children of 11 to 16 and Welsh to children in Welsh-speaking schools. The Secretary of State will lay down programmes of study, with attainment targets and assessment for children of 7, 11, 14 and 16.

What it means. Primary schools will need to pay more attention to science and technology. Secondary schools will need to ensure that all children follow a balanced curriculum until 16; it will no longer be possible for pupils to drop, say, modern languages or science at 13 or 14. The national curriculum is expected to take at least 70 per cent of the timetable for 14 to 16-year-olds.

Religious Education

Though religious education is not included in the national curriculum, a school must provide it for 'all registered pupils'.

What it means. In some respects, schools will have more freedom than under the 1944 Act. Though a daily act of worship is still required, it can take place at any time of the day, not just at the beginning, and it need not involve all pupils simultaneously.

Opting out

Schools will be able to opt out of local authority control and become grant maintained schools, funded directly from Whitehall.

What it means. All secondary schools and those primary schools with more than 300 pupils (about 10 per cent of the total) are eligible for grant-maintained status.

Though the paymaster will be different, grant maintained schools will receive the same money for current spending as they would receive under local authority control.

Open Enrolment

Parents will be able to enrol their children at any school that has physical capacity for them, provided this is appropriate for the age and aptitude of the child.

What it means. In many areas, the Bill will make little difference. But some, mainly urban, authorities have been setting maximum admissions limits below a school's physical capacity, in order to give all schools a fair share of pupils. Such authorities will have to change their procedures and the danger is that less popular schools will be trapped in a spiral of decline, with falling numbers of pupils and dwindling resources. Another danger is that white parents will manipulate their rights to keep their children out of schools that have large numbers of ethnic minority children, thus creating racial segregation.

Local management of schools

All secondary schools and primary schools with more than 200 pupils will receive budgets from the local authority, which they will be free to spend as they wish. The budget will cover the vast majority of their running costs, including staff salaries. Governors will have 'hire and fire' powers over staff.

What it means. Authorities will remain

2 The article appeared the day before the act became law.

technically accountable for spending ratepayers' money. But the schools will decide whether it goes on extra teachers or new staff-room furniture; at present, most have such flexibility only on day-to-day costs such as books and equipment.

Schools will operate rather as if they were small businesses. Income will depend on success in attracting custom.

Inner London Education Authority
The authority will be abolished and its powers transferred to the 13 inner London boroughs.

What it means. The ILEA has always involved a large-scale transfer of resources from richer boroughs, such as Westminster, to the poorer ones, such as Tower Hamlets. So the main danger is that schools in disadvantaged areas will get less money and fewer teachers than now; overall ILEA spending was already being reduced by the Government's rate-capping powers. The future of London-wide services, such as special needs, careers and child guidance, adult and further education, is uncertain. Parents, however, will still be able to choose schools across borough boundaries.

Polytechnics and colleges
All polytechnics, and those colleges with most of their work in higher education, will be taken out of local authority control. They will become free-standing corporate institutions, funded by a new Polytechnics and Colleges Funding Council.

What it means. The polytechnics and colleges will be in charge of their own payrolls and will have to set up financial control systems.

from the *Independent*, 28 July 1988

In an article which appeared in *The Times* in February 1988, John Clare reported an interview which he had held with the Secretary of State for Education responsible for the Education Reform Act (ERA), Kenneth Baker.

Here are some extracts from the article, in which Kenneth Baker explains his rationale for the National Curriculum:

'Our biggest mistake has been to demean and dismiss technological education as something to do with greasy overalls and dirty hands. That's where we missed out, by chilling the hopes and expectations of all those who would never be good at Latin or write great prose but who had an awful lot to offer.'

It leads him to one of his favourite Shakespearean quotations: 'The fire i' the flint shows not till it be struck'. 'One of the purposes of education is to strike the fire from the flint. Every boy and girl has something in them to be brought out, something they can do really well. But too many flints have not been struck. That's the real dreadful waste.'

That, says the Secretary of State for Education, is why he put computers into schools. That is why he is so proud of his nascent network of city technology colleges. And that is why technology is to be 10 per cent of every pupil's timetable under the national curriculum.

'I was given some carpentry lessons at school and a bit of metalwork, but you dropped them as quickly as you could because other things were supposed to be more important. Now, thanks to the Technical and Vocational Education

Initiative [TVEI] you see bright 16-year-olds who will be going on to university bending metal and making things that work.

'That's what I want all young people to have: a technological ability.' . . .

Technology is far from all Baker wants. He gladly subscribes to the thesis propounded by Chicago's Professor Allan Bloom that there is a core of knowledge all educated citizens should possess and which schools have a duty to impart.

'Part of it is teaching certain basic skills: literacy, numeracy and oracy. But over and above that, children should have an understanding of the literary and artistic background of this country as well as of the historical and geographical roots from which they come.

'That is why we must have a national curriculum. But there's nothing 1984-ish about it. One of the difficulties of the past 30 years has been that curriculum development has been too free-form, everyone doing their own thing. I sense a yearning among teachers for a more explicit framework, one which will limit the subjects pupils can drop.'

The subjects that worry Baker most are the three that will form the core of the national curriculum: English, mathematics and science. He describes English teaching as very patchy: 'There are too many young people who can read and understand only the simplest newspapers. That's very depressing.'

'I'll tell you what's wrong: not enough rigour, not demanding-enough teaching.' He quotes Browning on the 'reach exceeding the grasp, the grasp exceeding the reach'. 'Children must be extended and made to operate at the edge of what they think are their capabilities. Then they suddenly discover that it's not the edge, that they can do more than they thought.

'But that's not the way they've been taught. Instead, they're all roped together on the side of the hill to ensure that no one falls down and no one gets on the top. It's the convoy philosophy: keep them together instead of allowing them to go at their own speed and achieve things in their own way.

He says: 'It's like that other great struggle between those who think education is the acquisition of knowledge and those who say it's the application of that knowledge to life. But it's a false distinction. The basic skills have got to be taught first, and if they're taught intelligently you soon get into problem solving. Good teaching makes that transfer, bad teaching doesn't. It's that simple.'

from *The Times*, 18 February, 1988

Discussion points

What are your feelings about the so-called 'core curriculum'?

Do you think that compulsory testing of all children at key stages of their education is a welcome development?

Why do you think such strong emphasis has been placed on technological education? Is the emphasis right?

Do you agree with the setting up of city technology colleges?

Do you think that TVEI has been a successful development?

Do you agree with the principle of schools being allowed to opt out of local authority control?

Do you agree with the principle of parental choice over the school to which their child goes?

Can you see any pitfalls in the Local Management of Schools section of the ERA?

Do you feel that you have been extended enough in your education? If not, in what respects do you think you could and should have been extended more?

Writing/discussion suggestion

Devise your own 'ideal school', considering such issues as:

- the question of streaming, setting or mixed ability classes
- the degree of pupils' control over which subjects they should study
- the relative merits of public examination and continuous assessment courses
- the degree of stress on academic competition, through school exams, prizes, competitive marks for classwork, etc.
- the importance of fostering integration between pupils of different academic ability and home background
- the importance of individual attention in the classroom, and pastoral care outside it
- the role of senior pupils in maintaining discipline
- the use of corporal punishment
- the wearing of school uniform
- the importance of regular school assemblies.

Questionnaire

A questionnaire on education might be an interesting project for a few students to undertake. The questionnaire could be prepared and analysed, and a report on it written and printed for the rest of the class to discuss and evaluate, along the guidelines explained on page 134.
Here are a few possible questions for inclusion in a questionnaire:

1 What are the most important purposes of education:
   a to develop interests for later life;
   b to prepare for public examinations;
   c to develop skills which will be useful in later life;
   d to develop imagination and creativity?
   (List in order of importance.)

2 Which school subject do you find
   a the most interesting;
   b the least interesting? Say why.

3 Do you think that discipline should be more, or less, strict in the school
   you attend(ed)? Say in what way.

4 Do you think that homework is useful or not?
   Do you think you should get more, the same amount, or less
   homework than you do?

(Some of the questions on page 117 could also be framed for inclusion in the
questionnaire.)

Essay titles

a With the advent of the three- or four-day working week, should
   education be for leisure?

b Is educational equality a myth?

c What changes would you like to see in the educational system of this
   country?

d What do you think education is for?

e How far do you think students should have a say in the running of the
   school or college which they attend?

f Do schools try hard enough to develop pupils' creativity?

g Bearing in mind current trends, what kind of an education would you
   plan for a child born today?

h How far should education be used in an attempt to change society?

Bibliography

(The topic of education is so broad, and so many books have been written on
it, that there seems little point in attempting to make any specific suggestions
for further reading. The bibliography, therefore, simply lists the books
referred to in this chapter.)

Blishen, Edward, *The School that I'd like*, Penguin, 1969
Cox, C.B. and Dyson, A.E., *The Black Papers on Education*, Davis
   Poynter, 1971
Holt, John, *How Children Fail*, Penguin, 1964
Holt, John, *The Underachieving School*, Penguin, 1971
Macbeth, John E.C., *A Question of Schooling*, Hodder and Stoughton, 1976

Neill, A.S., *Summerhill*, Penguin, 1968
Newsom, John, *The Newsom Report: Half Our Future*, HMSO, 1963
Spock, Benjamin *Baby and Child Care*, Bodley Head, 1979

Advice on writing: preparing and presenting a questionnaire

For a questionnaire to yield meaningful results a number of factors must be taken into consideration.

Before you begin to prepare the questionnaire you must be absolutely clear about your aims, and be able to explain them clearly both when conducting the interviews and when writing up your report.

You must choose your sample carefully, as this is likely to influence the results of the questionnaire. For instance, you can only draw conclusions about the community in general from your data if the sample represents a cross-section of the community. Alternatively, you may wish to concentrate on particular groups, such as social class groups or year groups in a school, and correlate answers with these groups.

You might include a mixture of open- and closed-ended questions. The simplest form of closed-ended question just demands a 'yes'/'no'/ 'don't know' response. If you are collecting opinions or attitudes the interviewees might be given a statement and asked to respond in one of a number of given ways, the usual format being: 'strongly agree'/'agree'/'undecided'/ 'disagree'/'strongly disagree'. These can be numbered for ease of analysis. In the case of open-ended questions, interviewees are free to answer in any way they want. It is important that the questions are clear and unambiguous, and it is a good idea to show your completed draft questionnaire to someone else, to ensure that there is no ambiguity, and re-draft it if necessary.

When you are conducting your survey, it is important to explain to each interviewee exactly what it is about. A sample of 50 is generally considered to be the minimum required to achieve meaningful results, especially if it is to be subdivided into different groups.

The analysis of your questionnaire and the presentation of your report are likely to take much longer than the collection of your information. When you are analysing the answers to each question, it is simplest to put the questionnaires into separate piles according to the replies.

Your report should start with an explanation of the object and aims of your research, and of your research procedure. You should go on to explain the sample in terms of numbers and groupings. Each question should then be quoted, and the percentage response to the questions given. Significant trends in the answers should be explained, and particularly interesting answers to open-ended questions could perhaps be quoted. Finally, you should try to draw some conclusions from the questionnaire as a whole.

CRIME AND PUNISHMENT

Several aspects of the theme of crime and punishment are explored in this chapter: the viewpoints quoted are those of criminologists, psychologists, journalists, hooligans, prisoners, politicians and Jesus Christ. The chapter begins with a comprehension exercise on a provocative piece of journalism on the police.

Comprehension and comment

Read the following article carefully and answer the questions below. You are advised to spend about one and a half hours on this exercise.

a   Explain, in your own words, the 'lesser matter' introduced in the third paragraph.   *(3 marks)*

b   Give your response to paragraph 5 of the passage.   *(6 marks)*

c   Comment on each of the following aspects of the article, showing your reaction to them and how they are likely to influence the reader: the headline   the sub-heading   the picture and caption.   *(9 marks)*

d   Consider carefully the language and tone of the passage to show:
   (i)   its attitude to the Metropolitan police;   *(7 marks)*
   (ii)   its attitude to the Police Complaints Authority and Scotland Yard.   *(6 marks)*

e   Explain what the writer has to say about 'power' in paragraph 7.   *(4 marks)*

f   Why does the writer describe Scotland Yard's statement in paragraph 9 as 'shabby, deceitful words'?   *(5 marks)*

g   Write a letter to *The Times* offering your opinion of Bernard Levin's article.   *(10 marks)*

(50 marks total)

When there's more to black and blue than the bruises

Bernard Levin explains how racist thugs in uniform can be made to think twice before putting the boot in

POLICE COMPLAINTS AUTHORITY

Francis Morley

Last week, the general; today, the particular. Four black men have been paid damages in a civil process, totalling £20,000, by the Metropolitan Police. They had sued for assault, false imprisonment and malicious prosecution, and the Met settled out of court; the plaintiffs said they had been racially abused as well as physically ill-treated. In what has become standard conduct in policemen who have done wrong, the victims had earlier been prosecuted in the criminal courts; the magistrates dismissed all the charges as soon as the prosecution had finished; so obviously bogus were the cases there was no need for the defence to be called.

These upright benchers milked the Met for £7,500 in costs; the Met had to shell out another £3,000 in costs at the end of the civil action. There goes £10,500; not a bad rate I suppose, for an evening's entertainment, particularly since it is the taxpayer who has to foot the bill.

Before I explore the more significant aspects of these cases, there is one lesser matter to be considered. I do not know whether there is more police wrongdoing where racial matters are involved, or whether it only seems so because there is more public reporting and comment on such incidents. But there is disturbing evidence that the corner-cutting policemen are getting more stupid, a most dangerous combination.

The evidence for my claim lies in the nature of the people they pick on: not long ago I went into detail about a shocking case in which a black man was awarded a record £100,000 (reduced on appeal to £65,000) for having had drugs planted on him. The stupidity lay in the fact that the chosen victim turned out to be a teetotal, non-smoking lay preacher. But the coppers in the more recent case went a good deal further; the men they nicked were not only Seventh Day Adventists (you can't get more respectable than that), but they were returning from a religious retreat (there is reason to believe they were actually praying, in their van) when Plod decided to have his fun.

Don't misunderstand me; I like fun as well as any man, nor do I feel that the way I get it should be the only way permitted. If the Force like to while away an evening knocking a few darkies about, it is not for me to insist that they should give up the practice and try Wagner. But could not their superiors suggest that before kick-off they should pause to scrutinise the quality and identity of the kickees more closely?

Few will be surprised to learn that the policemen involved are still in the Met, and that the Police Complaints Authority may be ready to give its adjudication some time in the reign of King Charles the Fourteenth. But some may be surprised to learn that the total damages awarded in such cases quadrupled in 1988, and increased again

by a third in 1989. The overall total of the three years amounts to not much less than a million. And that is the damages only; costs must be added to the figure. It would be naive to suggest that the damages should come out of the wages of the miscreants and their superiors, but a compromise might be found; perhaps after such a case one of their helicopters or other expensive toys should be taken away from them.

Anyone with power will be tempted to extend it, and since there are people with weak characters in any organisation, there will be policemen who succumb to the temptation to extend their power. Anyone with extended power will likewise be tempted to abuse it, and since the same test governs the greater temptation, there will be policemen who abuse their increment of power. Anyone who abuses power is standing on a cliff-top of corruption, and it is well known that many of those who go near such cliff-tops lose their footing and fall over.

I do not know how to cure the disease of which these cases are the symptom, but I can see one form of treatment, widely applied, which so far from effecting a cure is making the disease worse. This poisoned pill was doled out lavishly in the case of the Seventh Day Adventists, as it has been in many other similar scandals. It is time

for the authorities to insist that the prescribing of it must cease, and any surplus supplies returned to the dispensary.

When the four black men had received their damages settlement and their costs, Scotland Yard put out a statement saying that the payments were made 'without any admission of guilt', and that 'it will be borne in mind that it is only necessary for the plaintiffs to prove a case on the balance of probabilities, and in considering whether an action should be settled, many matters are taken into account'.

These are shabby, deceitful words. Are we invited to believe that the Met shelled out £30,000 from nothing but a charitable impulse? Every word and nuance of that statement testifies to the extent of the rot, and a police force content to rely on such evasion of the truth has forgotten what truth is. There was no need for the Yard to say anything at all; yet it went out of its way to dig itself further into the mire. That, not the guilty policemen, constitutes the disease and the fatal prescription alike. How do the Met's leaders expect to restore public confidence in the police – a confidence that in recent years has suffered a catastrophic fall – if they demonstrate so clearly their inability to understand why such conduct erodes the confidence even further?

There is an obvious

reply, but it is dangerous, and the Met takes care it will remain dangerous. It is for those who have been wronged, and who have been offered compensation with the grubby string of 'no guilt' attached, to refuse a settlement which denies culpability. The danger, of course, is in our system of civil law; if a plaintiff refuses a sum offered and the defendent pays into court more than a jury subsequently awards, the plaintiff must pay the costs, often wiping out the damages.

There is, however, a way round that problem, and it has the extra merit of testing the Met's good faith. Let the Commissioner announce that from now on, if a plaintiff refuses to take a proffered settlement without admission of guilt, the question of damages shall be left entirely to the jury, with no attempt at a pre-emptive paying-in. The judges cannot be commanded; but I trust that the use of such weasel words would, when the plaintiff won, encourage the bench to increase the damages.

This will not by itself stop policemen ill-treating respectable black men for no better reason than that they haven't ill-treated one since the Thursday before last. But even that problem is soluble, if heed is paid to the advice I gave a few paragraphs back, where I urged the Met's higher ranks to persuade the men on the beat that they should have a good long look at the next man whom they feel like clouting. Otherwise, they will sooner or later march into the station dragging a black man 5ft 2in tall wearing very peculiar clothes, only to discover, after explaining that the prisoner had got his swollen eye, torn lip and lost front teeth from a misdirected conker, that they have booked, not to say bashed, Archbishop Tutu.

BERNARD LEVIN, *The Times*, August 1990

Juvenile crime

In this newspaper article, the sports journalist, Dudley Doust, reports an interview with a young Scottish football hooligan.

The article appeared in the *Sunday Times* in 1975. Over the years which followed, violence inside football grounds increased in frequency and intensity, until it died down again at the end of the 1980s, partly as a result of the 'closer surveillance' and the 'cages for fans' which 'Bobby' anticipates in the article. In other essential respects, the piece could have been written 15 years later.

It all ends with a kick in the face

Scotland's defeat in Czechoslovakia last week was reason enough to get drunk and Bobby McTear didn't rouse himself until noon next day. Gazing idly at the Ulster Volunteer Forces's poster and the King Billy portrait on the bedroom wall he dressed and then drifted down to the local pub near Bridgeton Cross in Glasgow. It was Bobby's first day back since he was jailed and fined £40 for assault and breach of the peace at the Aston Villa – Rangers match in Birmingham.

'Pleasure? No pleasure in throwing a bottle, man. Revenge is the word for it. When you throw the bottle you hope you'll hit some bastard, a polis, or a Catholic, a guy who's given you some shit about the Orange or Rangers or Glasgow.' His accent was as thick as porridge. 'There's always going to be fighting at Rangers matches. Aye, it's a good feeling to kick some guy in the baws. He's down and he's useless, and so you kick him in the face after that. That ends it.'

Bobby McTear is not the lad's real name, but his story is true. He is 17 years old. He looks younger. He has a spray of facial pimples and wears a scab, much like a signet ring, on his left little knuckle. He has also a knife-wound which, in the quiet of a nearby library reading room, he later pulled off his shirt to display; an ugly red welt under the shoulder blade.

'Parkhead,' he said. 'I didn't know what happened to me until I got home and was changing my shirt. Then I saw all this blood, and I went to the Royal Infirmary and got seven stitches. A week later we played the Celtic bastards again, and 16 of us got two guys on the London Road and we done 'em in. I took an open razor and did a guy's jaw. Seventeen stitches.'

In two seasons Bobby has been convicted on 11 charges of assault or breach of the peace following football matches. He has served two short spells in prison. 'I had my first football fight when I was 13,' he said. 'I was standing on the railway station after the Rangers – Aberdeen game, and a guy went like this to my dad, and told him to get out of the road. So my dad starts fighting him and I hit the guy over the head with a bottle. Out cold. Thirteen stitches.' Stitch-count is important in the language of violence.

Bobby was born in Bridgeton Cross, one of Glasgow's gloomy Victorian slums. His mother was born a Catholic in Northern Ireland and down the years her husband, who is sometimes a long distance lorry driver, has fought with her Catholic brothers. 'We all go to the Orange Order,' said Bobby. 'I'm a Protestant, and I'll always live up to my religion. I'll live up to it until the day I die.'

Rangers hooligans – indeed, even most of their orderly fans – have found comfort in the unblinking bigoted policy of the Rangers Football Club. During its 103-year history the club's proud tradition has been not to sign or play a Catholic in the side. That suits Bobby. Further, it is unlikely that he was shaken later when the club announced it was to drop its sectarian bias.

'A Catholic playing for Rangers?' he laughed. 'You gotta be joking. You'll never see a Catholic in the side, and if you do you won't see me supporting Rangers.' He sensed the irony of this ultimatum. 'Maybe that would be a good thing. Maybe if they brought in a Catholic on the side there'd be a lot less trouble because we guys, the trouble-makers, would be finished with Rangers.'

Bobby, however, foresaw a closer surveillance of alcoholic liquor at Ibrox; perhaps identity cards, cages for fans and even a lock-out for himself and his hooligan friends. He would like to see lounges and proper seating, he said, and then, in the way of a Glaswegian, he delivered a sudden, soft, piercing throw-away line – '. . . and give us more respect.'

Bobby left school abruptly at 15. 'If I'd finished school I might have been in some better place than this one,' he said with neither self-pity or remorse. 'I got expelled. I hit the teacher with a case of books.' He trained briefly as a bricklayer but, he says, due to his many criminal convictions he has been unable to get work. He drifts, steals, does a bit of house-breaking and, best of all, fights at football matches.

'I'm doing it because there's nothing else to do. There's not even a cinema or a dance hall down here at the Cross. Things might be a wee bit different if I had a job.' He smiled. 'But I'd still go to games and have a battle.'

The Villa battle followed a familiar pattern. Bobby and his mates, joined by three girls and half-a-dozen Rangers supporters from Belfast, boarded a chartered coach (£6 return) at Bridgeton Cross, at seven o'clock on Saturday morning. They had their standard battle gear: razors, screw-top bottles of beer, bottles of sweet Old English wine, blue and white Rangers scarves and, scattered across the occasional breast, the badge of the Red Hand of Ulster. 'If you don't have your gear ready, they'll be ready before you.'

On the coach, Bobby slept much of the way down the M6, and now and then joined in the songs exalting the beautiful Rangers and blaspheming the Pope. He was spoiling for the inevitable fight: 'If we get beat, we'll look for trouble. If we don't get beat, somebody else will look for trouble and we'll battle them back.'

The coach arrived at Villa Park just before noon. Bobby and his mates sent their girls into a pub with the purpose of enticing young Villa fans to the coach. The waiting Scots ambushed and 'mingled' the luckless English. Bobby stole £1.50 from one victim. 'You got to be half-drunk when this happens. If we weren't drunk? That's a hard question. I'll tell you, I wouldn't do it alone unless I had a bottle of wine in me.'

At the turnstiles, Bobby says, a young Villa fan taunted him: 'Go back to Glasgow, you yellow Orange bastards.' Bobby swung, missed and hit a brick wall. Trouble later broke out when Rangers went two down. Bobby and his mates swept into the passages under the stands. They smashed open a kiosk, went for the beer when 'this big polis started waving a stick at us. Then he dropped his stick and we jumped in and gave him a battering.'

Bobby was arrested outside the ground and after appearing in court on Monday ('fined £3 a week and I'm not paying it'), he wandered the Birmingham streets that night, stealing £20 from a newsagent and finally jumping on a train back to Glasgow without paying the fare. He slept under the seats to avoid the guard. What did his parents think of all this? 'They don't know. They don't know anything. My father just says, 'If you do daft things it's your own fault.'

Bobby one day may kill somebody. Would he be happy to kill anybody? 'No,' he said, 'I don't want to kill anybody. I want to hurt him bad, really mark the bastard, but I don't want to kill him. He has to go home to his mother and father. Same as me.'

Bobby was restless. He wanted to leave the library. But it was past 2.30 in the afternoon and the pub would be closed. So he went to a nearby snooker hall. One look at his face, and the attendant stopped the turnstile. The boy wasn't wanted. Bored and barred, Bobby walked back towards the street, pausing to urinate against the big oak door.

DUDLEY DOUST, *Sunday Times*, August 1975

Putting the boot in

In this extract from a *Times* article, the psychologist, Dr Sybil Eysenck, argues for harder sentencing of violent juvenile offenders.

My fear is that the escalation of crime, due to our unwillingness to take a firm stand and really enforce our laws, is leading to a far greater danger. This is the new public attitude to the police. For many generations there has been a strong unspoken rule concerning the police; nobody dared argue with them, never mind strike them. This taboo has slowly seeped away and assaults on the police are now not uncommon. Where the sight of a blue uniform once made a would-be criminal run, the new attitude is confrontation. Instead of chasing their suspects the police now reckon to have to put up a fight to restrain them.

There cannot be many people who did not feel truly alarmed by the riots in Bristol recently during which the police left the citizens to their own devices for four hours. If we expect police to protect the public, surely we should give them far more support and rather less criticism for their occasional indiscretions. Indeed, can we wonder at the lack of trust the police must feel towards the likes of soccer hooligans and demonstrators who so freely 'put the boot in' whenever they get within striking distance of a policeman? Maybe they have come to resent some members of the public and would return to the 'gentle bobby' image as soon as respect was restored for them. Magistrates too could do their bit; with £1,000 and six months' imprisonment as their maximum sentence for assaults on the police, why do they mete out a fine of £25 on average for such an offence? Nobody would welcome a 'chop off their hands' remedy for crime, but I for one would like to see a more determined effort to get to grips with the problem of lawlessness.

DR SYBIL EYSENCK

Analysis and discussion

The following questions can be answered in the form of a further comprehension and comment exercise, and/or as part of a general class discussion of crime and punishment.

1   Discuss the conflicting views of the police presented by Bernard Levin and Sybil Eysenck.

2   To what extent do you support Sybil Eysenck's views of the treatment of hooligans like 'Bobby McTear' by social workers, sociologists and magistrates?

3   From the evidence of 'Bobby McTear's' account of himself, what do you think are the main factors which have contributed to his becoming a juvenile delinquent?

4   Is there anything that could be done – socially, educationally or punitively – to persuade the 'Bobby McTears' of the world to behave with a greater sense of social responsibility?

The punishment of young offenders

Varieties of punishment

Magistrates courts have a number of options available when sentencing juvenile delinquents. These are some of the main ones:

a Prison sentences.

b Fines, or restitution to the victims of the crimes.

c Probation. The offender is assigned a probation officer, to whom he or she must report at regular intervals – normally a half-hour session once a week – for a specified length of time. During these sessions the probation officer tries to find out why his or her client committed the offence and whether there is anything that can be corrected. He or she also attempts to minimise the likelihood of the offender getting into trouble again.

d Intermediate Treatment (IT). Delinquents are 'sentenced' to 'treatment' intended to prevent them from reaching a stage where institutionalised care and control is needed. They are removed from their immediate home environment for a brief period or a succession of brief periods, often in company with non-offenders from deprived backgrounds. A 1972 government circular explained the rationale behind IT: 'It will be an important aim to secure the child's acceptance of his treatment, so that he does not resent it; and this aim is unlikely to be achieved if it involves activities which appear to set him apart from his contemporaries.' In practice this means 'treatment' such as compulsory attendance at youth clubs or other centres where social workers organise discussions and leisure activities and/or outdoor activities, not normally available to these delinquents, such as rock climbing, canoeing, art and drama.

e Residential care at Community Homes with education (CH(E)s). Offenders are 'sentenced' to an extended period in a Community Home concerned with counselling, discussion and therapy, a central feature of which is education at anything from remedial to public examination level, and job training.

f Community Service Order (CSO). Introduced in the 1972 Criminal Justice Act, the CSO means that courts could 'award from 40 to 240 hours of service to the community, normally to be completed over a period of not more than twelve months. This new idea of justice grew out of the voluntary service movement . . . The offender would be brought into direct contact with a variety of social needs in the community . . . There was also the hope that some offenders, having the experience of helping others, might want to continue such service to the community after the legal obligation had been fulfilled.' (Dennie Briggs: *In Place of Prison*.)

142

g   Borstal, and 'short, sharp shock' treatment. The latter 'treatment' was introduced in the late 1970s to provide brief periods of tough punishment, involving rigorous discipline and regular, intense exercise in detention centres, the aim of which is to instil a sense of self-discipline. Borstals, which have been in existence for several decades, are detention centres to which young offenders are sent for longer periods of military-style punishment.

Community Service Orders

To illustrate how one of these options can be made to work, here is an extract from the book *In Place of Prison*, by Dennie Briggs. The speaker is a young man of 22 called Dick Marshall, sentenced to a spell of Community Service.

I've spent time in borstal and in prison. I've had suspended sentences, fines and probation orders – I suppose you could say I've had all the alternatives to prison there are. In early 1973 I was due to go to court for 'theft'. Then I got into an argument with this full-time student when I was on day release to a college from the pits. I butted him and his teeth went through his tongue. I knew I had had it this time.

The probation officer told me about this new idea of CSO. I wasn't interested in helping people, but I didn't want to go to prison again. So, I said I'd like that, as a con. I just didn't want to go to the nick.

I made the right noises in court. The magistrate said this is my last chance as I had a very bad record. The probation officer said I was a good lad at heart. The magistrate finally gave me 200 hours which he saw roughly as seven months in the nick. He warned me that if I didn't do as I was told and stay out of trouble, he'd breach me and this time I'd go to prison.

The next day I went to see John Harding. He gave me this list of jobs that were available. Things like, you know, soup runs, painting and decorating, digging canals. Then there was a chance of doing youth work. I didn't fancy digging canals or painting. Maybe the youth club would have table tennis; I like that and I thought I could have a good time. I plumped for the youth club. I thought it would be an easy line. There was only one objection to this and that was that they might not want me because I had a record of violence and the animal description used by the magistrate stuck.

Next day I went to see my youth club leader. We got on straight away. He was a young guy with radical views. He ran an easy club and was dead against prison, wanted to open things up.

So I started at the youth club the following week. I was to go there two to three times a week. The idea of CSO is not to cram the hours up but to spread them out over time. I thought it would be a right doss, but that was soon knocked out of me. This particular youth club had the most under-privileged kids in town in it. There was no disciplining the kids, they didn't have to pay fees. There were a hell of a lot of them, all between 12 and 16.

I made the first mistake of giving one kid a piggy back ride. I didn't know what else to do. Then I had to give all of them a ride. I was grabbed by the kids to do things. I was so exhausted and pissed off after the first night, I didn't fancy doing 200 hours of this.

I liked the leader and got on with him. He had a tough job, but didn't seem to get discouraged. I carried on for a couple of months and got to liking some of the kids.

Then wham! I was called to court. I had been on bail for a previous charge. John Harding and the youth club leader both went to court and spoke up for me. The judge listened but he wouldn't hear of it.

'I fought for you in World War Two,' is the way he put it to me. Besides he said, 'What would others think if I let you off?'

'Six months,' he said. Off I went to the nick again. The youth club leader came to see me while I was in prison. We had some talks and he could see I had come around slightly. I probably could have got out of my CSO seeing I was doing six months. But I decided I'd go back to the club when I got out. I didn't know when I'd get out, as another old offence came up. While I was being arrested, a police officer hit me and broke my nose. I got mad and hit him. So I was called to trial and given another three months. I appealed and luckily won. Altogether I did five months.

When I went back to the youth club, things had changed, and I decided I needed a more definite role rather than just walking around and being grabbed to do any old thing. The most incredible thing happened, you wouldn't believe this. You see, there was another bloke who had got a CSO. While I was in prison the leader got another job. There was no one to run the club so they put this guy in charge. He was there when I got out. So I guess technically I reported to him. How about that – one ex-con in charge of another? We never worried about things like that, just got on with the job.

I organised a table-tennis team, and this gave me a role in the kids' eyes. The team started doing well and this gave me a sense of achieving something. After I came back the kids knew I was an offender. When they realised this, we got on even better. I became a regular with them and they were less wary of me. They could identify more with me now as they didn't see me as someone coming in to supervise them. I was the one being supervised you might say.

Most of the kids in that club had been in trouble, or were at the time. So were some of their families. Some of the 16-year-olds were in fact on bail. They began to talk to me about it and ask my advice. At first it was legal questions, how to talk in court and how to beat their cases. Then they wanted to know what it was like inside and what to expect if they got locked up. I began to feel more a part of the place, more like a counsellor, and didn't think of it as serving an order or sentence.

You know a funny thing happened. Somewhere along the line, I lost my card that had to be signed each night I went to the club and the number of hours recorded. Never thought about it. Then my year was up and only 177 hours had been recorded. I had done many times that amount but no one had kept track. So John Harding had to go back to court and get the order extended for another twelve months to make up the lost time. I didn't resent this, I was going to go on working there anyway.

I was lucky to get a youth club and that particular one. If I'd ended up digging a canal, I'd have been even more resentful and probably never finished it out. This youth club wasn't regulated. And John Harding said he didn't want me clocking-in like at a Detention Centre, but to get involved and perhaps continue on after my time was up.

Most of all it gave me a chance to prove to myself that I wasn't all what people had said I was: a thief, violent, couldn't stick with a job. 'You're a right bastard,' was the exact words one judge said to me in court. But just as bad, were the professionals who talk nice to you – you know underneath they really think the same.

DENNIE BRIGGS

Discussion/role play

1   Here is an imaginary situation:

Three youths are travelling on a bus at night, after an evening at the pub. A girl is also on the bus, alone. When she gets up, they do also; she panics, and they chase her down the stairs. The bus driver intercedes and the youths turn on him. Another passenger comes to his assistance. Both are injured, and the boys run away. The result of the incident is that the driver, after a brief spell in hospital, is traumatised by the incident, and is afraid to return to work; the passenger suffers from an eye injury which requires a series of operations over many months, and which leaves his eyesight permanently impaired, and the boys are arrested and appear at a magistrates' court, having been recognised by witnesses. During their trial, it emerges that one of them has several previous convictions for violence, vandalism and theft, the second has a single suspended sentence for theft, and the third has no previous convictions.

Which of the methods of punishment summarised on pages 142-3 would be most suitable for each of the three youths?

Do you know of any incidents of hooliganism in which the culprits were taken to court? What happened to them? What do you think caused the individuals concerned to become hooligans?

You might wish to analyse this case through role play. The situation will be a magistrates' court, with students playing the roles of the three defendants, the defence and prosecution lawyers, and the magistrates who discuss the most suitable punishment for each of the three offenders. Alternatively, you may wish to concentrate just on the magistrates' deliberations.

2 'Bobby McTear' has been arrested again for 'assault and breach of the peace' after a football match. A group of between four and six students should discuss the most suitable punishment for him, adopting the roles of magistrates, and assuming that all the information contained on pages 138-40 has been placed before them in court.

3 What is needed to stem the tide of juvenile delinquency: stricter punishment and stronger 'law and order', or more enlightened social policies to prevent delinquency from occurring in the first place?

The morality of punishment

The biblical viewpoint

The 'lex talionis' concept of retributive punishment ('an eye for an eye') goes back thousands of years. Two thousand years ago this ancient law was repudiated, and a very different view of punishment was expressed. Consider the following extracts from the Old and New Testaments (Authorised Version):

And he that killeth any man shall surely be put to death.
And he that killeth a beast shall make it good, beast for beast.
And if a man cause a blemish in his neighbour; as he hath done, so shall it be done
    to him;
Breach for breach, eye for eye, tooth for tooth: as he hath caused a blemish
    in a man, so shall it be done to him again.

(Leviticus 24 v 17–20)

Ye have heard that it hath been said, An eye for an eye, and a tooth for a tooth:
But I say unto you, That ye resist not evil: but whosoever shall smite thee on thy
    right cheek, turn to him the other also.
And if any man will sue thee at the law, and take away thy coat, let him have thy
    cloak also.

(St Matthew 5 v 38–40)

Jesus went unto the mount of Olives.
And in the early morning he came again into the temple, and all the people came
    unto him; and he sat down, and taught them.
And the scribes and Pharisees brought unto him a woman taken in adultery;
    and when they had set her in the midst;
They say unto him, Master, this woman was taken in adultery, in the very act.
Now Moses in the law commanded us, that such should be stoned: but what
    sayest thou?
This they said, tempting him, that they might have to accuse him. But Jesus
    stooped down, and with his finger wrote on the ground, as though he heard
    them not.

146

So when they continued asking him, he lifted up himself, and said unto them,
He that is without sin among you, let him first cast a stone at her.
And again he stooped down, and wrote on the ground.
And they which heard it, being convicted by their own conscience, went out
one by one, beginning at the eldest, even unto the last: and Jesus was left alone,
and the woman standing in the midst.
When Jesus had lifted up himself, and saw none but the woman, he said unto
her, Woman, where are those thine accusers? Hath no man condemned
thee?
She said, No man, lord. And Jesus said unto her, Neither do I condemn thee:
go, and sin no more.

(St John 8 v 1–11)

No large-scale society has ever adopted the view of punishment here
ascribed to Jesus Christ in the gospels of Matthew and John, though some
serious writers, like Leo Tolstoy, in his late work *What I Believe*, have
argued, on the basis of such New Testament passages, that society has no
right to stand in judgement on individuals.

Discussion points

Do you think that Christ really meant his words to be taken as a disavowal
of all forms of punishment, as Tolstoy understood them?

What do you think would happen if they were treated that way, and
societies acted upon them?

The prison system

Imprisonment has for centuries been the main means by which society deals
with adult criminals. For at least the past 200 years, however, questions have
been raised as to the purpose of prisons, and suggestions for prison reform
have been offered. In this section we will consider these issues.

First, some facts, figures and opinions about the prison situation in
Britain, taken from an article in *The Times:*

In spite of a slowdown in the number of people in prison in the early 1980s, the
prison population jumped by 3,070 last year to more than 47,303, although there is
provision only for 39,804 inmates . . .

Overcrowding has reached crisis proportions in most prisons throughout the
country and in at least three, Leeds, Oxford, and Leicester, the number of inmates
exceeds official capacity by 100 per cent . . .

Mr Cavadino[1] said: 'Overcrowding means that in many cases prisoners are held

1 Paul Cavadino, a spokesman for the National Association for the Care and Resettlement of
   Offenders (NACRO).

two or three in a cell built for one person in Victorian times. They have no access to proper sanitary facilities while locked up, only a bucket in the cell. It is degrading.'

The lack of adequate numbers of prison officials has led to more than 70 prison workshops and educational centres being closed, leaving prisoners up to 23 hours a day behind bars, according to Mr Colin Steel, national chairman for the Prison Officers' Association.

'The more we get people out of their cells, the easier it is to control them,' Mr Steel said. 'Lock a guy up for 23 hours a day, he is going to get a bit frustrated.'

He said: 'Signals are being picked up by all our members all over the prison system. The prisoners and the staff working overtime have had enough. If I hear those signals, I listen. If I am stupid, I ignore them.'

Although all sides agree that there is a problem, there is little agreement about how to tackle it.

'We are desperately short of staff,' Mr Steel said.

'We need at least 5,000 more prison officials and you cannot get them and train them overnight.'

'The answer is not in non-custodial service or in probation, because that merely delays the inevitable prison sentence,' he said.

Prison population at 30 June, 1985 (England and Wales)

Males	Pop.
Remand centres	3,748
Local prisons	17,207
Closed training prisons	13,159
Open prisons	3,404
Total	37,518
Females	
Open prisons	349
Closed prisons	1,019
Total	1,368
Closed youth custody centres	
Males	5,458
Females	120
Open youth custody centres	
Males	1,390
Females	89
Senior detention centres	1,016
Other detention centres	1,560
Total population:	48,519
Total capacity:	39,804

NACRO statistics

148

But Mr Cavadino argues that more prisons will not solve the problem. 'Trying to cope with such an increase by opening new prisons is like running up an escalator which is moving ever so rapidly downwards. Rather than open new prisons, the government must take the lead in calling for a reduction in the use of prisons,' he said.

A NACRO briefing paper, 'The Costs of Penal Measures', reports that the average weekly cost of keeping a person in prison in the financial year 1983–1984 was £234, ranging from £144 at open prisons to £478 in maximum security jails.

In contrast, the annual cost of a probation order in 1982–1983 was £580 and the average cost of community service orders was £310.

'With the prison population at a record level and widespread concern about acute overcrowding, a much greater use of non-custodial sentences makes practical sense,' the paper says.

Mr Paul Cavadino, of NACRO, said: 'At least two-thirds of those in prison could be given non-custodial sentences without danger to the public and with at least as good and perhaps a better chance of not being reconvicted for a crime.'

from *The Times*, 1985

In their book *The Growth of Crime*, published in 1977, Sir Leon Radzinovicz and Joan King explore the purpose and nature of imprisonment. Here are some extracts:

A time of disillusion

Today it is scarcely possible to mention prisons without bringing in the word 'crisis'. Recidivism, overcrowding, protest, have contributed to an atmosphere of mounting disillusion, even despair, about penal institutions.

This is in sharp contrast with the optimism that prevailed just before and after the Second World War . . . After the war [as a result of the Criminal Justice Act of 1948] administrative changes forged ahead. There were open borstals and open prisons. Prison welfare and after-care were reviewed and eventually put into the hands of probation officers, trained as social workers. There were various experiments designed to involve prison officers more fully in rehabilitation as well as custody. Prison hostels, or arrangements for employment outside, were introduced to pave the way for release for long-term prisoners. None of this, however, availed to stem the tide of recidivism.

Now virtually all the features that favoured prison reform and experiment in the thirties have been reversed; few prisons have any longer the elbow-room for improvement. They are crowded beyond belief, with nearly four times as many to hold as they had then.

Why do we still send people to prison?

Every other year the Institute of Criminology at Cambridge holds a Senior Course for people engaged in the practical tasks of dealing with criminals: judges, magistrates and their clerks, administrators, prison governors, senior officers of the police, probation and social services. One participant was recently heard to remark that, by the time they had finished discussing research about prisons, he had wondered why anyone was still being sent there at all. Yet, just afterwards, they had held a 'sentencing exercise', and had each been asked to say what sentence should be imposed upon certain offenders. And they had all found themselves deciding upon imprisonment as the only solution where the facts seemed to indicate that the convicted man was especially dangerous or had committed a deliberate and serious breach of trust.

People are not sent to prison primarily for their own good, or even in the hope that they will be cured of crime. Confinement is used as a measure of retribution, a symbol of condemnation, a vindication of law. It is used as a warning and deterrent to others. It is used, above all, to protect other people, for a longer or shorter period, from an offender's depredations. Yet there is a widespread idea that the trouble with prisons nowadays is that they are too soft, that 'rehabilitation' has been allowed to take over at the expense of both deterrence and security. No wonder prisoners get out of hand, goes the argument, no wonder they do not fear to go back, if they are allowed to associate with their cronies, have good meals, books, magazines, radio, television, little work, no responsibilities, even home leave before they go out. If prisons were a good deal grimmer, and the regime a good deal stiffer, it is contended, there would be fewer prisoners and less trouble with those there are.

Ironically, the very fact of rising crime and rising committals to penal institutions ensures that for most prisoners conditions remain quite sufficiently grim. More than half of all those sent to prison in England pass the whole of their sentence in the old general 'locals', where they are liable to spend 18 hours a day locked up in their cells – longer at weekends or if officers are too busy with other duties to supervise them outside.   LEON RADZINOVICZ and JOAN KING

So what actually *does* it feel like to be in prison? Here are some extracts from *The Man Inside*, a selection of interviews with prisoners and warders in traditional British 'closed' prisons, compiled by Tony Parker and published in 1973.

If you take the majority of the prison population, basically it's made up of only two kinds of prisoner – those who've got no skills whatsoever and are virtually unemployable, and those who could work if they wanted to, but prefer to live by crime. They've no intention of going straight when they get out, and all they think about while they're in is how to get away with it next time.

Principal Prison Officer (50)
20 years service

You can't be a person who works in a prison for long without realising what a terrible waste of time it all is, how men with brains and feelings and hearts are being ruined simply by the struggle to stay alive in the face of the stupid restrictions and regulations they're surrounded with. If only half the energy they had to devote to battling in their minds against that sort of thing could be put to some constructive use I'd say you might even get something worthwhile out of prisons. But under the present system there's not a hope: the important things are ignored and the petty things are all-important.

Prison Welfare Officer (32)
Seconded from Probation Service

No one learns anything that will be any help to them when they go out. I'm not aware, for instance, that there's an insatiable demand at good rates of pay for men who can scrub and clean and polish, or make roughly-fitting shoes or brushes, or boil hundredweights of cabbage and potatoes. Really it's beyond me why they don't do things like buying-up old motor cars and teaching men the rudiments of being garage mechanics, show them how to rewire a house, repair television sets, or make tables and chairs – anything that's got at least some connection with some sort of job they might get outside. Or it could be clerical work, book-keeping, filing, indexing, store-keeping. The ridiculous thing is it'd hardly cost them anything; there are plenty of men serving sentences themselves who could be put to teaching things like that, which they already know about, to others. So as well as passing on their knowledge they'd be usefully employed themselves while they were in, instead of being kept pointlessly occupied at the tax-payers' expense.

Walter C (54)
Offence: embezzlement
Sentence: 6 years

You're allowed to write one letter a week, but what the hell is there to write about? 'We scrubbed the corridor yesterday, it looks terrific. We had a great time in the tailoring shop last Tuesday, we made our one-millionth pair of prison-uniform trousers. I was walking round the yard on exercise today and I completed 17 circuits before it started to rain and we were brought inside.' You couldn't say it was exactly compulsive reading for someone who got it, could you? If you were honest all you'd write would be, 'Dear Blank, I hope you are well. I'm dead. Yours sincerely'. They could have a printed form to save you writing it, then everyone'd be saved a lot of time.

Ron G (26)
Offence: possession of drugs
Sentence: 4 years

I can't help it, I hate visits. I can't tell her not to come, I suppose she wants to, but I get choked. I mean I've got another eight years still to do, I don't want to hear about what's going on outside, what she said, what someone else said, how so-and-so is. It doesn't concern me, how can it possibly concern me? When she came today what she was talking about was the present, and that means nothing at all. She was saying things about what happened last week, what's going to happen next week: to her, and to people she knows. But nothing happened to me last week and nothing's going to happen next week, so what else could it be but a completely ridiculous one-sided conversation? The most I wanted was just to look at her, remind myself

151

what she looked like, not to talk or to listen. Now it's what, three hours later, I haven't the remotest idea of a single word she said.

Danny A (35)
Offence: armed robbery
Sentence: 14 years

The incredible way time seems to stop moving altogether, that was the thing I was least prepared for and haven't got used to even now. I'll be in the workshop and my mind'll be far away, thinking of the end of my sentence next year and all the things I'm going to do and the places I'm going to go, and then I suddenly come back with a jerk to where I am. I say to myself, 'Oh well, all that helped to pass a bit of time'. Then I look up at the clock, and I see the hand's moved on exactly one minute since I looked at it before.

Stuart H (24)
Offence: arson
Sentence: 4 years

All these places do for me is make me determined to hit back harder than ever when I get out. I've a chip on my shoulder, yes, but I don't think I had it so much when I first started being sent to prison. In those days I used to feel I probably deserved it. That's all gone long-since now though. All I've got is this big hatred for what's called straight society, and it's been going into prison such a lot that has turned me like that.

Les M (34)
Offence: housebreaking
Sentence: 6 years

The only sort of way I could tell you about myself, how I am doing this length of time, I suppose it would be to get a cup of water and float a burnt-out match on it and say sit and watch it, see how it got water-logged and gradually got lower and lower sinking under the surface, that'd be about it, how it is, that'd be me.

Len B (45)
Offence: manslaughter
Sentence: life

Over the past few decades there have been attempts to make prison regimes reformative rather than merely deterrent. The rationale behind these attempts is suggested in *The Growth of Crime:*

Since a prisoner has to do time, cannot that time be used constructively to get him to face and change the attitudes that lead him to commit crime? Why should not the various aspects of his life in prison – work, leisure, education, contacts with prison staff, contacts with family or friends outside, contacts with other prisoners, the social environment of the institution itself, be deliberately directed towards his reformation? Surely so much control over every aspect of life should be turned to good account?

LEON RADZINOVICZ and JOAN KING

Here are a few of the major 'reformative' ideas:

Vocational and industrial training

Prisoners are given instruction in work and life skills, in the form, for example, of factory units, where they are paid wages while in prison and where they learn trades which they could use to earn an honest living on release.

Individual welfare and 'treatment'

Psychologists, psychiatrists and social workers concentrate on the individual needs of prisoners, as a means of reform and rehabilitation, offering psychotherapy, or counselling to individuals, or group therapy, or regular contacts with prisoners' families.

Conjugal visits

Prisoners are allowed regular visits from partners in privacy, or periodic 'home leaves'.

While most prisons in Britain continue to be 'closed', with prisoners locked up and closely guarded, there are a number of 'open prisons', where there is a strong emphasis on 'reformative' measures. The aim of such prisons is to increase informality and opportunities for responsibility and self-determination. Typical features of such prisons are as follows:

Minimal security, in the traditional sense. Roll calls are reduced to a minimum and prisoners are often allowed to go for long unsupervised walks in the prison estates, where they may be engaged in market gardening.

Accommodation is likely to be in single rooms, or dormitories divided into cubicles, with unbarred windows. Prisoners may be allowed to decorate their rooms, or to have pictures, ornaments and radios.

Recreation is much more varied than the traditional exercise round the prison yard. There may be television rooms, snooker and table-tennis tables, a large, unsupervised common room, music rooms, a gymnasium, with squash and badminton courts and weight-training facilities.

Education programmes are provided, encouraging prisoners to develop hobbies and skills.

Resettlement programmes may be provided with prisoners allowed out to do voluntary work in the community prior to release.

On the following page is a newspaper report about the prison conditions of a particularly notorious murderer.

Fury over five-star luxury for Moors murderer

BRADY'S XMAS FEAST

Salmon, turkey, scampi and a Christmas pud

EXCLUSIVE
by Frank Corless

Moors murderer Ian Brady will be eating better this Christmas than thousands of decent Britons.

On his menu over Christmas and the New Year will be scampi, roast turkey, gamekeeper's pie, fresh salmon, sherry trifle, Christmas pudding and gateau.

He may even have his first glass of beer since he was jailed 19 years ago.

But the staff who serve him will only have sandwiches.

Brady is in Liverpool's maximum security Park Lane Hospital – the Broadmoor of the North – which has been criticised before for its five-star luxury.

Brady was transferred to the hospital from Leicester's Gartree jail three weeks ago.

Staff at Park Lane have been forbidden from speaking to the Press. But there was a storm of protest outside. Mrs Ann West, 56, the mother of Moors victim Lesley Ann Down, 12, who was murdered on a Boxing Day said:

'This makes me sick. Christmas is always a bad time for me – but this news will make it worse.'

Mrs Winifred Johnson, 52, whose son Keith Bennett is believed to have been a victim of Brady, said: 'I've got to work for my Christmas and he gets it all for nothing.

'I don't even know what scampi tastes like because I've never had the money to pay for it.'

from the *Daily Mirror*

Closed prison (above), open prison (opposite).

Studies of the actual results of such regimes in terms of the likelihood of prisoners 'going straight' after release from 'open prisons' have tended to be disappointing. Studies undertaken in Holland and Finland, where such prisons have been in operation over a long period, are summarised in *Open Prisons* by Howard Jones and Paul Cornes, published in 1977: 'treatment in an open institution hardly matters as regards later recidivism'.

155

Themes for discussion

Do you think that more prisons should be built to deal with the overcrowding in Britain's prisons, or do you think that more use should be made of non-custodial sentences for convicted criminals?

If the recidivism rate is the same amongst prisoners released from both 'closed' and 'open' prisons, can you see any value in spending extra public money on building more of the latter?

Do you think that the experimental American scheme, whereby first offenders, on probation, are taken into prisons to be lectured by 'lifers' about the reality of prison life, should be adopted in Britain?

Do you think first offenders should be kept separate from more experienced prisoners?

What are your thoughts about the *Daily Mirror* report on Ian Brady?

Which, if any, of the reformative measures outlined above do you consider valuable? What difficulties are likely to arise in the implementation of each?

Why do you think vocational training and work experience schemes in prison have had comparatively little effect on recidivism and employment prospects amongst prisoners?

Why, do you think, do most prisoners return to crime after being released from prison?

Research topics

1   Find out about conditions in two or three large prisons in Britain. Write a report to present to the group.

2   Find out about and write reports on countries where prison conditions are:
   a   more pleasant
   b   more unpleasant
   c   simply different
   in comparison with the normal conditions in British prisons.

The capital punishment debate

Capital punishment was abolished in Great Britain by Act of Parliament in 1964. Arguments about the morality of capital punishment and its value as a deterrent to murder have continued ever since, culminating in a parliamentary debate and a free vote, in 1983, on amendments to the law which would enable judges to sentence people found guilty of certain categories of murder to death. The amendments were defeated, and the law stood. The debate in society goes on.

Here are extracts from speeches by MPs, made in the House of Commons on 13 July, 1983, presenting opposing viewpoints on the issue:

. . . I want the House to understand my position clearly, that even were there evidence to demonstrate that capital punishment was a deterrent – such evidence does not exist – I shall still believe hanging to be wrong. I know that some people will argue . . . that hanging as retribution is right in itself and that in our society one can justify, shall I say as a matter of principle, the taking of the life of a man or woman who has himself or herself taken a life. . . . There is no moral or philosophical justification for that view. It is a cry for vengeance, and nothing except vengeance . . .

Even if the deterrent claim can be justified, its effect on the murder rate in Britain will be negligible . . . Time after time the hanging lobby repeats the old remedies and the venerable prejudices that capital punishment deters. I tell the hanging lobby what every informed person knows – that there is absolutely no evidence to support the view that capital punishment is in itself a deterrent.

If we compare abolitionist and retentionist countries and countries before and after abolition, we find that there is no evidence to prove that execution reduces the murder rate or reduces crimes of violence . . .

If the deterrent case is to be accepted, if we are to vote for capital punishment as a deterrent, we ought at least to be sure that it deters. If we are to hang men and women by the neck until they are dead, we ought to do it on more than a hunch, a superstition, a vague impression . . . Unless there is some positive proof that hanging deters, the case for hanging cannot be made even by its most sophisticated proponents.

They cannot provide that case. I must provide for them the other statistic, of which we are certain. Had hanging not been abolished in 1964, at least five innocent men would be dead today. That seems to me . . . the only statistic about which we can be sure in this entire debate . . .

I conclude as I began. Were all the practical or pragmatic arguments against capital punishment not to apply, I should still resist its introduction. Supporters of capital punishment insist on comparing crime rates before and after abolition, as though abolition itself had created a more violent society. The truth is something different. Violence has grown within our society during the past 25 years for many reasons. To legalise violence in the way proposed would make Britain not a more peaceful nation, but one in which violence had become accepted and institutionalised . . . By killing murderers we become like the murderers themselves. The whole community is lowered to their standards. For that reason I shall vote against the motion.

ROY HATTERSLEY
(MP for Birmingham, Sparkbrook)

The first duty of this House is not simply to debate what punishment we can place upon criminals. It is also to protect the lives of our people and to safeguard the innocent . . .

I was in the House when we abolished the capital sentence. We did so largely in the belief that life imprisonment would be an effective deterrent in its place. It has not worked out that way. On the contrary, violence and murder have increased rapidly . . .

When the capital sentence was abolished, the Police Federation warned the House that it would lead to a dramatic increase in the carrying and using of firearms. That is exactly what has happened. In the year before abolition, the number of guns used in crimes in London was 43; last year the number was close to 2,000. That is a 25-fold increase. Before abolition, when a professional gang planned a job the elder members frisked the younger members to ensure that they were not carrying guns. They did so because they knew, to put it in the vernacular, 'if you kill a cop we all get topped'. It is no longer that way. Today, it is the norm and not the exception for criminals to carry guns when they commit robberies. They do so for the simple reason that they know that their lives are not at risk.

There is also a new balance of risk for the police officer. When a policeman confronts a criminal with a gun, the odds are tilted against him. In that split second when the armed robber must decide whether to pull the trigger and shoot the policeman, the robber knows that if he surrenders he will go to prison for, perhaps, five to seven years for armed robbery. But if he shoots the policeman, he eliminates the witness and greatly improves his chances of getting away with the loot. And even if he is caught and convicted of murder the worst that can happen to him is life imprisonment. With remission that can mean little more than ten and a half years . . . I do not accept, and I doubt if the House would accept, that the difference between five to seven years for armed robbery and only ten years for murder is worth the life of a police officer . . .

There is a further consequence. Whereas, before abolition, unarmed police officers would not hesitate to tackle armed criminals because they knew or they believed that they were protected by the invisible bullet-proof waistcoat of the capital sentence, today even the bravest of policemen hesitates. He often sends for a gun.

What the Police Federation and I predicted when the House abolished the capital sentence has come to pass. We have put an end to the once-proud tradition of our unarmed police force. We therefore face the risk . . . that we have not succeeded in abolishing the capital sentence. On the contrary, it will be administered more and more not by due process of law and by courts, but by armed criminals and, on occasion, by armed police officers defending themselves and the public.

ELDON GRIFFITHS
(MP for Bury St Edmunds)

Questions for research and discussion

1   Both MPs, in the selected extracts from their speeches, concentrate on the question of whether or not capital punishment is a deterrent to murder and violent crime; both claim to draw upon the available statistical evidence, and yet they reach opposite conclusions. Who do you think is right? (To answer the question, of course, research will be necessary, possibly undertaken by a small group of students, who report back to the rest. You will need to work out exactly *what* evidence each MP is drawing on, find the relevant evidence and statistics, and present them to the class, before judgements about the viability of the opposing claims can be made.)

2   On what grounds does Roy Hattersley argue that capital punishment is morally indefensible? Do you consider that he is right when he argues that, 'even were there evidence to demonstrate that [it] was a deterrent, capital punishment would be wrong'?

3   What do you think Eldon Griffiths meant when he said, 'we have not succeeded in abolishing the capital sentence'? Do you think that there is any fundamental difference between the kinds of 'death sentence' he is talking about in the last quoted paragraph of his speech, and capital punishment carried out by legal process?

4   According to one of the speakers in the debate, Albert McQuarrie (MP for Banff and Buchan), 'an estimated 87 per cent of the total adult population have called for capital punishment to be made available to the courts again'. Yet the House of Commons voted against the restoration of capital punishment. Is this democratic?

Essay titles

a   Vandalism – inevitable social evil?

b   The European Court decided that birching is an offence against human rights. What is your opinion?

c   Punishment should fit the crime.

d   'All punishment in itself is evil.'

e   In defence of discipline and order.

f   Can and should society do anything about anti-social behaviour?

Bibliography

Non-fiction

Briggs, Dennie, *In Place of Prison*, Temple Smith, 1975

Evans, Peter, *Prison Crisis*, Allen and Unwin, 1980

Fitzgerald, Mike and Sim, Joe, *British Prisons*, Blackwell, 1981

Gowers, Sir Ernest, *A Life For A Life: The Problem of Capital Punishment*, Chatto and Windus, 1956

Jones, Howard and Cornes, Paul, *Open Prisons*, Routledge and Kegan Paul, 1977

Lea, John and Young, Jock, *What Is To Be Done About Law and Order?*, Penguin, 1984

Parker, Tony, *The Courage of his Convictions*, Hutchinson, 1962

Parker, Tony, *The Man Inside*, Michael Joseph, 1973

Pearson, Geoffrey, *Hooligan: A History of Respectable Fears*, Macmillan, 1988

Radzinovicz, Sir Leon and King, Joan, *The Growth of Crime: The International Experience*, Hamilton, 1977

Fiction

Koestler, Arthur, *Darkness at Noon*, Penguin, 1969

Malamud, Bernard, *The Fixer*, Penguin, 1966

Orwell, George, 'A Hanging' in *The Collected Essays, Journalism and Letters*, Vol. I, Penguin, 1970

Sartre, Jean-Paul, 'The Wall' in *Intimacy*, Panther, 1960

Sillitoe, Alan, *The Loneliness of the Long Distance Runner*, Granada, 1985

Advice on writing: note-making technique

Whether you are making notes in lessons, or from books, there are various methods which you can use to simplify and clarify your note-making.

As you can see, the points are themselves set out in note-form; this is intended to illustrate an effective note-making format in itself.

I   Making notes in lessons/lectures

1   Don't try to write down everything.
2   Concentrate on main points.
3   If possible, try to make sure you understand an idea before writing it down.
4   Use a system of abbreviations:
    a   miss out unimportant words like 'a', 'the'

   b use abbreviations for as many words as possible:
- (i) common abbreviations, e.g.:
  1. ∵ – because
  2. ∴ – therefore
  3. + – and
  4. c.f. – compare, remember in this context
  5. i.e. – that is
  6. N.B. – note well

  etc.

- (ii) personal abbreviations: work out as many as possible, e.g.:
  1. sim. – similar (to)
  2. diffic. – difficult
  3. diff. – different
  4. poss. – possibly
  5. prob. – probably
  6. char. – character

  etc.

- (iii) use initial letters for names of characters and titles, e.g.:
  1. O – *Othello*
  2. P.I. – *A Passage to India*

   c N.B.: never use abbreviations in writing intended to be read by someone else.

II Making notes from books

1 Decide first whether book is suitable:
   a skim over chapter(s)
   b concentrate on headings + 1st + last paragraphs of sections.

2 Make notes by one of the following methods:
   a using a pencil:
- (i) read through a section
- (ii) re-read, underlining or marking in margin relevant points in pencil
- (iii) write out marked sections, trying to use own words

   b relying on memory:
- (i) read through a section
- (ii) re-read, pausing over each key point
- (iii) make notes from memory, as far as possible
- (iv) check back to book whenever necessary in making notes

3 Use format illustrated here in setting out notes:
   a use indentations for major and subsidiary points
   b mark points with letters and figures, if it makes notes clearer
   c use colour, underlinings, etc. to emphasise key points
   d use new page for each new set of notes

III   Note-making as an exam exercise

1   Read through passage as many times as is necessary to understand main argument
2   Underline each main point
3   Write points in note-form, but without abbreviations, a new line for each point, with sub-headings if this would be helpful

IV   Making revision notes

1   Don't just keep re-reading your notes
2   Organise your revision:
   a   Take a theme or a character in literature
   b   Read through your notes, jotting down in *brief summary form*, with page reference if relevant, each important detail relating to theme or character
   c   Re-order your summary notes into a logical pattern
   d   Learn your summarised points, looking back to original notes and/ or book for amplification when necessary
3   Write out a realistic revision schedule for each day up to the exams
4   Answer exam questions in note-form, as part of revision

V   Conditions for note-making

1   Try to make notes in a quiet, well-lit and comfortable place.
2   Don't start if you have something on your mind which will distract your concentration.
3   Have regular breaks (but avoid watching television during them!).
4   Always have a clear end in view for each work session.

WOMEN

The question of women's role and identity in the modern world has become, over the past two decades, an issue which few people of either sex in the Western world are able to ignore, and it is the theme of this chapter.

The chapter begins with a comprehension passage from the most influential feminist book of the early 1970s, *The Female Eunuch*, by the Australian writer and journalist, Germaine Greer. The chapter is then divided into sub-themes, each of which is followed by discussion questions. The themes are explored largely through extracts from books written in the 1980s and 1990s by women.

There is no particular reason to tackle the sections and questions in order; in fact, the questions themselves could well be ignored altogether, and a free-ranging discussion conducted after the chapter has been read as a whole. Alternatively, the sections can be discussed separately, without specific reference to the questions, or particular issues suggested by some of the questions can be discussed. The questions provide plenty of scope for research by students of other disciplines, ranging from history and sociology to music and art, but the only essential requirement is to read and consider the extracts themselves.

Comprehension and comment

Read the following passage and answer the questions which follow it. You are advised to spend about one and a half hours on this exercise.

Energy is the power that drives every human being. It is not lost by exertion but maintained by it, for it is a faculty of the psyche. It is driven to perverted manifestations by curbs and checks. Like the motive force that drives the car along the highway, when it meets with an obstacle it turns to destructive force and shakes
5   its source to pieces. It is not too hard to point out to the averagely perceptive human being that women have plenty of the destructive kind of energy, but far

fewer people can see that women's destructiveness is creativity turned in upon itself by constant frustration. Nervous diseases, painful menstruation, unwanted pregnancies, accidents of all kinds, are all evidence of women's energy destroying

10 them. It extends beyond them, wreaking havoc with the personalities and achievements of others, especially their husbands and their children. That is not to say that women must hate all their relatives, but that if children are presented to women as a duty and marriage as an inescapable yoke, then the more energy they have the more they will fret and chafe, tearing themselves and their dependants to

15 pieces. When children are falsely presented to women as their only significant contribution, the proper expression of their creativity and their lives' work, the children and their mothers suffer for it.

The adult woman has already established a pattern of perversity in the expression of her desires and motives which ought to fit her for the distorted

20 version of motherhood: it will not disappear if she is allowed alternatives. Any substituted aim is likely to be followed in a 'feminine' way, that is, servilely, dishonestly, inefficiently, inconsistently. In most cases women are not offered a genuine alternative to repressive duties and responsibilities: most would happily give up unskilled labour in a factory or the tedium of office work for the more

25 'natural' tedium of a modern household, because their energies are so thwarted by the usual kinds of female work that they imagine even housework would be a preferable alternative. Women who are offered education are offered a genuine alternative, insofar as they are offered genuine education, a rare commodity in these days of universal induction. And yet, when they were offered education at

30 first the result was not the creation of an instant race of superwomen. This is one contemporary's account of the first female undergraduates, and university teachers will recognise a familiar phenomenon:

'At lectures women students are models of attention and industry; perhaps they even apply themselves too much to carrying home in black and white what they

35 have heard. They generally occupy the front seats because they enter their names early and then because they arrive early, well before the beginning of the lectures. Only this fact is noticeable, that often they merely give a superficial glance at the preparations that the professor passes round; sometimes they even pass them on to their neighbours without even looking at them; a longer

40 examination would hinder their taking notes.'

What this rather prejudiced observer noticed is real enough: the girls were diligent, even too diligent, but their efforts were expended on mistaken goals. They were anxious to please, to pick up everything that they were told, but the preparations handed around by the lecturer were the real subject of the lecture, and in that they

45 were not interested at all. Their energy is all expended on conforming with disciplinary and other requirements, not in gratifying their own curiousity about the subject that they are studying, and so most of it is misdirected into meaningless assiduity. This phenomenon is still very common among female students, who are

forming a large proportion of the arts intake at universities. It is not surprising then
50 that women seldom make the scientific advances, but rather serve men as
laboratory assistants, working under direction: it is merely a continuation of the
same phenomenon that we observed in their undergraduate days.

   By the time they have come to apply for entrance to a university the pattern of
their useless deflection of energy is already set. In the very great majority of cases
55 they have not retained enough drive to desire to qualify themselves any further; the
minority who go to university do so too often as a response to guidance and
pressure from their mistresses at school, still not knowing what the real point is, still
not interested in developing their own potential: we are not surprised to find that
many of them think of even their professional life either as a stop-gap or an indirect
60 qualification for marriage.

   All the blanket objections to women in professions may be understood as ways
of stating this basic situation. They may appear to be the judgements of prejudice
and, insofar as they adduce no other case than sex, we must admit that they are.
However, unless feminists admit that the phenomena described by critics of
65 women's performance in industry, offices, schoolrooms, trade unions and in the
arts and sciences are real, they must fail to identify the problem, and therefore to
solve it. It is true that opportunities have been made available to women far beyond
their desires to use them. It is also true that the women who avail themselves of
opportunities too often do so in a feminine, filial, servile fashion. It must be
70 understood that it will not suffice to encourage women to use an initiative that they
have not got, just as it is useless to revile them for not having it. We must
endeavour to understand how it is that women's energy is systematically deflected
from birth to puberty, so that when they come to maturity they have only fitful
resource and creativity.   GERMAINE GREER

a Explain the point of the simile of the car. (lines 1–5)   (*3 marks*)

b Why is the word 'feminine' in inverted commas? (line 21)   (*3 marks*)

c What is the writer's purpose in quoting the 'account of the first female
    undergraduates'? (line 31)   (*4 marks*)

d Why is it 'not surprising that women seldom make the scientific
    advances' (lines 49–50), according to the writer?   (*4 marks*)

e Explain the writer's attitude to 'the blanket objections to women in the
    professions'. (line 61)   (*4 marks*)

f Give the meaning of the following phrases as they appear in the passage:
    (i)   'a faculty of the psyche' (line 2);
    (ii)   'a pattern of perversity' (line 18);
    (iii) 'meaningless assiduity' (line 47-8);
    (iv)   'filial, servile fashion' (line 69).   (*6 marks*)

g Consider the implications of the final sentence.   (*4 marks*)

h Comment on the tone of the passage. *(6 marks)*

i Do you consider the passage 'well written'? You should make clear your criteria of assessment. *(8 marks)*

j To what extent do you agree and/or disagree with the overall view of women presented in this passage? *(8 marks)*

(50 marks total)

Background to feminism

The modern 'feminist' or 'women's liberation' movement has its origins in 19th-century women's rights organisations. First sketched out by Mary Wollstonecraft in her book, *Vindication of the Rights of Women*, published in 1792, the feminist cause was taken up more concretely in Europe and America in the late 1840s and early 1850s, as British sociologist Ann Oakley explains in *Subject Women:*

The 'Declaration of Sentiments' and 'Resolutions' adopted by the first American women's suffrage convention in 1848 summarised the outlines of women's position in many countries of the world at that time. It stated the feminist grievance in no uncertain terms:

> The history of mankind is a history of repeated injuries and usurpations on the part of man toward woman, having in direct object the establishment of an absolute tyranny over her . . .
> He has never permitted her to exercise her inalienable right to the elective franchise . . .
> He has made her, if married, in the eyes of the law, civilly dead.
> He has taken from her all right in property, even to the wages she earns . . .
> He has so framed the laws of divorce, as to what shall be the proper causes and, in cases of separation, to whom the guardianship of the children shall be given, as to be wholly regardless of the happiness of women – the law, in all cases, going upon false supposition of the supremacy of man, and giving all power into his hands . . .
> He has monopolised nearly all the profitable employments, and from those she is permitted to follow, she receives but a scanty remuneration.
> He closes against her all the avenues to wealth and distinction which he considers most honourable to himself. As a teacher of theology, medicine, or law she is not known.
> He has denied her the facilities for obtaining a thorough education, all colleges being closed against her . . .
> He has endeavoured, in every way that he could, to destroy her confidence in her own powers, to lessen her self-respect, and to make her willing to lead a dependent and abject life . . . ANN OAKLEY

The first women's suffrage society in Britain was formed in 1865, and by the end of the century the suffragette movement was intensely active, under the forceful leadership of such women as Emmeline Pankhurst, becoming organised in 1903 in the Women's Social and Political Union. During the First World War women were encouraged to undertake a whole range of jobs and skills for which they had previously been considered incapable or unsuitable, and, as a result of this as well as the fierce and persistent suffragette activity, women were at last given limited access to the franchise in Britain in 1918.

After that, for over 40 years, the feminist movement fell into abeyance, to be revived in the early 1960s by women's liberation organisations in Britain and America, coming to the forefront of public consciousness once more in 1968.

The significance of the arrangements for men and women in Western society before their recent modifications is suggested by the British philosopher Janet Radcliffe Richards in *The Sceptical Feminist:*

The facts are stark, but beyond any question. All social arrangements, institutions and customs which defined the relative position of the sexes were designed *to ensure that women should be in the power and service of men.*

This no doubt sounds like pure feminist rant, but it is not. It is proved by many quite incontrovertible facts about the formal devices which, for most of history, were employed by men to make sure that women were kept in their power, and involves no recourse to extravagant assertions about the general moral turpitude of men . . .

To see the position of women in this way is to see clearly what femininity traditionally was. Feminine characteristics were the ones needed for making a success of the position into which women were forced, and roughly, therefore, to be feminine was to be pleasing to men. The whole essence of femininity is, or at least traditionally was, the limiting of all endeavour and activity to a confined end. Ideal femininity has never consisted in weakness and incompetence (contrary to much popular opinion, which seems to confuse descriptive and prescriptive femininity at this point as at many others); no man ever wanted a total loss of a woman. The idea was only to direct all abilities to being useful to men and their offspring, using a great deal of skill (the more the better) but always carefully directing it so that it presented no threat to men's position. It was unfeminine of women to want to study at universities or have the vote because in doing so they were showing that they had ideas about stepping beyond their allotted sphere: higher education and political power were not among the requirements for being a devoted wife and mother, and to seek them was to want to compete with men and become independent of them, rather than to remain in service to them.

JANET RADCLIFFE RICHARDS

The advances made by women in the twentieth century away from this enforced domesticity and subservience owe much to advances in contraception, offering a control over reproduction which was never previously possible. As the French philosopher and novelist Simone de Beauvoir points out in her classic study of women, *The Second Sex:*

One of the basic problems of woman . . . is the reconciliation of her reproductive role and her part in productive labour. The fundamental fact that, from the beginning of history, doomed woman to domestic work and prevented her taking part in the shaping of the world was her enslavement to the generative function. In female animals there is a physiological and seasonal rhythm that assures the economising of their strength; in woman, on the contrary, between puberty and menopause nature sets no limits to the number of her pregnancies . . . Contraceptives have been in existence since antiquity, . . . but [they] were practically unknown to the Middle Ages in Europe; scarcely a trace of them is to be found up to the 18th century. For many women in those times life was an uninterrupted succession of pregnancies . . .

  [Birth control and abortion] are of tremendous importance for women in particular; she can reduce the number of her pregnancies and make them a rationally integral part of her life, instead of being their slave.   SIMONE DE BEAUVOIR

Discussion points

Why do you think the situation of women in Europe and America summarised in the 1848 American women's suffrage convention was as it was?

What were the original conditions for female suffrage in the 1918 act? Why do you think these restrictions were imposed? When were they removed?

What happened to most of the women who were employed in 'men's' jobs at the end of the First World War? Why?

Why do you think the women's movement died down after 1918? Why did it revive in the 1960s?

Women's inferiority in the arts and sciences

Compared with men, there have been very few women of recognised genius. Many people feel that this is because women as a sex are generally intrinsically less capable of inspiration and more narrow in their range of feeling and thinking than men.

  Simone de Beauvoir takes up this point:

The anti-feminists obtain from the study of history two contradictory arguments:
1   women have never created anything great; and
2   the situation of women has never prevented the flowering of great feminine personalities . . .

168

The women who have accomplished works comparable to those of men are those exalted by the power of social institutions above all sexual differentiation. Queen Isabella, Queen Elizabeth, Catherine the Great were neither male nor female – they were sovereigns. It is remarkable that their femininity, when socially abolished, should have no longer meant inferiority: the proportion of queens who had great reigns is infinitely above that of great kings. Religion works the same transformation: Catherine of Siena, St Theresa, quite beyond any physiological consideration, were sainted souls; the life they led, secular and mystic, their acts, and their writings rose to heights that few men have ever reached.

It is quite conceivable that if other women fail to make a deep impression upon the world, it is because they are tied down in their situation. They can hardly take a hand in affairs in other than a negative and oblique manner.

SIMONE DE BEAUVOIR

The British writer Bryan Magee takes a different viewpoint in this extract from an article which appeared in *The Guardian* in November 1989. He challenges the feminist claim that women 'haven't had a chance' to achieve greatness in the Arts, and offers his own explanation for the absence of any great women painters, composers and playwrights.

To put it crudely, I think women are more people-oriented than men, and men more inclined to look at things in other ways, including abstractions and generalities (which, be it said, are not at all subtle or refined for the most part, but rough and ready, and nearly always self-serving). Thus if a man and a woman form a passionate attachment to each other, it usually becomes the central preoccupation of the woman's life; and if she then discovers that it is not the central preoccupation of the man's, she is uncomprehending and resentful.

I think this general difference between the sexes is one of the things that helps to explain why their most gifted members tend to shine in different spheres, and it is salutary to remember now that we are talking about one in a billion of either sex, at a level of accomplishment that excludes nearly all of us.

The creative art in which women have conspicuously excelled is the one the very stuff and substance of whose subject matter is personal relationships; namely the novel (as against drama whose stuff and substance is conflict). It explains why several women are to be found at the top level in the social sciences and the life sciences, but not in mathematics or physics; though even there we have had Marie Curie, the joint discoverer of radium who, having won a Nobel prize for physics, then won another for chemistry.

BRYAN MAGEE,
The Guardian,
November 1989

Themes for discussion

How were musicians and painters generally financed in Europe, up to the 19th century? Does this have any bearing on the lack of notable women musicians and painters in earlier times?

Why was George Eliot so called? What does this show about the problems of aspiring women writers in the 19th century?

How many great 19th-century British writers were women? How many of them were married, with children?

In what fields have women generally achieved fame and distinction in the 20th century? Why these, rather than others?

Does the comprehension passage from Germaine Greer's book help to shed any light on the reasons why women continue to be outshone by men in the arts and sciences? What other reasons are there to explain this phenomenon?

Do you agree that women are 'more people-oriented than men', as Magee says? If so, would you agree with Magee's conclusions about the spheres of human endeavour in which women have excelled?

Biology or conditioning?

The most intense controversy between feminists and anti-feminists concerns *the nature of women.* Most men, and many women, tend still to argue that the sexes are by nature psychologically different because of their biological make-up. Post-war feminist writers, on the other hand, have generally contended that these differences are simply or largely the result of conditioning and that there are no fundamental differences between the sexes, beyond the obvious physical ones. Girls, it is argued, are conditioned to think of the future preeminently in terms of wife and motherhood, by being given dolls to play with and being expected to stay in the home to help with household chores, and by being taught such subjects in school as cookery and needlework, whilst boys are prepared for their future role as breadwinners and decision-makers by being given toys like guns, being encouraged to be aggressive and independent, and being taught technical subjects from an early age.

Janet Radcliffe Richards attempts to shed some light on this endlessly contentious issue:

Common beliefs about the differences between the sexes are still usually based only on differences between men and women as they appear. Men are seen to be interested in politics or business while women tend to talk about homes and men and babies; men are seen to have mechanical or business abilities while women are baffled when confronted with the engine of a car and don't know what to make of bank statements, and so on. But even to the extent that propositions such as these stem from impartial observation (which is true of by no means all of them), they are still not enough to show that women and men really are different by nature. You cannot tell the nature of anything just by looking in a casual and unsystematic way at how it appears, because whenever something is observed, it is in some environment or other, and the total phenomenon results not only from the nature of the thing under observation, but also from the environment it is in. If, therefore, two things appear different, they may not be different in nature at all: they may simply be in different environments. And this, of course, is what most feminists claim about many of the alleged differences in nature between men and women . . .

The feminist argument is that there are all kinds of systematic differences in the environment of men and women which are so subtle, or so universally taken for granted, that they have gone completely unnoticed or are underestimated. It is only relatively recently, for instance, that we have noticed that boy and girl children are treated differently almost from birth, or understood how radically people's performances are influenced by what is expected of them . . .

Recent discoveries of the extent and significance of systematic differences in environment between men and women are indeed enough to prove that most of the evidence people thought they had about the natures of men and women is totally inadequate to support the usual conclusions. However, it is important to realise that that is all they do. We may know that traditional views are almost certainly wrong, but it does not follow that we know which views are right.

When we find the environmental differences between two things are probably enough to account for their appearing to be different from each other, it certainly follows that they may be intrinsically alike in nature, but not that they certainly are. For instance, the difference in social expectations of the behaviour of men and women is enough to account for the fact that women show emotion far more readily than men do; even if they were precisely the same by nature this would account for different behaviour. It does not, however, prove that they are the same by nature. Perhaps women really are, by nature, more inclined to show emotion, as well as being socially encouraged to do so. Or again, the fact that women have, during most of history, been forced by their biology (and men) to spend nearly all their time in the care of small children is a perfectly sufficient condition of their having made relatively little impact on the history of the world; if men had had to do the same they would not have had time for other things either. However, it does not follow that men and women have the same inherent capacities.

Perhaps women are inherently different; perhaps nature made them less interested in other things to ensure that they would be sufficiently inclined to care for their children.

Of course, our ignorance is lessening. In several areas we have made a great deal of progress, and have certainly shown that women are capable of acquiring skills traditionally thought beyond them, as soon as they are given the opportunity. In the most complicated areas, however, dealing with innate desires, temperament and so on, it is very difficult to find out how different men and women are. In the first place, social customs are so deeply entrenched that there are relatively few natural variations in environment we can watch, and manipulating society for the purpose of experiment is difficult . . .

The reason why it is important for feminists to study history and anthropology is that knowing how women acted in different times and under different circumstances gives us a greater understanding of their natures than seeing them only here and now.

This is a kind of work which must be carried forward with care and perseverance if we are to find out about the raw material we have to work with in planning our ideal society. And in the meantime we can certainly argue strenuously that traditional ideas about women and their differences from men are founded on totally inadequate evidence, and ought to be abandoned forthwith.

JANET RADCLIFFE RICHARDS

Themes for discussion

Do you think that there are any differences between men and women which we can be *fairly certain* are biological differences in the nature of the sexes?

Is the possibility that most of the apparently natural differences between the sexes may be produced by conditioning sufficient reason to treat the sexes equally, since differences *do* exist, whatever the cause?

What areas of employment have recently ceased to be exclusively male preserves? Is there any good reason why any of them should have always been reserved for men before?

Should positive discrimination in favour of women be introduced, to help women to overcome their traditional disadvantages? If so, in what areas?

What anthropological evidence has come to light about 'primitive' societies in which men and women do not behave according to their traditional sex roles? Is it of any significance?

Should parents try to avoid guiding their children into conventional sex roles? Would social and peer group influence have the effect of conventional gender differentiation anyway?

Should schools treat boys and girls equally in the choice of school subjects?

Men's attitudes to women

There can be little real doubt that throughout history men have treated women as their inferiors, and regarded feminine traits with contempt. In the late 1960s the phrase 'male chauvinist pig' was coined to describe men who allowed their prejudice to show, and masculine assumptions of superiority led some of the more radical women's groups to advocate avoidance of all dealings with men. This attitude can be seen, for instance, in the women's peace camp at Greenham Common, from which men were discouraged on the grounds that as soon as men take part in activities with women they attempt to take over.

Let us look at what some modern women writers have to say about sexual attitudes and their implications. First, another extract from *The Sceptical Feminist:*

It must be said on behalf of feminists who are inclined to resist any differences in function, convention and expectation between the sexes that they have one very strong argument on their side in men's quite astonishing record of downgrading whatever is associated with women. Margaret Mead commented that in every known society, men's activities were regarded as more important than women's, quite irrespective of what those activities were. 'Men may cook or weave or dress dolls or hunt humming birds, but if such activities are appropiate occupations of men, then the whole society, men and women alike, vote them as important. When the same occupations are performed by women, they are regarded as less important.'

That is very striking, but even without any special knowledge of all known societies we have a pretty good idea of what an uphill struggle we should have, even within our own, if we tried to establish respect for what has traditionally been associated with women. The average woman is very pleased if she has any understanding of any such male terrain as the engine of a car, but there are still a good many men around whose claim not to know where to find anything in the kitchen is really a boast about their never demeaning themselves with women's work. Women on the tube are happy to be seen reading city newspapers, but no man would dream of knitting in public as some women do. It is quite unthinkable that the general relaxation of conventions of dress which has led to women's wearing trousers might have resulted in men's taking to skirts, for reasons having nothing at all to do with the relative comfort of the two. Girls in schools are doing more science and metal work, but most people are still slightly shocked at the thought that boys might learn to sew. And as Michael Korda in his book on male chauvinism quotes Jules Feiffer as saying: 'Whatever ground woman manages to establish for herself man abandons, denying its importance.' It is not at all difficult to understand the point of view of feminists who see that in any difference there lies potential inequality, and who suspect that wherever there is potential inequality men will contrive to make it actual.

However, not all women are willing to give up the struggle just because they are not very optimistic about the moral improvement of men. There are feminists who think that to abandon feminine things just because men are determined to downgrade them is to give in altogether, and what we should be doing is demanding respect for whatever deserves respect, feminine or not.

JANET RADCLIFFE RICHARDS

The alternative to ignoring male prejudice for women with ambitions in male-dominated areas of work – aping men – is discussed by the American

writer Betty Friedan in a magazine interview from *The Sunday Times*, with
Rosemary Wittman Lamb:

> 'I had lunch with a group of women executives, and I was horrified,' she
> told me. 'They were so grim, so dressed-for-success. And they told me:
> 'We have to be hard-headed, like the men, and get rid of all vestiges of
> femininity.'

In the area of love and marriage, many feminists argue that only a genuine
feeling of equality between the partners can engender mutual respect which
is necessary if love is to last. Here is a fairly radical view of love and marriage
by the British journalist and writer, Jill Tweedie, from her book *In the
Name of Love:*

It is a bitter irony for men that their insistence on women's inferiority, their refusal
to grant her a place in the sun, has robbed them of the only chance they have to be
loved properly. They cannot love women because they have made women
unequal and forced them into all the unloving patterns of inequality. And women
cannot love them because the inferior do not properly love their masters, they only
prostrate themselves or live vicariously through them. Contrary to the old wives'
tales, the real joy of love lies in the knowledge that your lover could manage
without you, that he or she has no *need* of you but simply feels a great deal happier
that you are there.

   With unequals you must always lie a little, if only to save them pain. Equals know
that pain is part of growing and believe each other strong enough to stand what is
necessary for growth. This applies as much to the minefield of outside sexual
encounters as anything else. True love accepts that one person cannot provide
everything for another – indeed there is a kind of obscenity in the very notion.
Besides, what have you gained if you force anything, even faithfulness, on another
person? Their presence, perhaps, but who wants a body with a mind elsewhere?
What is the point of trying to coerce what cannot be coerced? Love does not
'allow', 'permit', or 'forbid' or it is not love.

JILL TWEEDIE

Discussion points

Why do you think that women have tended to accept the idea that their
activities, whatever they may be, are less important than those of men?

Should women try to develop the kind of toughness and aggressiveness
normally associated with men in order to compete with them in the job
market? What is the alternative?

Do you agree that a feeling of equality between partners is the strongest
basis for marriage? How possible is it to achieve?

Do you think it is right for married partners to separate if they no longer feel in love?

The beauty question

For centuries it has been the convention for women to adorn themselves with make-up and ornaments of various kinds. This reflects the age-old conception of women as the 'beautiful' sex, and women's enhancement of their beauty as a source of pleasure and enjoyment for both sexes.

Recently, however, many women have come to regard the concern of both sexes with women's 'beauty' as an unhealthy obsession, with serious and even destructive consequences for women. This view is taken by the American writer Naomi Wolf in her book, *The Beauty Myth*.

Wolf sees the root of the problem in the constant pressure on women to think of themselves in terms of their appearance, in a way that is not expected of men. She sees this pressure reflected in women's magazines:

In providing a dream language of meritocracy ('get the body you deserve'; 'a gorgeous figure doesn't come without effort'), entrepreneurial spirit ('make the most of your natural assets'), absolute personal liability for body size and ageing ('you *can* totally reshape your body'; 'your facial lines are now within your control'), and even open admissions ('at last you too can know the secret beautiful women have kept for years') they keep women consuming their advertisers' products in pursuit of the total personal transformation in status that the consumer society offers men in the form of money.

She sees one of the results of this as an unhealthy competitiveness in terms of appearance:

'Men look at women. Women watch themselves being looked at. This determines not only the relations of men to women, but the relation of women to themselves.' Critic John Berger's well-known quote has been true throughout the history of Western culture, and it is more true now than ever.

Many women tend to resent each other if they look too good and dismiss one another if they look too bad. Ironically, the myth that drives women apart also binds them together. A wry smile about calories, a complaint about one's hair, can evaporate the sullen examination of a rival in the fluorescent light of the ladies' room.

Wolf sees another result in women's increasing obsession with their weight, seen at its most disastrous in the growing number of women suffering from the so-called 'slimmers' diseases', anorexia and bulimia:

The hunger cult has won a major victory against women's fight for equality if the evidence of a 1984 *Glamour* survey of 33,000 women is representative: 75 per cent of those aged 18–35 believed they were fat, while only 25 per cent were medically overweight; 45 per cent of the underweight women thought they were too fat. But more heartbreaking in terms of the way in which the myth is running to ground hopes for women's advancement and gratification, the *Glamour* respondents chose losing 10–15 lb above success in work or in love.

Wolf's conclusion is that when women regard their personal appearance as a source of anxiety rather than pleasure, then their beauty is imprisoning; it is from this that they must escape:

The real problem isn't whether women wear make-up or don't, gain weight or lose it, have surgery or shun it, dress up or down, make their clothing and faces and bodies into works of art or ignore adornment altogether. The problem is their lack of choice.

The problem with cosmetics exists if women feel they are invisible without them.

Whenever we ignore a woman on television before we hear what she is saying, simply because we don't like her make-up or hairstyle, the beauty myth is working.

NAOMI WOLF

Andrea Dworkin, radical feminist writer (top left); Sinead O'Connor, Irish singer/songwriter (above); Naomi Wolf (left).

Discussion points

Are women inclined to think about their appearance significantly more than men? In what ways?

What pressures are women under to worry about their appearance?

Why are an increasing number of women suffering from the 'slimmers' diseases'?

Do you think that it is true that women have limited choice about spending more time and money on their appearance than men?

Look at the photographs on page 176. Write down your instinctive reactions to each of these three pictures, and then discuss them. Do your responses have any bearing on the points made by Naomi Wolf?

A woman's place: at home, at work, or both?

Arguments have raged, since the renaissance of the feminist movement in the 1960s, about the extent to which home and family should dominate a woman's life. At the one extreme is the traditional view that a woman fulfils her biological destiny as a mother and housewife, and that no other role can fulfil her as a *woman*. At the other extreme is the radical feminist rejection of the family, which is seen as a means of repressing women and keeping them in subjection, and preventing them from achieving their fulfilment as *people*, which can only come through the pursuit of an independent career. Housework, according to this view, is seen as a dreary and endless routine, as was colourfully expressed by Simone de Beauvoir in 1949: 'Washing, ironing, sweeping, ferreting out fluff from under wardrobes – all this halting of decay is also the denial of life; for time simultaneously creates and destroys, and only its negative aspect concerns the housekeeper'.

Writers in the 1940s and 1950s developed the image of the happy housewife, competent in a wide range of domestic skills, providing sympathy and support for her breadwinner husband, and creatively bringing up her children in a loving home environment.

The first English-speaking writer to emphasise the discontent felt by many women with this role, evidenced by the large number of housewives dependent on tranquillisers, was Betty Friedan, in her book *The Feminine Mystique*, published in 1963. She called it, 'the problem without a name', and characterised it thus:

It was a strange stirring, a sense of dissatisfaction, a yearning that women suffered in the middle of the 20th century in the United States. Each suburban housewife struggled with it alone. As she made the beds, shopped for groceries, matched slip cover material, ate peanut butter sandwiches, chauffeured Cub Scouts and

177

Brownies, lay beside her husband at night, she was afraid to ask even of herself the silent question: 'Is this all?'

Many feminists in the late 1970s and 1980s, Betty Friedan included, have arrived at a kind of synthesis, arguing that most women need both work and family in order to be fulfilled. In *The Second Stage*, published in 1982, Betty Friedan takes this viewpoint:

Personal choices and political strategies of women today are distorted when they deny the reality of both sets of needs: woman's need for power, identity, status and security through her own work or action in society, which the reactionary enemies of feminism deny; and the need for love and identity, status, security and generation through marriage, children, home, the family, which those feminists still locked in their own extreme reaction deny. Both sets of needs are essential to women, and to the evolving human condition . . .

The enemies of feminism insist that woman's move to equality, self-realisation and her own power in society is destroying the family, which they feel is woman's real focus of power. Many feminists insist that the family was, and is, the enemy, the prime obstacle to woman's self-realisation. There are pieces of the truth in these interlocking fears, shadows of conflicts that were insoluble in the past. I believe that the first stage, woman's movement to equality and her own personhood, was, in fact, necessary for the survival and economic/emotional health of the family, and that the second stage can, and must, transcend these conflicts. For I believe, from all we know of human psychology and history, that neither woman nor man lives by work, or love, alone: the absolutely powerless, the denigrated, the self-abnegating ones are too hungry for power, too lacking in self, to love and nurture; the loveless crave power because they lack both love and self. The human self defines itself and grows through love and work.

Why are some women so afraid, on either side of this conflict, to put to the test of personal reality our own needs for power in the world and for love and family?

Such a choice can, of course, cause immense practical problems, especially when childcare facilities are lacking and husbands are not supportive in the home. Betty Friedan interviewed many working mothers before writing *The Second Stage*. Here are two typical *cris de coeur*:

A young woman in her third year of Harvard Medical School tells me, 'I'm going to be a surgeon. I'll never be a trapped housewife like my mother. But I would like to get married and have children, I think. They say we can have it all. But how? I work 36 hours in the hospital, 12 off. How am I going to have a relationship, much less kids, with hours like that? I'm not sure I can be a superwoman. I'm frightened that I may be kidding myself. Maybe I can't have it all. Either I won't be able to have the kind of marriage I dream of or the kind of medical career I want.'

'The worst problem for women today is trying to juggle it all,' said a 38-year-old lawyer in Chicago, a mother of two. 'Wanting to get ahead in your career, wanting to have a perfect marriage and really be with your husband, wanting to do all the right things about your kids, and not giving up any of it. The guilt, because you can't really do all these things and do each one perfectly.'   BETTY FRIEDAN

For many women, of course, there is no dilemma. In this letter to the *Guardian*, Ann P. Heaton expresses her feeling of fulfilment in having adopted the traditional role of homemaker and mother:

I like being a housewife. It is 30 years since I left university, but I hope my mind has not been completely atrophied by staying at home to look after my family. Bringing up my family has been a joyous occupation for the most part, and far more satisfying and entertaining than any of the jobs I held before. I have always had time for them and for my husband, and have not missed any of their childhood. Now that I am older I have time for myself and the freedom to do what I choose. I certainly don't feel like a dodo, or a parasite for that matter.

Similarly, for many women who *do* seek outlets for their creativity beyond their traditional role, the experience of bringing up children remains their greatest source of satisfaction and achievement. The Nigerian novelist, poet and television playwright, Buchi Emecheta, expressed this view in an article in *New Internationalist*, in 1985:

I had my photograph taken once in my 'office' where I do my writing. The photo-journalist was a staunch feminist, and was so angry that my 'office' was my kitchen and that packets of breakfast cereals were in the background. I was letting the women's movement down by allowing such a photograph to be taken.

But that was where I worked, because it was warmer, because it was convenient for me to be able to see my family when I put my typewriter to one side. I tried in vain to tell her that, in my kitchen, I felt I was doing more for the peace of the world than the nuclear scientist: in our kitchens we raise all the future Reagans, or the future Jesuses. In our kitchens we wash for them and cook for them. In our kitchens they learn to love and to hate. And we send them out from our kitchens to be grown men and women.

What greater work is there than that? I do not think it low. A mother with a family is an economist, a nurse, a painter, a diplomat, and more. Those who wish to control and influence the future generation by giving birth and nurturing the young should not be looked down upon. If I had my way it would be the highest-paid job in the world.   BUCHI EMECHETA

Despite two decades of women's liberation, many people continue to take the stereotyped sex roles for granted. Here are some instances:

A son to carry on the family name, and share in all the excitement of cheering on his dad's favourite football team, or a daughter who will dress in pretty frocks, borrow mum's make-up and raise the next generation? That's what every parent wonders about when a baby's on the way. And it's the biggest mystery in the world.   from *Sunday* magazine, 1985

He's earned the sort of millions that could provide a life of super luxury. Yet Paul McCartney has not forgotten his working-class roots, insisting that his wife Linda does the laundry, washes the dishes and rises at seven to cook the family breakfast.

from *Woman* magazine, 1984

If the good Lord had intended us to have equal rights to go out to work, he would not have created man and woman.   PATRICK JENKIN, MP

Discussion points

Do you think it is better if women stay at home while their children are young?

Do you think that most women with children who work do so mainly in the interest of personal fulfilment or financial security?

How realistic do you think it is for a woman to attempt to pursue a demanding full-time career while bringing up young children?

Do you think that employers should be compelled by law to provide crèche facilities for the children of female employees?

Women at work

In the 1970s in Britain two acts were passed – the Equal Pay Act of 1970 and the Sex Discrimination Act of 1975 – aimed at ending discrimination against women in employment.

Many fields of employment opened up for British women in the 1970s, but in terms of pay the results of these Acts have not been as dramatic as might have been expected.

The main reason for this is the continued existence of 'women's jobs', which tend to be low-paid occupations, as is made clear in a 1983 Low Pay Review: 'Women represent 39.5 per cent of Britain's total workforce (Equal Opportunities Commission Annual Report, 1981) but three-quarters of all the low paid . . . In a quarter of all occupations in which women work they outnumber men nine to one.'

The wage gap does seem to be gradually closing, however, as the April 1990 New Earnings Survey shows: 'Average weekly earnings for women increased to £201.50, up by 10.5 per cent in the year to April, compared with a 9.7 per cent increase to £295.60 for men . . . Average earnings for men working a full week in non-manual jobs came to £354.90, which included £27.40 overtime pay, incentives and other extras. Women in white collar jobs averaged £215.50, including £10 on top of basic rates.'

The country which has gone furthest in legislating for equality between

men and women in employment is Sweden. Here is a report by Anuradha
Vittachi on the Swedish system and its effects at the beginning of the 1980s:

Officially, women in Sweden are more liberated than anywhere else in the world.
'It's socially unacceptable in Sweden today to think women are anything less than
the equal of men,' I was told by a young male teacher in one of Stockholm's
suburbs. 'Male chauvinists here have to retreat to the frozen North.'

In every country, rich and poor, the biggest barrier to equality for a woman is
her burden of 'bearing and caring' for children. That is why you cannot travel in
Stockholm now by bus or train without being confronted by government-
sponsored posters promoting the idea that men should share fully in the task of
bringing up their children. 'Father's freedom to be with children', reads the caption,
'it's natural. Make the most of your rights'.

Now under Swedish law men can take as much as six months 'paternity leave'
when a child is born, without loss of pay or job security. Or men and women can
decide to share 'parenthood leave.'

Men and women can also take up to three months leave at any time before the
child's eighth birthday if they feel the need to spend time with a son or daughter –
for example during the settling-in period at the start of school.

Men as well as women can take up to 12 days a year leave when their children
are sick – and they do. On several occasions in Stockholm I found my appointments
postponed because the men concerned had to go home to look after an ailing child.

Swedish law also gives couples the right to share one job so they can be free to
look after their children equally. Nor can a father of a young child be legally refused
his right to work a six-hour day. And there is mounting pressure to pay him for the
two hours he spends at home. All these changes mean men have more time for
sharing family duties.

To back up these changes there have been other reforms to help equalise the
sexes. The retirement age is the same for men as for women. Free abortions are
available up to the 18th week of pregnancy. Free contraception counselling services
are available to all. Husbands and wives are taxed separately. Wives are no longer
classified as 'dependents'. Marriage is seen now as just one form of 'voluntary
cohabitation between individuals.' Custody of children following a divorce may be
shared between parents and is not automatically awarded to the mother.

'There's a big crisis in Sweden now and it's a crisis for the men,' I was told by Lars
Nilsson, a young journalist. 'The men have to face the problem of changing their
traditional role to keep up with changes in society and the demands of women.
The man who can't change loses all the time. He is stuck, like Superman where
there is Kryptonite about.'

Even men with traditional views of the submissive and domesticated wife can find
their expectations shattered by the matter-of-fact acceptance of equality of
women.

'My parents had pretty conservative ideas about men and women,' said the
owner of a small business in his late 30s. 'But not so my wife. So when I got married
I had a problem. It forced me to change. Now my wife and I take care of the

business and the children, and the cleaning. At first it was unusual for me – especially the laundry. But now at home we share 50–50, and I'm happy my 14-year-old son takes sharing for granted. He's been cooking dinners all week' . . .

So the foundations seem to have been laid for achieving equality between the sexes in Sweden. But there is still a long way to go. Cooking and childcare classes for boys and metalwork for girls may be compulsory at school, but 86 per cent of students in technical courses are still boys, and girls still flock to nursing and pre-school training colleges. And although men have been entitled to parenthood leave since 1974, less than 10 per cent of fathers have been taking advantage of their rights.

Women may earn equal pay, but their access to equal work is only theoretical. The labour market is split between 'men's jobs' in heavy industry and 'women's jobs' in the service sector. Three quarters of all gainfully employed women work at only 25 different jobs – and it can be no coincidence that these jobs are badly paid. Even in female-dominated professions, the top jobs usually go to men. For instance, teachers tend to be women, but headteachers tend to be men. The management of the hotel I stayed in was almost exclusively male, but invariably my bed was made and my room cleaned by women.

Sweden's radical idea whereby the 'time-cake' of men and women would be carved into four equal portions – one for paid work, one for family, one for community service, and the last for leisure – is still a dream. But things are on the move. Where else in the world could a woman feel within her rights to complain that her husband 'only' took two months leave to look after the baby?

ANURADHA VITTACHI, *New Internationalist*, 1980

Discussion points

Why do you think the Equal Pay and Sex Discrimination Acts have not had a greater impact on removing the discrepancies in pay between men and women?

What do you think of the various methods outlined above for promoting equality of employment prospects between the sexes?

Do you think the traditional division between men's jobs and women's jobs should or could eventually be broken down?

Do you think that day-care centres or crêches at workplaces should be available to all working mothers? Is it feasible to legislate for this?

Some final thoughts

In a magazine interview in *The Sunday Times* in November 1981, the American journalist, Nora Ephron, looked back on the women's liberation movement in the USA in the 1970s:

My point is, we started out in the 1960s with this great burst of energy, and then degenerated into *massive* divorce. In 1973, 1974, 1975 the basic feminist act was to get divorced. In 1973 it seemed to me that five million women turned around and said: 'I divorce you! I divorce you! I divorce you!'

The one thing that happened in 1972 was that all these men cleared the table. That was what everyone got their husbands to do. They all screamed and yelled about household chores and made lists about who did what and the men said: 'Okay, I'll clear the table', and then looked round as though they deserved a medal. And they hoped it would all go away. And it did. It all went away. Their wives went away, everything went away. And they found someone else and they went back to being princes.

So many of us in that period were trying to sort of smash feminism into our marriages. We ended up absolutely drained.   NORA EPHRON

A magazine article in *The Sunday Times* in November 1978, written by Anna Coote, ended thus:

Will men's liberation be the movement of the 1980s, a natural successor to women's liberation? I doubt it. I am sure men are ultimately oppressed by their own machismo; but that is the price of power and most men are willing to pay it. Rarely, if ever, has any power group willingly surrendered power.   ANNA COOTE

Discussion points

Has the women's liberation movement been essentially beneficial or damaging in its effects on the lives of men, women and children?

Do you think that a 'men's liberation movement' is needed? What might its goals be? Are there any signs of men's attitudes to their position in the world radically changing?

Will the 1990s see the establishment of the 'new man', sharing the work in the home?

Women in the Third World

The whole of this chapter so far has been concerned with the situation of women in the developed world. In large parts of the developing world the very idea of women's liberation is meaningless, as women continue to cope in the same ways as they have for centuries with the effects of male assumptions of women's inferiority and subservience.

In many areas of the Third World women are forced to play a major role in agriculture as well as child-rearing and home-making, and often gain little or no recognition for their contribution to the economic and domestic life of the family. The situation of women in developing countries is, however, far too varied for brief analysis. Instead, we will take a glimpse into the life of just one woman in Latin America, whose story has been repeated across the world countless millions of times over numberless centuries. She comes from the state of Rio Grande do Norte, in north-east Brazil, where rural mothers have an average of more than seven living children. She was met by Paul Harrison while he was researching for his book *Inside the Third World*, from which the extract is taken:

You often meet women like Luisa Gomez, a slight, small 39-year-old. She married at 14. Since then she has been pregnant 16 times, once every 18 months. For half of her adult life she has been pregnant, and for the other half breast-feeding the most recent addition. Only six of those 16 are still alive. There were three stillbirths and seven died in their first year. Ten wasted pregnancies. Seven and a half years of drain on an already weak organism, for nothing. Worse than nothing, for all the anxiety, all the care, all the concern, and then the grief.

Life goes on like that. Before the first one is even on its feet, the next is on the way. Housework becomes a crushing burden with no labour-saving devices to help out. Feeding the family is like cooking for a works canteen. And with each successive birth the figure collapses a little further, the breasts sag and a paunch develops, making the women look pregnant even when they are not. Privacy, time to yourself, time to rest even, is an unheard-of, undreamed-of luxury. Bearing and rearing children, every girl is told, is a woman's only function. And because to believe otherwise would be to condemn herself to utter despair, the woman accepts the idea: and teaches it to her daughters.

PAUL HARRISON

Discussion points

Research and discuss some of the religious and cultural traditions which affect women in different countries and areas of the world.

Is it possible to envisage a time in the future when men and women all over the world will treat one another as equals at home and at work?

Essay titles

a '. . . most women nowadays expect to marry, have children and work.'

b 'Room at the top, but not for women!'

c 'Women's liberation has resulted in men's enslavement.'

d Is the status of women in our society still unsatisfactory?

e 'Marriage is still a woman's best investment!' Discuss.

f Do you think it desirable or undesirable that men and women should maintain separate and clearly differentiated roles at home and at work?

g To what extent can male supremacy in commerce and industry be justified?

h How far have we got in equalising opportunities for the sexes, and how much further should we go?

i 'Literature is the only art form in which women have excelled.' How far do you agree?

Bibliography

de Beauvoir, Simone, *The Second Sex*, Penguin, 1983
Friedan, Betty, *The Feminine Mystique*, Gollancz, 1971
Friedan, Betty, *The Second Stage*, Michael Joseph, 1982
Greer, Germaine, *The Female Eunuch*, Paladin, 1971
Millett, Kate, *Sexual Politics*, Virago, 1977
Neustatter, Angela, *Hyenas in Petticoats: A Look At Twenty Years of Feminism*, Penguin, 1990
Oakley, Ann, *Subject Women*, Robertson, 1981
Radcliffe Richards, Janet, *The Sceptical Feminist*, Routledge and Kegan Paul, 1980
Seager, Toni and Olsen, Ann, *Women of the World: An International Atlas*, Pan, 1986
Spender, Dale (ed.), *Feminist Theorists*, The Women's Press, 1983
Tweedie, Jill, *In the Name of Love*, Jonathan Cape, 1979
Wolf, Naomi, *The Beauty Myth*, Chatto and Windus, 1990
Wollstonecraft, Mary and Mill, John Stuart, *Vindication of the Rights of Women/Subjection of Women*, Everyman, 1982

Advice on writing: using facts, figures, and sources in essays

It is perfectly possible to write a satisfactory argumentative essay with very little precise factual content, as was illustrated in Chapter 1. Facts and figures, however, give substance and conviction to an argument and it is sensible to learn a good deal of 'hard' information in preparation for an examination language essay. The degree to which this information needs to be detailed and exact is largely a matter of common sense. It may be helpful, nevertheless, to give some examples of the kinds of factual information which do and do not need to be exact.

Quoting sources of information is sometimes important, but it's obviously not necessary to give the source of every piece of information you include in an essay. If you are offering general information which is common knowledge, or is the kind of information which could be checked from a number of sources, such as details of the paternity-leave system and parenthood reforms in Sweden, there is no need to quote your source.

If you are giving precise figures, on the other hand, such as the percentage of the world's resources consumed by the USA, or the drop in the price of a commodity on the world market over a specified period, you ought to quote the source of the figures. The date when figures were issued also needs to be given sometimes, as when quoting the projected world population in the year 2000, since such projections are likely to change. Equally, if you quote an opinion, rather than presenting it as your own, you should be precise about the source of the opinion. For example, if you quote the opinion of Paul Cavadino, given on page 149, about the suitability of non-custodial sentences for two-thirds of the people now in prison, the point would gain much more bite and conviction if you quoted his name and official position, instead of saying 'as has been suggested recently' or some similarly vague phrase. Sometimes it may be necessary to be *very* explicit in giving your source, for instance, in the case of information about the living conditions of Bolivian tin miners' families mentioned on pages 77-8. If you merely quote the source as Domitila Barrios de Chungara, without mentioning who she is, and the title of her book, it will simply seem obscure. In this case you also need to quote the year of publication of the book, since the conditions referred to may have entirely altered since it was written. Generally speaking, however, there's no need to mention the actual book from which information or ideas are drawn, as long as the author is reasonably well known.

Exact figures and details should be given if doing so will clarify the point being made. In the case of historical background, for instance, precision is important. If you are mentioning acts of parliament, such as the Equal Pay Act, you should learn the date. If you mention the capital punishment debates in parliament, it is useful to know the years in which they took place. A proper historical perspective on events can only be given if you can quote dates; the year in which women achieved the vote, for instance, or the year when Mary Wollstonecraft achieved publication of the first feminist book.

Drawing comparisons between different groups of people in some particular respect is another case where precise back-up information is helpful. For instance, if you are arguing that women often earn less than men for similar work, despite the Equal Pay Act, you need at least to specify in which areas of work this is so, even if you can't quote figures. Similarly, if you are making the case that one of the reasons for women's wages being lower than men's on average is that many jobs are still heavily female-dominated, the statistic that women outnumber men nine to one in a quarter of all occupations in which women work will add considerable strength to

186

your argument. In this case, since the figures are not particularly well known or recognised, it would be useful to quote your source.

In general, exact facts and figures can often make an otherwise vague point precise and persuasive. A statement about Britain's prisons being seriously overcrowded is a case of point. If you could refer to the fact that prisoners are often held two or three to a cell built for one in Victorian times, you would establish the point convincingly. Greater detail than this, such as *how* often and in which prisons these conditions exist, is unnecessary. Here the source is less important, since the information is generally known and admitted. If you are mentioning famous people and places, you should try to make sure that you can give their names; instead, for instance, of referring to 'the headmaster of a progressive independent school' when discussing the ideology of Summerhill, you should be able to mention A.S. Neill and Summerhill by name.

Very often, of course, points can be made perfectly convincingly without precise facts and figures; you can, for instance, make the point that, despite anti-sexist legislation in Sweden, the great majority of students on technical courses there are boys, without needing to quote an exact figure. Common sense is ultimately the only guide in this matter.

RACE

For centuries, Britain has been a multi-racial society. Only recently, however, has 'race' become an issue, owing largely to the influx of easily identifiable black and Asian immigrants, which began just after the Second World War. Racial tensions, simmering since the late 1950s, boiled over in the early 1980s in a series of riots which shocked the whole of Europe and the English-speaking world. This chapter will concentrate largely on the racial situation in modern Britain. It begins with an exercise for summary of an article concerning the virtual absence of black and Asian journalists in Fleet Street.

Summary skills

The article which follows, which was written by Yasmin Alibhai, appeared in the *Guardian* newspaper in September 1990. Read it carefully, and answer the following question.

> Summarise the writer's comments on the policy of British newspapers with regard to the employment of black and Asian journalists. Your summary should not exceed 200 words in length.　　　*(40 marks)*

You are advised to spend about one hour on this question.

Still papering over the cracks

'Are you not just creating the problem by asking these questions?' enquired the voice of the spokeswoman (Department of Human Resources) from that vast media archipelago, News International. The problem under discussion was the employment of ethnic journalists on national newspapers and weeklies. I explained all I wanted to know was how many staff reporters were black or Asian: ('We don't know, to us they're all just reporters'); whether monitoring was done in this area ('No'); and how people were recruited for editorial jobs ('I wasn't told you wanted to ask that question. I'll have to get back to you').

Later I was told they had about 10 to 15 such journalists; that they had a very good relationship with the Race Relations Board (sic) and that recruitment was through contacts and approaches, though some senior posts were advertised.

Most other spokespeople were equally coy and defensive. Charles Burgess, managing editor of the *Independent*, thought there were maybe three Asian black journalists on staff, but said they did not look at things in that way. Nor does the *Observer*, which has an all-white editorial team of 100 except for one foreign correspondent.

The newspapers show a similar dearth. The *Sunday Correspondent* has no general black or Asian reporters, but one on the City Desk; the *Independent On Sunday* has none. *The Guardian* has two black reporters, a black sub-editor and had an Asian reporter on work experience. The *Sunday Telegraph* seems to have a couple. The *Evening Standard* has one and the *Mirror*, according to Bill Berentemfel, the editorial manager, has very few, 'two to three out of 200'.

Three quality weeklies – the *Listener, The Economist* and the *New Statesman and Society* – cannot conjure up one black staff reporter between them. Exceptionally the *Financial Times* has six – mostly sub-editors.

The Black Journalists Association (which includes Asian journalists) is currently carrying out a more comprehensive study, but its findings are unlikely to show anything but a thoroughly discouraging picture if this random survey is anything to go by.

The BJA held a meeting on Saturday with newspaper and magazine editors at the London School of Economics to air their concerns.

The situation seems to have arisen not out of conspiracy, but inertia. Traditional methods such as word-of-mouth recruitment and old boy net-works are known to militate most against those who come from under-represented groups. The Commission for Racial Equality recommends certain formal procedures to extend access and counter subjective factors. But the message remains anathema to the newspaper industry, even though the arguments for change are common-sensical. How can the papers harvest exciting new talent with diverse views and perspectives by

sticking so rigidly to the safety of clones?

It is common to see rivulets of guilt and concern trickling down the powerful foreheads of television chiefs, even if it is for PR purposes. But to date no newspaper editor has been heard to speak out on the issue. In five years, television has transformed itself. On the BBC recently, Peter Kenyatta, the deputy Editor of Current Affairs, sat suitably contrite when asked why more had not been done to recruit and promote blacks and Asians in key departments. Independent companies such as LWT and Thames have pursued aggressive policies to redress the balance through open advertising and the results are striking, with talented journalists like Trevor Phillips and Zeinab Badawi fronting prestigious news and current affairs programmes.

Changes in the television industry were spurred on by the Campaign Against Racism in the Media and other black groups. The inadequate television coverage of the Brixton and Southall street disturbances also exposed the need for ethnic reporters with an intimate knowledge of what was going on in the communities.

Newspapers have not displayed any such self-criticism. All describe themselves as equal-opportunity employers but have never sought to examine if the description is justified. Most editors/managing editors I spoke to felt they operated a genuine meritocracy and that they did not think in terms of special groups. No one, however, came up with any convincing explanations why there were so few ethnic staff journalists on their papers.

Berentemfel said that changing recruitment practices would be difficult. 'We employ people we know. We cannot afford to train anyone. They come to us from provincial papers, and they have to come up to scratch.'

But he agreed that change was necessary: 'It broadens the reporting spectrum. We should have not only ethnic minorities but perhaps Germans and French, too, as we go into Europe.'

This is good sense. Most white journalists do not have good contacts within black and Asian communities and have little genuine awareness of their lives, concerns and conflicts. It took over three months, for example, for papers to pick up on the abducted Southall baby – still missing – an event which came a few days after the Griffith baby abduction. Ethnics only exist when they riot, burn books, arrange marriages or dope deal. And yet many significant media events in the past few years have involved black and Asian Britons as this country tries to establish a multi-racial identity.

'Consciousness raising does need to be done,' said Peter Fiddick, editor of the *Listener*. 'We need to diversify and become more sensitive. The reasons why change is not taking place is apathy rather than not caring about it. Like women, ethnic minorities should speak out.

Trevor Grove, editor of the *Sunday Telegraph*, is also sympathetic. 'Members of these communities must not think that this is a closed shop. We believe in a meritocracy, and if they are good, race should not be an issue. It may be a positive plus. But what you don't want is to be a token figure, someone who is always typecast as the expert on these matters.'

But, if it is all right to have chess and wine correspondents, why not have race or community correspondents? Experts whose reports would have depth instead of being trite and superficial as they so often are at present.

Many black and Asian journalists do not want to be pushed into that particular box because they see it as an under-valued area of expertise and because they want to work in general interest areas. But most are not so choosy. As one young black journalist put it: 'I would love to be a token. Just tell them to give me a chance.'

David Walker, the Deputy Editor of the *Financial Times*, urged more journalists from under-represented groups to apply for jobs. 'When the UK Press Gazette did a similar article a few years ago, there was a flurry of applications,' he said. 'It was the only time we had any. Maybe these journalists are setting their sights too low, and their perceptions about jobs on the paper are negative.'

Shyama Perera, almost unique at present as an Asian woman journalist who has worked on major national papers, including *The Guardian*, is not convinced by the paucity argument. 'It is true that there were not enough of us initially. That's not the case now, but historical prejudices run deep. Editors are loath to try out this talent. And one barrier curiously is the desperately colour-blind approach – "I am a Liberal: I have done India. I frequent Mauritian fish restaurants so I cannot be racist."'

This barrier of self-righteousness is less easy to break than overt prejudice. The *New States-man and Society*, a paper for which I worked, had no other black journalists then and has none now. The *Daily Mail* on the other hand, not well known for its anti-racism, can boast that it has given space and high-profile positions to many black and Asian journalists such as Baz Bamigboye and Hal Austin.

Tariq Modood, principal officer at the Commission For Racial Equality, says: 'It is very disappointing to note the absence of ethnic minority people in newspaper journalism. When one looks at the way the issues of ethnic minorities are so poorly reported – usually too late and from the point of view of the outsider – one would have thought that papers would be desperate to buy in understanding and expertise.

In a recent article on these pages, John Pilger wrote of how the British media and its narrow, predictable coverage of issues has helped to insulate the status quo. He quoted the Runnymede Trust report, which says the press 'plays a very significant part in maintaining, justifying and strengthening racism at all levels of society, providing a cover for racist activity, especially racist violence.'

This is true of all the papers. You can do as much damage through exclusion and miscomprehension as you can through misrepresentations and falsehoods. How many Afro-Caribbean writers reported or commented on Broadwater Farm? And would the whole picture of that story have been different if they had done so? How long will white journalists on pilgrimage to Bradford continue to be amazed that young Muslims are not waiting to flee from the prisons of their lives? The ethics of racist reporting will only effectively be challenged when there is a core group of ethnic reporters on every paper.

Other vistas need to be opened, too. There are hardly any ethnic book, film or television reviewers, and no staff columnists.

There is a whole world out there, from cinema to commentary, waiting to be tapped.

YASMIN ALIBHAI,
The Guardian,
September 1990

What is 'race'?

Before we can talk sensibly about 'race', it is necessary to establish what we mean by the term. This definition of 'race' is taken from *A Dictionary of Race and Ethnic Relations* edited by E.Ellis Cashmore:

Physical anthropologists used to speak of human 'races' in the sense of sub-species, the most common scheme being the great tripartite division of mankind into Negroid, Mongoloid, and Caucasoid. Over the last forty to fifty years, however, it became increasingly clear that no meaningful taxonomy of human races was possible. Not only were numerous groups not classifiable as belonging to any of the three main groups, but physical anthropologists could not agree with each other as to where the genetic boundaries between human groups were to be drawn, or even on how many such groups there were. Humans have migrated over large distances and interbred extensively for thousands of years. Especially with the maritime expansion of Europe starting five centuries ago, this process of interbreeding has greatly accelerated, thereby blurring 'racial' boundaries, and contributing more than ever to the genetic homogenization of our species.

A 'race' can also mean a group of people who are socially defined in a given society as belonging together because of physical markers such as skin pigmentation, hair texture, facial features, stature, and the like. To avoid the confusion, some people specify 'social race' when they use 'race' in this meaning. Nearly all social scientists only use 'race' in this sense of a social group defined by somatic visibility. It is important to stress here that any resemblance with the first usage is little more than coincidental. For example, 'blacks' in South Africa and in Australia, although they occupy somewhat similar social positions in their respective societies, are no more closely related genetically to each other than each of them is to the 'whites.'

E. ELLIS CASHMORE

So, when we talk about 'races' in this chapter, we will simply be talking about groups of people of different skin colour. For the sake of simplicity, the term, 'black' is used to cover all dark-skinned people of Asian, African and West Indian origin.

It should be borne in mind, of course, that tensions between groups within societies arise from factors other than simply 'race', and in some societies different factors are paramount. Antagonism between Protestants and Catholics in Northern Ireland, or Sikhs and Hindus in India, stem from cultural and religious, rather than 'racial' distinctions, while in many nations of Africa conflict arises principally from tribal divisions.

Immigration: some facts

There have been black people in Britain for centuries. It was only after the Second World War, however, that immigration from black Commonwealth countries became at all significant. The background to the influx of black Commonwealth immigrants which began in the late 1940s, and which was originally mostly from the West Indies, is explained by Peter Fryer in *Staying Power:*

Ten years after the 'Empire Windrush'[1] there were in Britain about 25,000 West Indians who had come since the end of the war.

British industry gladly absorbed them. In some industries the demand for labour was so great that members of the reserve army of black workers were actively recruited in their home countries. In April 1956 London Transport began recruiting staff in Barbados, and within 12 years a total of 3,787 Barbadians had been taken on. They were lent their fares to Britain, and the loans were repaid gradually from their wages. Even this number was not enough and in 1966 London Transport would begin to recruit in Trinidad and Jamaica too. The British Hotels and Restaurants Association recruited skilled workers in Barbados. And a Tory health

---

1 The ship on which the first Commonwealth immigrants from the West Indies sailed to Britain in 1945.

minister by the name of Enoch Powell welcomed West Indian nurses to Britain. Willing black hands drove tube trains, collected bus fares, emptied hospital patients' bed-pans.

From the early 1950s, Britain's other black community – the hitherto tiny community from the Indian sub-continent – also began to grow as rural workers from India and Pakistan came to work in Britain, again with official encouragement. By the end of 1958 there were in this country about 55,000 Indians and Pakistanis.

All these West Indians and Asians were British citizens. The 1948 Nationality Act had granted United Kingdom citizenship to citizens of Britain's colonies and former colonies. Their British passports gave them the right to come to Britain and stay here for the rest of their lives.

In their own countries there were strong incentives to take advantage of their right to settle in Britain. In the Indian sub-continent, millions had found themselves adrift from homes and jobs when Pakistan and India went their separate ways after independence. Emigration to Britain offered the prospect of a new life unthreatened by flood, famine, or the miserable poverty that was their countries' chief legacy from imperial rule. In the British West Indies, the cost of living had almost doubled during the war. There was large-scale unemployment, and those without work were desperate. There was no relief of any kind: no dole, no children's allowances; no social security at all. 'No one knows exactly how the jobless live', wrote Joyce Egginton in 1957. She added: 'It is not surprising that thousands have left the West Indies. The surprising thing is that so many have stayed.'

PETER FRYER

This 'open door' immigration policy for Commonwealth citizens lasted for a decade and a half, but by the early 1970s it had been entirely reversed. The following passage from *Racial Disadvantage in Britain* by David J.Smith explains how and why:

Government policy in the early stages of the immigration has been described as laissez-faire; that is, there was no policy. Bowing to increasing pressure, given further weight by racial disturbances in 1958 and 1960, the government introduced immigration control through the Commonwealth Immigrants Act of 1962. By this time about half the present minority population had already entered the country. One of the effects of control was to stimulate an enormous increase in immigration over the 18 months before the Act became operative. Another was to help switch the balance of immigration from the Caribbean to India and Pakistan, though it was not entirely clear how this came about.

Controls were tightened in 1965 within the framework of the existing legislation. The previous controls were superseded by the Immigration Act of 1971, which gives the 'right of abode' to people it defines as patrial. The definition of this term is complex, but essentially it means people who, as well as being Commonwealth citizens, or citizens of the United Kingdom and colonies, have some substantial connection with the UK; for example, they were born in the UK, or acquired UK citizenship by naturalization or registration, or one of their parents or grandparents acquired UK citizenship in one of these ways. Those who are patrial have the right of free entry. Those who are not may enter only if they are granted a special voucher. Thus in three stages from 1962 onwards the right of entry to Britain has been withdrawn from most of the population of the New Commonwealth countries, and a strict control of immigration has been imposed. Since 1971 most of those granted entry under the voucher scheme have been the dependents of people already living in Britain.

It is worth noting that over the whole period, immigration policy has been taken to mean finding a way of limiting the flow of immigration.

DAVID J. SMITH

Discussion points

What factors do you think influenced various British governments to abandon the original post-war 'open door' immigration policy, and to tighten immigration controls?

Why do you think the distinction between Commonwealth and non-Commonwealth citizens was effectively withdrawn in the 1971 Immigration Act? Do you agree with the Act?

Do you consider the current immigration controls too severe, about right, or insufficiently severe?

Black people in Britain

An ever-increasing proportion of black Britons have spent all their lives in this country. But their experience of life in Britain depends to a large extent on their country of origin; their cultural background has an enormous bearing on their attitudes and aspirations.

In the extract which follows, from a book edited by E. Ellis Cashmore and Barry Troyna entitled *Black Youth in Crisis*, the term 'black' is used to mean people of West Indian origin, as distinct from 'Asian', which refers to people of Indian, Pakistani and Bangladeshi origin.

As the 1970s drew to a close, apprehension mounted in regard to black youth in England. Maybe they were expected to exhibit docility, indifference to what was going on about them, resign themselves to social circumstances. If there was optimism about their ability, or inclination, to integrate fully into the society that had played host to their parents, it faded as the years passed by . . . The futility of technical measures directed at avoiding the type of furores caused by blacks in the USA in the 1960s became apparent as unemployment grew disproportionately amongst this group, street offence and theft convictions spiralled ominously, feelings of disengagement intensified . . .

Perspectives on the problematic nature of young blacks were provided by simple comparison with another major ethnic group – Asians. Studies suggested that the first wave of Asians to England were materially in the same position as West Indians; further, they housed similar expectations as to what they might get out of the new society: a relatively smooth reception, better living conditions, possibly an accumulation of wealth followed by a return to the homeland. Objectively, the position of Asians was in alignment with that of West Indians; both groups crystallised in the less salubrious regions of urban centres where housing was most available but least desirable.

Discernibly, the Asians made most inroads in the commercial sphere, establishing small businesses, retail outlets, wholesale and manufacturing services, and many grew to prosperity. West Indians, on the other hand, seemed anchored. Young Asians, highly motivated by their parents to work steadfastly at school and maximise the benefits they might receive from formal education, improved quite dramatically. The emphasis on education in Asian culture had its effect on them and, by the late 1970s, they were comfortably in range of white school-children in terms of actual achievements.

The picture was very different for black youth, very, very different. Study after study led to the depressing conclusion that young blacks were making little or no impression. Continually, they achieved less than both whites and Asians and there were utterly no grounds for expecting a change. If anything, black youths seemed to be reinforcing their own lack of achievements by consciously promoting an attitude of rejection of education. Whether the lack of achievement bred the loss of affiliation or vice versa is a chicken-and-egg conundrum; for the moment, however, we rest with the observations that young blacks did not do well at school and their orientations to education were such that they gave no cause for believing they would do better in the future. In brief, they did not want to know.

Depicted is a scene where Asian youths, supported by their parents, entertained positive orientations towards education and improved steadily in terms of actual achievements. The importance of formal education as a route to social mobility and material gain was not lost on Asians as it seemingly was on blacks. Their collective attitude towards education was captured nicely by a black youth whom one of us encountered whilst engaged in research in the late 1970s: 'Education. What good is that to the black man? Qualifications? Them mean nothing so long as you're black.'[2]

E. ELLIS CASHMORE and BARRY TROYNA

2   A newspaper report on 12 January 1992 suggests that this situation is at last beginning to change:
    'For the first time, researchers have discovered evidence that the brightest young Afro-Caribbean children outshone their white classmates in Britain's primary schools. A new study commissioned by the School Examinations and Assessment Council, the official watchdog on school standards, challenges traditional views that Afro-Caribbean pupils are "trapped" by under-achievement and low expectations almost from birth. It found 10% of black seven-year-olds gained the top grade in mathematics and 19% in science, compared with 6% and 18% for whites.'

Generalisations about human beings always distort to some extent. But some experiences and personal conflicts are extremely common to black people living in Britain.

In the extracts which follow, which appear in a book called *'Race' in Britain*, edited by Charles Husband, two young men, one of West Indian and the other of Indian origin, talk about their lives in this country:

A West Indian/British male

Ever since I can remember, and this is going way back, early 1960s, from being very small I was always aware of being dark – black – and for a six-year-old it wasn't very pleasant being called 'darkie' and 'monkey'. Because if you're dark then you're stupid – a fool – and I wasn't stupid, I wasn't a fool, but I was quiet and different. I remember wanting to be white when I grew up because being black was something bad and awful, and in all my dreams I was white and I'd go round in space from planet to planet in my spaceship doing good deeds and rescuing people. Then we moved to Leeds and Leeds was a big frightening place . . .

I remember the first day I went to school in Leeds. I don't know why – perhaps it was because I spoke differently or looked different but this white kid came up and started to pick on me. All the resentment, all the fear and frustration of coming to Leeds just came out and I found myself attacking him. I'd never done anything before like that in my life and I haven't since, but I had to be dragged away. Since then nobody ever picked on me, which was surprising because there were kids who were stronger than me who got picked on and cowed. I still wanted to be white and most of my friends were white, I suppose, and then we moved to junior school which was just across the playground. There I had to be much more aware of black kids because we all seemed to be lumped together in the same class, and I suppose because we were all black we just got on – it wasn't a question of making friendships but I still went around with my white friends. I felt I didn't belong to either group – white or black. I was in a sort of limbo of my own . . .

The weird thing was that, although I had this attitude in me that I wasn't going to be a 'blackie' no matter what, the people I used to go round with used to come out with 'nigger' jokes. It was okay because I was supposed not to mind, 'It's all right, he doesn't take offence', I was part of their group so I had to accept it. I did mind, but I didn't say, because it was something apart from me, I wasn't what they were talking about – I was almost like them. It was a really strange attitude when I look back on it now – I don't understand it – but at the same time I wasn't going to conform to what other people wanted me to be. I wasn't going to be a 'happy nigger' or an athlete, or a footballer, I wanted to be something that everyone else was – everyone white that is. As far as I could see there were no black guys doing A levels and writing essays, they were all playing football – and I wanted to be somebody . . .

Racism doesn't exactly help you feel secure as a person. I've been followed by the police and I don't look your sort of heavy dread guy. I've had the police follow me in a car all the way up Roundhay Road at ten o'clock at night, just cruising by the side of me not saying a word. It was really eerie and I just carried on walking, because I knew that if I stopped or jumped over a wall or something they'd have got me and there'd have been no witnesses. And I've had people in the middle of town trying to run me over and other people don't believe it. Patti and I have suffered abuse from people – it happens all the time, and when we tell people they're so amazed. Drivers have made U-turns to come back at me, shouting 'you wog, you bastard, you nigger' and people just walk on – I just walk on, I mean I'm so hardened to it now. I've been attacked in Safeways in Headingley and nobody did a thing – and that was when I was out with one of the children from the home where I work. You can't go into a shop without being the focus of attention because people expect you to steal something. If you go into a restaurant for a meal then you are shunted off into a corner where you won't offend the other all-white clientele.

Being a mixed couple we tend to move in racially mixed circles when we can, except where we have to move in all-white ones because of work or colour reasons. This means that for a lot of the time we are with a lot of white people and we stand out. We have to fight continuously against people's stereotyped ideas about us as a racially mixed couple. When you are out, you are always aware of people because they are always aware of you. They are always staring and making comments and you learn to sum people up in one go, because you have to for your own survival otherwise you could be walking straight into trouble. You learn to read body language – you immediately know if someone is being friendly or not, then you have to decide how to deal with it . . .

Younger generation blacks who don't know us would feel that it was a promotion of the sexual stereotype – perhaps some of those who do know us as well – but most of them accept us for what we are. The same with our white friends, but for the majority of white people who see us in the streets, we just fulfil their idea of the sexual stereotype – white girls who go with black men must be of 'loose morals', just looking for sexual excitement.

I'm a lot more secure now in my black identity than I have ever been, but it took a long time getting there, through a lot of stages. I didn't go through what some would term the 'ethnic road' of, say, youth cult groups. For white kids there's always been teds, skins, mods, rockers, punks, but for black kids there's never been anything they could really identify with, that was really culturally theirs, until Rasta came along. Like, it was embarrassing to be black – for me anyway – I didn't even speak patois, I didn't want to sound like an ignorant 'wog'. It was easier to get along without any hassle by conforming to a stereotype because you were being what people expected of you, whereas it was harder and more threatening if you were something that was close to them. If you acted like the jolly buffoon or the thicko who was good at sports you were then conforming to all the stereotyped attitudes that are around, of black people being musical, good dancers etc., but not very intelligent. If you wear a wooly hat and spend your time building a sound system then you also conform to the stereotype, but if you aspire to be something else, a substitute white, an imitation white as they see it, wanting to study and do well, then

you are threatening because you have the ability to take people's jobs away and be in a position of telling other people – especially white people – what to do. But in doing that you don't feel comfortable on either side of the fence because you're not black and you're not white . . .

Black people tend to be more accepting than white people and Patti often feels a lot easier in all-black gatherings than I do in all-white ones. White people often forget that black people have to face this every day of their lives, yet if the situation was reversed they would feel a lot less confident. A white friend of mine is a good example of this – he says he feels uncomfortable if there are a lot of black people and he is the only white, yet he never expects me to mind being in all-white situations . . .

Most of the things I've been talking about are psychological – how people see themselves and how they see other people. Black people in Britain in my opinion are still slaves, but the chains are not on their bodies but on their minds, and black kids especially need someone to help them break out of these chains, because otherwise they've got no future, they've got nothing. They've got to learn, but more important, white people have got to learn to accept them for themselves, then perhaps we can learn to accept each other.

A young Gujerati/British male

Being about five years old when I came to England, I had few memories of India – I had not formed my Indian identity. Having emigrated to England, I was to form two

198

identities alongside each other: that which my family and community socialised me into, and that which the white society wanted.

My first real encounters of racial violence were when I moved into secondary school. Gangs of white youths used to go around 'Paki-bashing'. Only when this persisted did Indians form gangs and retaliate. However, by now I had some idea of the British class structure and knew that these 'troublemakers' were from the lowest rungs. I was convinced and knew that the 'others' were not like them. Though objectively I was from the same class as they were, I differentiated myself from them and identified myself with those above me. I aspired to their good, commonsense way of life, values, attitudes, etc.

By now I was about 15 years old and I was becoming well integrated into the white culture. It was about at this age that I realised that I was leading two lives, that of an Indian at home, and the black man with a white mask outside. I realised that I was experiencing culture conflict and had difficulty in identifying with either and coming to a compromise. I now realise that in the few years before the age of 15, when I thought I was going through the normal phase of being a rebellious teenager, that they were really acts which manifested the internal cultural and identity crises that I was going through.

Difficulties arose when, for example, the norm in the white society was in the belief of 'individualism'. Youths were expected to drink, smoke, have girlfriends, etc. This was not the case in the Indian culture. The family was a tightly knit and integrated unit with the Indian community. The belief was that of 'collectivism': life was with the people.

This presented real problems to me because on the one hand, I was expected to conform with my white friends and their culture, and on the other hand, with my family and the Indian community culture . . .

There were frequent periods of confrontation with my family when it became apparent to them, from my behaviour, that I was slipping away from them, rejecting the Indian culture and becoming totally immersed in the white culture. These confrontations often served to bring me into a state of equilibrium. From there, I would again try the futile pursuit of trying to find a compromise between the two cultures, for this seemed the only logical way ahead. It seemed to me that my parents wanted me to succeed in the white society, yet retain my identity as an Indian; and the white society was making demands upon me to fully incorporate myself into their culture and only then would I be accepted. In a sense, they were ready and waiting with their arms to embrace me.

It was when I started to date white girls and generally go out with them that I realised that this was not so. The malicious and contemptuous looks and abuse that were received made me realise that, although I wanted to be fully integrated into the white society, the white society would only let me at a superficial level. Thus, underneath the surface the divisions were to be maintained and reinforced. The purity of the Indian culture and race was insisted upon by my parents. Whereas before I felt that this was not the case for the white man, (for he could 'understand' the culture conflict and be more 'liberal' minded), I was to change my mind. Any notion that I had of being fully integrated, finding a compromise, or marrying a white girl in society, had to be rejected. I was in a situation where, should I marry a white girl, I would be excommunicated from my Indian community and be virtually in the same situation with the white society. Thus, the cost outweighs the benefits . . .

So I set out positively to form a white identity. This resulted in a conflict and a period where I was in search for a compromise. This leaves one in a precarious and difficult situation. This leaves the vast majority of Indians (including myself) being forced to go back and identify with their Indian culture. For I am in a situation where I cannot integrate fully into the white society, and, not wanting to be rejected by both, opt for the safest and surest way of identifying with my Indian culture more.

Perhaps the majority of my generation will take this route, because to some extent we are still able to identify with the poor social and economic conditions with which they started when arriving as immigrants. So, we also suffer from a guilt complex in that we feel our parents have given their lives and suffered so that we would be better off, and yet here we are repaying them by denouncing everything they believe in and have worked for. Their blood, sweat and tears have been worthless.

However, the children of my generation will hopefully not suffer too much from the cultural and identity crises. At least my generation will have a better understanding of the acculturation processes that their children will be going through and the crises that will confront them. Thus I hope the assimilation processes will be a little easier for them, for the pressure from Indian parents will ease a little. But I doubt very much if the same will happen with regards to the white man's view on integration.

Themes for discussion

What factors do you think might have influenced the differing general responses of people of West Indian and Asian origin to life in Britain?

What do you think of the idea of 'positive discrimination' in employment, such as legislation demanding that a certain proportion of vacancies in factories must be filled by people of ethnic minority background?

Do you think that more should be done in schools in Britain to make education genuinely multi-cultural, so that children of different ethnic backgrounds can be helped to understand and appreciate one another's cultures better? Alternatively, do you think special schools should be set up for children of ethnic minority ancestry, paying more attention to their cultural and linguistic background?

What is your attitude to 'mixed marriages' between people of different racial origins?

Do you think that black and white people will ever 'learn to accept each other'?

Racial prejudice

Though support for the overtly racist political parties like the National Front has waned slightly since its zenith in the late 1970s, prejudice and violence against black people has remained a constant feature of life in racially mixed areas of Britain.

Its growth over the past 25 years is traced in *Sociology* by Anthony Gittens:

In 1968, while Parliament was discussing race relations, Enoch Powell (then Conservative front-bench spokesman for defence) delivered a speech in Birmingham in which he envisaged an extraordinary growth of the non-white population: 'like the Romans, I seem to see "the River Tiber flowing with much blood".' A Gallup poll showed that 75 per cent of the population were broadly sympathetic to Powell's views.

The end of the 1970s and early 1980s witnessed increasing unemployment in Britain concentrated particularly among the ethnic minorities. There were waves of unrest, with racial clashes in Brixton, Handsworth and Tottenham in London, Toxteth in Liverpool and St Paul's in Bristol.

In a 1985 survey, nine out of ten British whites said that they believed there is prejudice against Asians and blacks. The survey also revealed that over a third of whites openly admit to being racially prejudiced themselves (a far higher proportion than in similar surveys in the United States). Men are more likely than women to admit to prejudice, as are older people and those in working-class jobs or the unemployed. Although the whites surveyed were sceptical of the claim that the level of racial prejudice had increased over the past five years (it had), they were generally quite ready to believe that racial prejudice in Britain is likely to grow rather than diminish.

ANTHONY GITTENS

Racial prejudice is born largely of ignorance and insecurity. In his book *Black Testimony: The Voices of Britain's West Indians*, Thomas J. Cottle explains some of the most widespread misconceptions concerning black people in Britain:

During the last few years, I have spoken with people in Great Britain who, never having met families from the West Indies, were in doubt of the languages spoken by West Indians . . . I have heard estimates of the number of blacks in Great Britain reach as high as 25 per cent of the population. It was not uncommon for people to believe that fewer than 5 per cent of England's black citizens were English born.

In point of fact, some 2,000,000 blacks live in England, 40 per cent of whom were born in this country.[3]

THOMAS J. COTTLE

3   At the end of the 1980s, six per cent of the population were officially classified as non-white; approximately half of these were born in the UK. (Gittens, *Sociology*, 1990)

Here are some of the most commonly-heard complaints of white Britons against blacks and vice-versa, taken from *Learning to be Prejudiced* by Alfred Davey:

'They don't fit in.'
'They take the houses needed by the whites.'
'They won't learn the language.'
'They don't like us, they just tolerate us because they have to live here; they should ship them back.'
'They don't mix; they pretend to be tolerant but they're not.'
'There's too many of them.'
'They do their toilet in the street; they take houses and turn them into slums.'

'Blacks seem to be synonymous with barbarians.'
'Too many black kids are relegated to ESN schools; they see us as inferior.'
'Parliament pays lip-service to equality; we are dominated by whites; they treat us like second-class people.'
'They say we take their jobs; they think only of themselves.'
'We're picked on by the police.'

Prejudice can take horrifying forms, as was illustrated in a BBC radio *File on 4* programme, in which Janet Cohen interviewed residents of the East End of London:

Cohen: Teachers, too, complain of growing racial hostility in the classrooms. J., a teacher, who is considering joining a vigilante group, says he faces a daily tide of abuse from his pupils.

J: Oh, it affects me all the time.

Cohen: How?

J: Because they call me, you know, 'Paki' and 'Paki out', and they scrawl on the door of my teaching room. I mean, I've been in the school for seven years but now things are deteriorating. They may say, well, we're doing it for a laugh or something like that, but then they are influenced by the older people, you see, because in that area where I live there are, you know, lots of demonstrations organized by the British Movement.

Cohen: You know it's the British Movement, do you?

J: They write on my blackboard, they write BM, and then they have these Nazi signs, you know, under their lapel and they show it to me and they ask me to read their leaflets, they carry them around. Oh yes, I know – the leaflets from these various movements, the New National Front, the National Front, the British Movement, kids now start saying to me, oh, you have taken our job; suddenly they have found that I have taken their job, so why don't I go back, you Paki, you see, they shout.

| Cohen: | Many black families don't even feel safe at home; in the heart of the East End one family claims their house has been attacked 35 times. White gangs, they say, have aimed bricks, bottles and air-gun pellets through their front windows. The glass is now protected by two layers of metal grilles, sheets of plywood, and then shutters. The police have advised the three adults and ten children to move into the two back rooms of the house. But the attacks continue and they aren't limited to the home. This man, who's too frightened to broadcast his name, fears for his and his brother's children; all of them have been threatened and assaulted on the streets . . .

Today's violence takes place against a background of rising unemployment. In some boroughs, one person in seven is out of a job. A report published today claims that blacks are more likely than whites to lose their jobs in the economic recession, but skinheads on the streets don't see it this way. Their heads shaved, their trousers cropped six inches above their ankle, their faces pinched in the cold, they feel the blacks are stealing their jobs. As for violence against the ethnic communities: |
|---|---|
| 1st skinhead: | Do I condone it? Yes. They've got no right to be here. |
| Cohen: | That families should have bricks thrown through the window, airgun pellets, that kind of thing? |
| 1st skinhead: | Well, only blacks like, and Jews, yeh. White European race, right, is the superior race and always will be. |
| Cohen: | Is it really fair that families should be intimidated; after all, they are people? |
| 2nd skinhead: | Yes, course it is. They're not people, they're parasites, they're just poncing off us . . . |
| 3rd skinhead: | The fact is, right, ordinary people don't like 'em moving in round the East London environment round there, right, and they want 'em out. |
| Cohen: | But is it fair to attack these families? |
| All skinheads: | Yes, it is. |
| 3rd skinhead: | It's the only way isn't it, I mean the government ain't doing nothing are they, nobody's doing anything, are they? |
| 1st skinhead: | It takes 10 years for a bill to get through Parliament, right, and nothing happens, right, so if you give them like a good dig and all that like, it might just send a couple of them home; you know what I mean. They might think, oh, you know like, we've had enough like, we're going to get home. So we're doing our little bit. |
| 4th skinhead: | We believe that the blacks are taking over our country, the Yids are taking over our country. |

Cohen:	So how much violence do you think there is around here, then, towards . . .
All skinheads:	There's a lot more, there's a lot more, there should be a lot anyway. There is, there's a lot going around.
Cohen:	It's gangs of youths like those who are blamed for the growing number of racial assaults, but where in some boroughs immigrants make up 14 per cent of the population, members of the older generation, too, say they understand the powerful feelings of the young, even if they don't support the violence.
1st man:	Well, it's out of order, isn't it? Everyone's entitled to live, you know, you know, there's a little bit of racial in everyone, but there you go. Especially if we're sort of, we're inundated with them, ain't we, it's getting overcrowded. I mean you've got to admit, even though the housing problem's enough, isn't it?
2nd man:	I think, quite honestly, the economic situation today forces them into this: you get kids who are left on the streets, they haven't got any work or anything like that; they've got to take their anger out on somebody, so they take it out on the unknown. It'll certainly take years before we sort the problem out, we'll probably have to go through the sort of problems that America has suffered before we can really sort it out.

Themes for discussion

Why do you think that white people have stereotyped views of what black people are like? Do you think other minority groups are stereotyped in a similar way?

Consider the list of complaints by whites against blacks and blacks against whites, and discuss the reasons for them.

How do you explain the degree of hatred of black people expressed by the skinheads in the *File on 4* interviews?

Do you think that racial tension in Britain is increasing or decreasing? Do you think that the government could or should do more to promote racial harmony?

Research suggestion

Write a brief report on British government legislation to combat racial discrimination, and its effectiveness.

Racial tension in America

In his novel, *Go Tell it on the Mountain*, the black American writer, James Baldwin, explores the feelings of black people in the 1960s living in a society in which racial prejudice is deep-rooted and often intense. Here is an extract from the novel, which forms, in effect, a short story:

Go Tell it on the Mountain

She lived quite a long way from Richard – four subway stops; and when it was time for her to go home, he always took the subway uptown with her and walked her to the door. On a Saturday when they had forgotten the time and stayed together later than usual, he left her at her door at two o'clock in the morning. They said goodnight hurriedly, for she was afraid of trouble when she got upstairs – though, in fact, Madame Williams seemed astonishingly indifferent to the hours Elizabeth kept – and he wanted to hurry back home and go to bed. Yet, as he hurried off down the dark, murmuring street, she had a sudden impulse to call him back, to ask him to take her with him and never let her go again. She hurried up the steps, smiling a little at this fancy: it was because he looked so young and defenceless as he walked away, and yet so jaunty and strong.

He was to come the next evening at suppertime, to make at last, at Elizabeth's urging, the acquaintance of Madame Williams. But he did not come. She drove Madame Williams wild with her sudden sensitivity to footsteps on the stairs. Having told Madame Williams that a gentleman was coming to visit her, she did not dare, of course, to leave the house and go out looking for him, thus giving Madame Williams the impression that she dragged men in off the streets. At ten o'clock, having eaten no supper, a detail unnoticed by her hostess, she went to bed, her head aching and her heart sick with fear; fear over what had happened to Richard, who had never kept her waiting before; and fear involving all that was beginning to happen in her body.

And on Monday morning he was not at work. She left during the lunch hour to go to his room. He was not there. His landlady said that he had not been there all weekend. While Elizabeth stood trembling and indecisive in the hall, two white policemen entered.

She knew the moment she saw them, and before they mentioned his name, that something terrible had happened to Richard. Her heart, as on that bright summer day when he had first spoken to her, gave a terrible bound and then was still, with an awful, wounded stillness. She put out one hand to touch the wall in order to keep standing.

'This here young lady was just looking for him,' she heard the landlady say.

They all looked at her.

'You his girl?' one of the policemen asked.

She looked up at his sweating face, on which a lascivious smile had immediately appeared, and straightened, trying to control her trembling.

'Yes,' she said. 'Where is he?'

'He's in jail, honey,' the other policeman said.

'What for?'

'For robbing a white man's store, black girl. That's what for.'

She found, and thanked Heaven for it, that a cold stony rage had entered her. She would, otherwise, certainly have fallen down, or begun to weep. She looked at the smiling policeman.

'Richard ain't robbed no store,' she said. 'Tell me where he is.'

'And *I* tell you,' he said, not smiling, 'that your boyfriend robbed a store and he's in jail for it. He's going to stay there, too – now, what you got to say to that?'

'And he probably did it for you, too,' the other policeman said. 'You look like a girl a man could rob a store for.'

She said nothing; she was thinking how to get to see him, how to get him out. One of them, the smiler, turned now to the landlady and said: 'Let's have the key to his room. How long's he been living here?'

'About a year,' the landlady said. She looked unhappily at Elizabeth. 'He seemed like a real nice boy.'

'Ah, yes,' he said, mounting the steps, 'they all seem like real nice boys when they pay their rent.'

'You going to take me to see him?' she asked of the remaining policeman. She found herself fascinated by the gun in his holster, the club at his side. She wanted to take that pistol and empty it into his round, red face; to take that club and strike with all her strength against the base of his skull where his cap ended, until the ugly, silky, white man's hair was matted with blood and brains.

'Sure, girl,' he said, 'you're coming right along with us. The man at the station house wants to ask you some questions.'

The smiling policeman came down again. 'Ain't nothing up there,' he said. 'Let's go.'

She moved between them, out into the sun. She knew that there was nothing to be gained by talking to them any more. She was entirely in their power; she would have to think faster than they could think; she would have to contain her fear and her hatred, and find out what could be done. Not for anything short of Richard's life, and not, possibly, even for that, would she have wept before them, or asked of them a kindness.

A small crowd, children and curious passers-by, followed them as they walked the long, dusty, sunlit street. She hoped only that they would not pass anyone she knew; she kept her head high, looking straight ahead, and felt the skin settle over her bones as though she were wearing a mask.

And at the station she somehow got past their brutal laughter. (*What was he doing with you, girl, until two o'clock in the morning? – Next time you feel like that girl, you come by here and talk to me.*) She felt that she was about to burst, or vomit, or die. Though the sweat stood out cruelly, like needles on her brow, and she felt herself, from every side, being covered with a stink and filth, she found out, in their own good time, what she wanted to know: he was being held in a prison downtown called the Tombs (the name made her heart turn over), and she could see him tomorrow. The state, or the prison, or someone, had already assigned him a lawyer; he would be brought to trial next week.

But the next day, when she saw him, she wept. He had been beaten, he whispered to her, and he could hardly walk. His body, she later discovered, bore almost no bruises, but was full of strange, painful swellings, and there was a welt above one eye.

He had not, of course, robbed the store, but, when he left her that Saturday night, had gone down into the subway station to wait for his train. It was late, and trains were slow; he was all alone on the platform, only half awake, thinking, he said, of her.

Then, from the far end of the platform, he heard a sound of running; and, looking up, he saw two coloured boys come running down the steps. Their clothes were torn, and they were frightened; they came up the platform and stood near him, breathing hard. He was about to ask them what the trouble was when, running across the tracks toward them, and followed by a white man, he saw another coloured boy; and at the same instant another white man came running down the subway steps.

Then he came full awake, in panic; he knew that whatever the trouble was, it was now his trouble also; for these white men would make no distinction between him and the three boys they were after. They were all coloured, they were about the same age, and here they stood together on the subway platform. And they were all, with no questions asked, herded upstairs, and into the wagon and to the station house.

At the station Richard gave his name and address and age and occupation. Then for the first time he stated that he was not involved, and asked one of the other boys to corroborate his testimony. This they rather despairingly did. They might, Elizabeth felt, have done it sooner, but they probably also felt that it would be useless to speak. And they were not believed; the owner of the store was being brought there to make the identification. And Richard tried to relax: the man *could* not say that he had been there if he had never seen him before.

But when the owner came, a short man with a bloody shirt – for they had knifed him – in the company of yet another policeman, he looked at the four boys before him and said: 'Yeah, that's them, all right.'

Then Richard shouted: 'But *I* wasn't there! Look at me, goddammit – I wasn't *there*!'

'You black bastards,' the man said, looking at him, 'you're all the same.'

Then there was silence in the station, the eyes of the white men all watching. And Richard said, but quietly, knowing that he was lost: 'But all the same, mister, I wasn't there.' And he looked at the white man's bloody shirt and thought, he told Elizabeth, at the bottom of his heart: 'I wish to God they'd killed you.'

Then the questioning began. The three boys signed a confession at once, but Richard would not sign. He said at last that he would die before he signed a confession to something he hadn't done.

'Well then,' said one of them, hitting him suddenly across the head, 'maybe you *will* die, you black son-of-a-bitch.' And the beating began. He would not, then, talk to her about it; she found that, before the dread and the hatred that filled her mind, her imagination faltered and held its peace.

'What we going to do?' she asked at last. He smiled a vicious smile – she had never seen such a smile on his face before.

'Maybe you ought to pray to that Jesus of yours and get Him to come down and tell these white men something.' He looked at her a long, dying moment. 'Because I don't know nothing *else* to do,' he said.

She suggested: 'Richard, what about another lawyer?'

And he smiled again. 'I declare,' he said, 'Little-bit's been holding out on me. She got a fortune tied up in a sock, and she ain't never told me nothing about it.'

She had been trying to save money for a whole year, but she had only thirty dollars. She sat before him, going over in her mind all the things she might do to raise money, even to going on the streets. Then, for very helplessness, she began to shake with sobbing. At this, his face became Richard's face again. He said in a shaking voice: 'Now, look here, Little-bit, don't you be like that. We going to work this out all right.' But she could not stop sobbing. 'Elizabeth,' he whispered. 'Elizabeth, Elizabeth.' Then the man came and said it was time for her to go. And she rose. She had brought two packs of cigarettes for him, and they were still in her bag. Wholly ignorant of prison regulations, she did not dare to give them to him under the man's eyes. And, somehow, her failure to remember to give him the cigarettes, when she knew how much he smoked, made her weep the harder. She tried – and failed – to smile at him, and she was slowly led to the door. The sun nearly blinded her, and she heard him whisper behind her: 'So long, baby. Be good.'

In the streets she did not know what to do. She stood awhile before the dreadful gates, and then she walked and walked until she came to a coffee shop where taxi drivers and the people who worked in nearby offices hurried in and out all day. Usually she was afraid to go into downtown establishments, where only white people were, but today she did not care. She felt that if anyone said anything to her she would turn and curse him like the lowest bitch on the streets. If anyone touched her, she would do her best to send his soul to Hell.

But no one touched her; no one spoke. She drank her coffee, sitting in the strong sun that fell through the window. Now it came to her how alone, how frightened she was; she had never been so frightened in her life before. She knew that she was pregnant – knew it, as the old folks said, in her bones; and if Richard should be sent away, what, under Heaven, could she do? Two years, three years – she had no idea how long he might be sent away for – what would she do? And how could she keep her aunt from knowing? And if her aunt should find out, then her father would know, too. The tears welled up, and she drank her cold, tasteless coffee. And what would they do with Richard? And if they sent him away, what would he be like, then, when he returned? She looked into the quiet, sunny streets, and for the first time in her life, she hated it all – the white city, the white world. She could not, that day, think of one decent white person in the whole world. She sat there, and she

208

hoped that one day God, with tortures inconceivable, would grind them utterly into humility, and make them know that black boys and black girls, whom they treated with such condescension, such disdain, and such good humour, had hearts like human beings, too, more human hearts than theirs.

But Richard was not sent away. Against the testimony of the three robbers, and her own testimony, and, under oath, the storekeeper's indecision, there was no evidence on which to convict him. The courtroom seemed to feel, with some complacency and some disappointment, that it was his great good luck to be let off so easily. They went immediately to his room. And there – she was never all her life long to forget it – he threw himself, face downward, on his bed and wept.

She had only seen one other man weep before – her father – and it had not been like this. She touched him, but he did not stop. Her own tears fell on his dirty, uncombed hair. She tried to hold him, but for a long time he would not be held. His body was like iron; she could find no softness in it. She sat curled like a frightened child on the edge of the bed, her hand on his back, waiting for the storm to pass over. It was then that she decided not to tell him yet about the child.

By and by he called her name. And then he turned, and she held him against her breast, while he sighed and shook. He fell asleep at last, clinging to her as though he were going down into the water for the last time.

And it was the last time. That night he cut his wrists with his razor and he was found in the morning by his landlady, his eyes staring upward with no light, dead among the scarlet sheets.   JAMES BALDWIN

Discussion points

Why do you think Richard committed suicide in the story?

Do you think Elizabeth's attitude to white people is racist?

Suggestions for writing

Write two newspaper articles about the arrest, acquittal and suicide of Richard. In the first one, tell the story from a position sympathetic to the attitudes of the policeman and the shopkeeper. In the second, make your report and comments those of a reporter in sympathy with Richard and Elizabeth. The articles should include details of the court case, interviews with the people involved, and, possibly, conclusions and recommendations for action.

Research suggestions

Write a brief report to present to the class on the history of relations between American Indians, whites and blacks in the USA.

Write a brief general report on relations between American Indians, 'mestizo' (people of mixed racial origin) and white people in Latin America.

Essay titles

a   Colour.

b   'Race relations have little to do with race itself.'

c   Problems and opportunities in a multiracial society.

d   How do you think racial harmony can best be achieved in Britain?

Bibliography

Audio-visual materials and pamphlets

Divide and Rule – Never (Film and support materials)
Racism the Fourth R (VHS cassette made for BBC2 *Open Door* programme)
(both issued by All London Teachers Against Racism and Facism, Room 216, Panther House, 38 Mount Pleasant, London WC1X 0AP)

Roots of Racism and *Patterns of Racism* (both issued by the Institute of Race Relations)

Non-fiction

Cashmore, E. Ellis (ed.), *A Dictionary of Race and Ethnic Relations*, Routledge and Kegan Paul, 1984

Cashmore, E. Ellis and Troyna, Barry (eds), *Black Youth in Crisis*, Allen and Unwin, 1982

Cottle, Thomas J., *Black People in Britain: The Voices of Britain's West Indians*, Wildwood House, 1978

Davey, Alfred, *Learning to be Prejudiced: Growing up in Multi-Ethnic Britain*, Edward Arnold, 1983

Fanon, Frantz, *Black Skins, White Masks*, McGibbon and Kee, 1968

Fryer, Peter, *Staying Power: The History of Black People in Britain*, Pluto Press, 1984

Gittens, Anthony, *Sociology*, Polity Press, 1990

Husband, Charles (ed.), *Race in Britain: Continuity and Change*, Hutchinson, 1982

Osler, Audrey, *Speaking Out: Black Girls in Britain*, Virago, 1989

Segal, R., *The Race War: The World-Wide Conflict of Races*, Penguin, 1966

Smith, David J., *Racial Disadvantage in Britain*, Penguin, 1977

Fiction

Baldwin, James, *Go Tell it on the Mountain*, Corgi, 1984
Ellison, Ralph, *The Invisible Man*, Penguin, 1965
Icaza, Jorge, *Huasipungo*, Dennis Dobson, 1962
Wright, Richard, *Uncle Tom's Children*, Harper and Row, 1965
Wright, Richard, *Native Son*, Penguin, 1972

Advice on writing: illogical argument in essays

Logicality of argument is obviously one of the absolute essentials of language essay writing. A basic logical flaw can invalidate a whole line of argument, with disastrous results. The purpose of this section is to help students to recognise varieties of false reasoning.

One of the most damaging errors of logic in essay writing is to stray from the point at issue into a discussion of something which has no direct relevance to the essay title. An absolutely cardinal rule of essay writing is to keep the point at issue constantly in mind, and the simplest way to do that is to glance back at the title frequently, and check whether the argument which is being developed is relevant to it. All manner of irrelevancies can creep into essay writing. Here are a couple of typical examples. You are writing an essay on crime and punishment, the title of which reads: 'The only way to reduce the crime rate is to make punishment more severe.' If you have strong feelings about capital punishment, it would be easy, if you were not careful, to enter into a discussion of the morality of capital punishment, making a case for its restoration on the 'eye for an eye' principle. This is a different issue altogether from the question of whether or not the restoration of capital punishment would reduce the crime rate, which would be the only valid reason for mentioning it. Similarly, if you were writing an essay on education with the title: 'What changes would you like to see in the educational system of this country?', it would be irrelevant to discuss the relative merits of the comprehensive and selective school system, unless you concluded the discussion by relating it precisely to the question; by arguing, for instance, that you would like to see comprehensive or selective schools abolished entirely.

Failure to define terms used in an essay is another error which can have a damaging effect on the validity of an argument. This is particularly the case when you are dealing with abstractions such as 'freedom', or 'democracy', or 'communism', or 'equality', which can have different meanings for different people or in different contexts. Many words are simply ambiguous, and it is impossible to argue sensibly about them without defining what you understand by them. When a term about which you are writing has a straightforward, generally recognised meaning, on the other hand, there is no point in wasting time and effort on defining it.

A further problem can arise when you *do* attempt to define the terms you are using. If you define a term or an issue too *narrowly*, then the subject becomes oversimplified. For example, if you are answering the question: 'Is educational equality a myth?' you should consider a variety of possible ramifications of the term 'equality'. If you see the issue simply in terms of the debate over comprehensive and selective school systems, and/or over the abolition of private education, and concentrate exclusively on inequality of access to a 'good' education, higher education and top jobs, you are limiting the range of the question unduly. Aspects of 'equality' such as natural aptitudes for and parental attitudes towards education, ethnic factors, and so on, should also be considered. Oversimplification is a particular danger when discussing politics, especially since political propaganda relies on gross oversimplification. If politicians sometimes use terms like 'totalitarian' to mean states which are ruled by a 'communist' system, and 'the free world' to mean all the states which are not, you should avoid falling into the same error.

Generalisation is another pitfall to be wary of in essay writing. However common a particular phenomenon may be in a particular human group, there are virtually always exceptions which invalidate a sweeping generalisation. Some quite frequently repeated generalisations, such as the assertion that 'women are illogical' are themselves patently illogical. Generalisations about foreigners are particularly common. Many West Indians, for instance, are good dancers, but it would be absurd to state baldly: 'West Indians are good dancers'. Generalisations are often introduced by phrases such as 'It is a known fact that . . .' and 'History proves that . . .' Such expressions do not make dubious statements any more convincing, and should always be avoided. A particularly common and dangerous variety of false generalisation is the error of arguing from the particular to the general. This commonly takes the form of drawing general conclusions from personal experience. An example of this would be to argue that your own education was lacking in creativity, and to draw from this the spurious conclusion that British education generally is insufficiently creative. Newspaper 'scandal' stories frequently give rise to unwarranted generalisations. A report of a prison where the inmates are allowed to watch colour television and wander in the extensive grounds, for instance, might lead the unwary to the conclusion that prisons in Britain generally resemble 'holiday camps'.

A similar error of logic is that of drawing conclusions from selected evidence, and ignoring the evidence which tends to point in the opposite direction. A classic illustration of this is in the popularity of newspaper horoscopes, which depend to some extent on people's willingness to ignore predictions which are *not* fulfilled and take notice only of the ones which *are*. Literary criticism, at its worst, is prone to this error, when critics select quotations from a text to support their theses, and conveniently ignore quotations which tend to refute them.

False analogy is a further common flaw in logical reasoning. Its most popular form is in drawing irrelevant conclusions about human behaviour based on observation of other species. Darwin's theory of 'the survival of the fittest', for example, is used as 'proof' that human affairs are most effectively conducted on a competitive, 'dog eat dog' principle, taking no account of the complexity of human social evolution.

Essays which specifically ask for arguments for and against some premise can easily lead to another error. Students sometimes argue an apparently personal case for the proposition, and then present the opposite case in such a way as to suggest that they agree also with the arguments *against* it. Care must be taken to avoid appearing to agree with incompatible viewpoints.

Care must also be taken to distinguish between opinions and facts. The former should never be presented as the latter. You should never make statements, for example, like this: 'The fact that the government has allowed in too many coloured immigrants is one of the major causes of racial tension in this country'. This is a value judgement, not a fact.

Finally, care should be taken over the use of statistics. It has become an axiom that statistics can be used to prove anything, and assessing the validity or otherwise of published statistics requires some understanding of the complexities of statistical method. Probably the best advice that can be offered with regard to statistics is that they should be used with caution, and should never be offered as proof of any contention. Statistics showing that crimes of violence have increased dramatically since capital punishment was abolished, for instance, should not be treated as a proof that abolition was a mistake, since the increase could equally be attributed to other factors. Likewise, statistics showing that world population and deaths from starvation have both increased alarmingly over the past 30 years do not prove that the population explosion is the cause of starvation. Other factors may in fact be more significant.

Many other types of false reasoning could be mentioned, but if you can succeed in avoiding all of the ones discussed here, you're unlikely to lose marks in an essay because of invalid argument.

THE NEW TECHNOLOGIES AND THE FUTURE

12

Computers provoke extreme reactions. For many, the very word 'computer' provokes scorn or fear; to many others they are objects of veneration. There can be no doubt that the microtechnological revolution will have profound effects on the lives of everyone living in the developed world in the last decade of the twentieth century, as dramatic an impact as the agricultural and industrial revolutions of the past, according to some analysts. The purpose of this chapter is to explore the implications of this new branch of science, through a series of extracts from recent books on the subject.

The chapter begins with a passage for comprehension from Christopher Evans' book, *The Mighty Micro*.

Comprehension and comment

Read the following passage, and answer the questions which follow it. You are advised to spend about one and a half hours on this exercise.

1   What if computers tell us something we do not like or do not want to know about the universe? If we create super-intelligent computers to probe the mysteries of the universe, then we should be prepared for the possibility that what they have to tell us may be intellectually shocking or emotionally unacceptable. It is true that even
5   through routine, non-computerised science we always risk finding out horrific or alien facts, and it might be argued that we have already survived quite a few of these shocks. The realisation that the earth was not the centre of the universe rocked quite a few people at the time, as did the discovery of our planet's stupendous age, the fossil record of prehistoric life and Darwin's insight into the
10 origin of Man. But momentous though these discoveries have been, they have unfolded at a discreet and manageable pace. Assuming that the universe contains further shocks, doubtless of a far more unsettling kind, are we not in danger of having them thrust quite brutally upon us?

It could be argued that the true nature of any apocalyptic facts will only be

214

15 obvious to the super-intelligences of the computers, in the way that some of the
paradoxes of space and time are comprehensible to us but would be quite
meaningless to a chimpanzee. There may be some comfort in this view, that the
computers, as we have frequently pointed out, will turn out to be excellent tutors,
capable of teaching us everything that we want, or even that we don't want, to
20 know. Equally the reverse may hold, and the more we find out about the universe
the more benevolent it will turn out to be, in which case the computers will be
doing us a favour by hustling the news along. Somehow I doubt it. The best we can
hope for from the universe, I fear, will be supreme indifference. But whatever
happens, we will soon be in danger of finding out.
25   Since the foundations of social life Man has been aware of his special role on
earth, and until the significance of the Darwinian thesis began to sink home, he
considered himself to be unique in the universe, second only in status to God. But
even when identifying himself with the animals, he has still been able to convince
himself – justly – of his uniqueness. The evidence has been that he is the possessor
30 of intellectual powers vastly superior to those of his closest rivals within the animal
kingdom. There is no doubting the importance that we all assign to this sense of
intellectual dominance, and of our pride in human endeavour and success. Most
creative art is committed to glorifying or dramatising those aspects of humanity
which emphasise this special place in nature and our implicit claim to divinity.
35 Furthermore, ingrained in our unconscious minds is a psychologically potent self-
image which helps us to accept our role in a frightening and mysterious universe.
This self-image has been tarnished – the Inquisition, Passchendaele and Belsen did
little to keep it polished – but never seriously doubted. The coming of the
computer may be the event that first calls it into question, by casting doubt on the
40 assumption that problem-solving, thinking, even creativity are exclusively human. If
these talents can be shown to be within the domain of computers, then this self-
image may be shaken or destroyed. The problem will be compounded if we find
ourselves not just equalled, but surpassed in these areas.
     The situation will be roughly analogous to that arising if, after the fashion of the
45 movie Close Encounters of the Third Kind, the earth was suddenly visited by
extraterrestrial life forms who possessed a science and technology of
overwhelming, almost incomprehensible power. In the movie, incidentally, far too
little was made of the culture shock which would ensue, and humans trotted
amiably in and out of the alien spaceship as if all that was necessary to ensure instant
50 and complete détente was a linguaphone course. But the appearance of
intelligences greatly superior to our own, whether they come from outer space or
from within computers of our own creation, would pose some tremendous
problems.
     How will we, as a species, feel if all our endeavours, all our scientific
55 knowledge and expertise, all our philosophical deliberations, all our artistic
and cultural strivings are suddenly revealed as shallow and inconsequential?
And how will we feel at the realisation that the gap between ourselves and

60 the Ultra-Intelligent Machines is unbridgeable, and that any advances we
make will be easily outdistanced by their superlative endeavours? This may
explain why, if the universe is teeming with intelligent life, we have not,
despite all the testimony of Ufologists, been contacted by aliens. The
culture-shock, as the highly advanced aliens must know, would be too much
for us to handle. As long as the UIMs are solidly under our control, we
ought to be able to prevent them from flinging us into a terminal case of
65 culture-shock. Even so, we shall have to re-appraise our role, our goals, our
future and, so far as this is possible, our purpose in the universe.

a   With reference to paragraph 1:
   (i)   In what ways do you think that the 'facts' discovered by 'non-
         computerised science', outlined in lines 7–10, caused 'shocks' to
         people in earlier eras?   (6 marks)
   (ii) What do you think the writer might mean by his suggestion that the
         'further shocks' which computerised science will make will be of 'a
         far more unsettling kind'? (line 12)   (5 marks)

b   Explain the parallel between men and chimpanzees in paragraph 2.
                                                                    (4 marks)

c   With reference to paragraph 2:
   (i)   Explain the nature of the writer's 'fear'. (line 23)   (3 marks)
   (ii) Do you tend to share his 'fear', or do you take a more optimistic
         view of the discoveries which computers will enable us to make
         about the universe?   (4 marks)

d   Consider the section which begins 'Furthermore . . .' (line 35) and ends
    '. . . doubted' (line 38):
   (i)   What do you think the writer means by 'This self-image has been
         tarnished . . . but never seriously doubted'?   (4 marks)
   (ii) Give two examples of your own of events which have tarnished our
         'self-image'.   (3 marks)

e   What point is the writer making by his reference to *Close Encounters of
    the Third Kind?* For what does he criticise the film?   (6 marks)

f   Explain why, according to the writer, 'if the universe is teeming with
    intelligent life, we have not . . . been contacted by aliens'. (lines 60–1)
                                                                    (4 marks)

g   What do you think the writer might mean by the final sentence?
                                                                    (3 marks)

h   Comment briefly on the way the argument is presented.   (8 marks)

                                                              (50 marks total)

A brief history of the computer

The effects of the microcomputer are already being felt by everyone living in the Western world. Yet in the mid-20th century, when the earliest computers were being developed, no one, not even the experts, had the slightest conception of how, within another quarter of a century, computers would be all-pervasive. The development of the silicon chip means that hundreds of thousands of circuits can be concentrated on a single finger-nail-sized piece of silicon, and the microtechnological revolution is upon us.

These developments are explained by Alan Burkitt and Elaine Williams in their book *The Silicon Civilisation:*

When it was invented, the computer – often nicknamed an electronic brain – was so totally a tool of the mathematician that only a brave or foolhardy person dared suggest there might ever be other uses. Alan Turing, the Englishman who developed the idea of controlling computers with stored instructions or programs, and who worked on the wartime decoding machines, thought that Britain would never need more than three computers. There were not enough mathematicians to operate more, he reasoned. A similar prediction was made in America . . . not only because of a shortage of mathematicians, but also because machines would be so expensive to build and operate that they could only be justified economically in a few applications . . . As we know, computers have not been so limited. Today they are found in the factory, running machine tools and complete production lines. Small firms keep their accounts on them. Linked to a typewriter, a computer can write letters. It can operate trains, control oil refineries, fly aircraft. A computer records sales in a supermarket and orders replacement stocks; a miniature computer can monitor the pollution in a car's exhaust and regulate the engine to bring it within the law; an even tinier computer can control a washing machine. Giant installations can store, and supply to anyone, more information than the Encyclopaedia Britannica.

The reason can be expressed in two words: silicon chip. When computers were built of valves they were expensive, large, greedy in terms of energy, and, by our standards, not very intelligent creatures. The transistor brought down the cost and size, reduced their energy consumption, and provided enough computer power to make computers easily programmable. No longer did they have to be tended by mathematical geniuses. In the 1970s the integrated circuit completed the revolution. The microcomputer arrived, and each was more powerful than one of the earliest giant valve models.

. . . And price is what makes modern computers so attractive and so ubiquitous. A machine tool fitted with a microcomputer costing a few thousand pounds can make parts so quickly and so accurately that the extra cost is soon recouped.

A microcomputer can pay for itself within months when it saves energy running a building's heating and air conditioning. Some applications would not be possible for valve computers – such as in washing machines, car engines or automatic typewriters – but no one would have considered using electronics if the cost was still that of the valve era. The cheapness of silicon integrated circuits means such previously outlandish proposals are now completely practicable.

ALAN BURKITT and ELAINE WILLIAMS

Exercise and discussion suggestion

List all the things affecting your life which use microcomputers. Compare your list with other people's.

On the basis of the facts which emerge from this comparison, discuss the importance of microcomputers in the lives of ordinary people in Britain at the moment.

The social effects of the new technologies: optimistic and pessimistic views

In his book *The Microchip: Appropriate or Inappropriate Technology?*, Alan Burns devotes a chapter to 'Two Views of the Future'. In it he presents the views of both an imagined optimist and pessimist about the social effects of microtechnology. Here are some extracts:

The optimist

No element of traditional home life will be spared the helping hand of the micro; . . . Some homes in the USA are already heavily computerised, and systems such as central heating or cooking which can be activated via the telephone, from outside, are on sale now in the UK. The optimist's home will be a completely controlled but personalised environment where every need (well, almost) will be anticipated and fulfilled in a totally relaxed atmosphere, which is just as well, as considerable amounts of time will be spent there.

Work

'Once computers infiltrate a society, their virtues override any intrinsic objections to their use, and their continued infiltration and ultimate domination is from that point inevitable. They achieve their subtle take-over by demonstrating first their usefulness and, when that has been established, their indispensability. The laws of survival in the modern world apply and those companies that employ computers to their maximum effectiveness will achieve a monumental economic advantage. Those that reject or ignore them will sooner or later find themselves in ruins.' (Evans)[1]

1 See Bibliography, page 232.

218

That computers will take over work is irrefutable, and this must be to our eventual benefit even though, at first, large-scale redundancies, short-time working and early retirement will bring a host of social problems. Boring work, by definition, is repetitive, and repetitive work is just what robots are good at; therefore the unattractive jobs in our society will become the forte of the machine. Similarly, dangerous work will become increasingly unacceptable, and automated systems in the mines and chemical plants will become the norm.

No area of work will remain unaffected by the micro; manufacture will be undertaken by robots, and data handling by automated information systems; even the professions will eventually be superseded by intelligent machines that will organise education, diagnose illness, and adjudicate in legal disputes. Whether this means the end of work as we know it or just a radical restructuring, with other jobs being created to replace the redundant ones, is still not clear, but obviously the role of work will never be the same again. It will no longer dominate our lives, in terms of hours spent or significance given . . .

Education and health

These two pillars of society, which in Britain have formed the basis of our welfare state, will change out of all recognition by the turn of the century. Teaching machines ranging from hand-held dictionaries to complete classroom systems will, to a great extent, replace the human teacher. Schools themselves may decline in importance when the home information system supplements, or even supersedes, traditional methods of education. It is not, however, only the children that will need or require education; all ages in a rapidly changing society will be demanding retraining and refresher courses. This demand will be impossible to satisfy if the potential of automated computer-aided teaching is not fully utilised.

In health care changes will be even more significant. When a patient arrives at the local GP surgery, she or he will not be met by a nurse or a receptionist but by a computer terminal linked to a national data processing network. This computer will contain complete records of the patient, and built into it will be routines for undertaking the preliminary diagnosis. Having done this it will produce a report and recommendations to the doctor who will then decide on the course of treatment. Few GPs can have a working knowledge of the complete range of drugs currently available for prescription; the computer system will have such knowledge and will be able to advise the doctor on the most apposite medication for each patient.

Possible side-effects of drugs can be monitored by the national network; if a new specialised drug is brought into use today, perhaps only one or two patients per doctor would be prescribed it. This sample is too small for all but the most obvious and consistent side-effects to be noticed. With an overall medical monitor, detrimental effects could quickly be highlighted and the drug taken out of use. When everything else is equal the cheapest form of the tablet or medicine would be recommended, and with computerised dispensing equipment the exact quantity of drug could be given. These two facts alone would probably pay for a national computer in only two or three years.

Doctors and surgeons of the future will be trained by computers that have learnt from previous experts in the field. This ability of intelligent machines to learn from interacting with humans may even be put to good use in psychoanalysis:

> 'Current experiments with computer-interviewing . . . suggest that patients can strike up a surprising rapport with the computer, particularly in sensitive areas such as those involving psychosexual or emotional problems. Might not the very much more powerful machine intelligence of the late 1990s, trained to respond to every nuance of a patient's voice, patterns of speech, hesitancies, even his facial expressions and eye movement, provide exceptional relief and, perhaps, therapy?' (Evans)

One area in which the micro is already providing considerable help is in the development of aids for the handicapped. The automated home will be a boon to people who have limited mobility, and 'intelligent' wheelchairs with many robotic features will have a similar role outside. In addition, individuals who suffer from visual and hearing disabilities will find an increasing number of electronic aids on the market, particularly voice-controlled equipment. Some injuries, such as a severed nerve, may even be bypassed by some appropiate microelectronic appliance.

In the long term the micro may well find more of a role in preventive medicine. External apparatus will continually monitor the somatic functions and broadcast alarm at any irregular or inadvisable behaviour. Internal probes equipped to sense malignant cells may be implanted in patients at risk so that the earliest warning of possible cancer growth can be given. There is really no limit to the number of uses that the micro can be put to in health care.

The government

International organisations and governments will become more dependent on computers to fulfil their administrative and political objectives. Economic planning will be almost entirely taken over by sophisticated computer controlled analysis which will finally make economics an exact science. Democratic control will be maintained by 'instant elections' and referenda in which the people are asked, via their viewdata communication network, to give their opinions on whatever is the subject of the moment.

As computers become more intelligent – the generic term for future computers is UIM, Ultra Intelligent Machines – they will systematically gain control over functions and roles currently considered exclusively human. For instance, Professor J. McCarthy of the Artificial Intelligence Laboratory at Stanford University has remarked: 'What do judges possess that we cannot tell a computer?' A UIM would contain detailed knowledge of the defendant's previous convictions, if any, and would have access to a vast store of case history upon which to base its decision. New laws would be instantly accommodated and might even be initiated by a UIM suggestion. The important thing to remember is that judgements would be correct ... As a further aid to crime-fighting, personal identifiers based upon a single communication chip will enable the police to check the whereabouts of all citizens at all times.

The basis of this optimistic view is that if change is inevitable, as appears to be the case, then there is no reason why it should not be for the better. As people in an information society gain more knowledge they will have greater control over their own lives and more freedom from the state. But to get the most from this technical revolution, attitudes must change and quickly; society must be sufficiently adaptable so that this image of a golden future will be realised. In particular, the wealth created through the widespread use of efficient microelectronic basic machinery and services must pass to the population at large, who will then buy the goods and use the services necessary to sustain the economy. A truly brave new world is ahead.

The pessimist

The pessimistic view is based upon a resignation to the inevitability of a continued exponential growth in the electronics industry, and a fear that the social changes needed to meet the resulting cultural upheavals will not happen at anywhere near the rate necessary. Technology growth will continue because the primary users and the technology manufacturers have a vested interest in it doing so; the remaining population have no say in how the machinery should be controlled and gains little direct benefit from its deployment ...

Two issues which provoke great concern, and form the foundation of the pessimistic outlook, are the future of work and the fear of the Big Brother State.

Work

'The people who develop and control technology are not interested in the quality of our lives; they are only interested in increasing profits. So instead of building a new world of freedom and leisure, new technology is bringing the fear of mass unemployment to the hearts of millions.' (Counter Information Service Report, 1980)

From car manufacture to chocolate packing, the most labour intensive element of production is the assembly of the final product, and that is therefore where most effort will be focused in the introduction of new systems. Manufacturers find themselves caught in a Catch 22 position; to employ the same number of workers they must retain their share of the market by remaining competitive, but if other firms are increasing their efficiency by the use of new technology, then the only way to remain competitive is to make similar rationalisations by laying off staff. Companies are forced to either cut their labour costs or to go out of business altogether.

221

Though factory workers are quite familiar with the pressing demand for greater productivity and have accommodated new skills in order to achieve it, office personnel have been working in an industry that has changed very little over the past fifty years. The situation will not continue, for electronic equipment is already revolutionising the office. Copy typing will disappear, filing will be done automatically as will data processing, and all communications will be carried out by electronic mail. A vastly diminished flow of business letters will lead to refinements in the telephone system resulting in increased reliability and automation. The impact of this upon employment will be devastating; clerical work (traditionally female) will virtually vanish and the Post Office, being the largest employer in Britain, must suffer considerably from this 'progress'. Another alarming aspect of the communications revolution is that office work can easily be transferred around the world. This will lead not only to manufacturing taking place in the Third World, for cheaper labour, but also data processing and document preparation. This would exacerbate unemployment in the developed world whilst being of little real benefit to the emergent nations.

The net result of all these effects will be gross and permanent unemployment on a scale as yet unknown. It may be that, in the long term, attitudes to work will alter, but the protestant work ethic is deeply rooted in our society and will not be removed overnight. In the interim we face the prospect of having many millions of 'second class citizens' who may not be happy just to sit back and accept this role.

Big Brother is watching!

Unemployment, however bad, is not a new phenomenon in our society, even if in the future it will be of unparalleled severity. By comparison, the use of sophisticated electronics to monitor an individual's every move is a new and sinister development which will have far greater effect on our way of life in the so-called post-industrial society.

In the future it will be possible for security forces to record each person's movements, wherever they may be, by making it compulsory for everyone to wear a communication beacon. This development would be considered by most people as an infringement of civil liberties, and it is unlikely that this situation could actually arise in a democratic society. There are, however, examples of company systems that come close to these ideas. Computerised factories are currently in operation where all personnel must carry an identification card to gain access to each area of the factory through electronic locks. This card does not just unlock the door, it also records the event, therefore a worker's progress around the buildings can be followed, and such activities as clocking on and off are done automatically at the main gate.

Computerised cash registers are becoming a familiar feature of the modern supermarket; they work efficiently and have a number of special functions not available on the standard till. One of these enables the operations of the person working the register to be timed . . . New technology word-processors are also capable of automatically measuring the work efficiency of typists in a manner not known or understood by the typists themselves.

The office and supermarket are only two examples of what could be a general application of microprocessor-equipped tools. If one's job has anything to do with a microcomputer then it is possible, and in many instances likely, that your ability to work with the machine will be continually recorded for your employer. It is rare for any job to consist entirely of interacting with a computer, therefore to take just one measurement as an evaluation of overall performance and, moreover, to do so without the knowledge of the employee is a gross misuse of an employer's power.

In an information society all data, including personal records, is kept in computerised data bases. These computers will be linked together to form networks and give the effect of there being just one enormous file containing information on every member of society. This file will be open to local and national government officials, tax officers, the police and security forces. Additionally, unlawful and unsanctioned access to the file will make a mockery of any concept of privacy in tomorrow's society, for no matter how modern the equipment, there are always means of 'getting into' the data bases, especially if you have the backing of expertise and equipment.

The pessimistic consequences of computerising personal information are high-lighted by the following questions: Is it reasonable for your employer to have access to your medical and possible criminal records? Should a credit firm be able to check all your bank accounts? Is it right for tax inspectors to automatically have knowledge of every financial transaction you make? Would you be happy for commercial organisations to know that you have not bought a television for five years nor taken a holiday abroad for three, and to be sent unsolicited advertising because of that knowledge? Should the police know where you spend your money, how much you have and how much you earn? Should government officers have access to all your personal records?

There is at least one more disquieting feature of this technology that should be related; the libraries of the future will not be collections of printed books but visual display units where all reading material can be obtained, from a novel to a government report. It is not unheard of for books to be banned and the mere possession of sensitive material to be an offence. Even with technology currently available it would be possible to restrict access to material and monitor the reading habits of the nation. In the name of national security, will such data be used to draw political conclusions about individuals? Freedom of information has a somewhat hollow ring to it when its consequences are fully appreciated.

The ownership of technology

The electronics business is one of the world's fastest growing industries, and this will presumably continue to the end of this century and beyond. IBM, the gigantic computer manufacturer, can amass over £5 billion[2] gross profit per year and spend £1 billion of that on research and development. The rewards from this area may be

2   five thousand million.

high, but so too is the cost of taking part. Small firms cannot compete in the production of 'new technology', and the faster this technology changes the more likely it is that manufacture will be concentrated in just a few large multinationals, based either in the USA or Japan . . .

If a government cannot control the use and distribution of computer technology and microelectronics, what chance does an individual have? Information technology will rationalise most aspects of everyday life and make it virtually impossible for anyone to contemplate any alternative lifestyle. In a cashless society you must have a direct-debit card and an 'open' bank account or you will not even be able to use the local shop. If all information comes from a VDU linked to a central system, then failure to have this equipment will prohibit one's access to books, magazines, newspapers and government data; it may even eliminate one's democratic right to vote in elections. To work, pay taxes or visit the doctor will necessitate computerised data files being kept on you. There is no choice; if you are a member of society you must play the game.

ALAN BURNS

Discussion suggestions

How do you react to the various predictions in this section? You might consider them one by one:

The short-term disappearance of jobs in various areas of employment:
  (i)   assembly line work in factories
  (ii) dangerous jobs
  (iii) office work

The longer-term possibilities either of new types of jobs being created to replace redundant ones, or of 'gross and permanent unemployment'.

Teaching machines replacing teachers and 'home information systems' superseding schools.

Computers taking over the functions of lawyers and judges.

The use of microtechnology in medicine:
  (i)   national computerised monitoring of drugs
  (ii) psychoanalysis by 'intelligent machines'
  (iii) preventive medicine by micro

The role of computers in politics and economics:
  (i)   'instant elections' by 'viewdata communication network'
  (ii) economics becoming 'an exact science' by computerisation

The use of 'personal identifiers' enabling the police to check everyone's whereabouts constantly.

Built-in efficiency records on word-processors.

The availability of personal records on 'data bases' available for official scrutiny.

The replacement of printed books by 'visual display units'.

Overall, do you take an optimistic or pessimistic view of the effects of the increasing computerisation of society?

Leisure and home life in tomorrow's world

For good or evil, there seems little doubt that leisure will become much more important that ever before in the years ahead. In his book *The New Revolution: The Impact of Computers on Society*, Barrie Sherman suggests some of the implications of this:

Many forecasters believe that unemployment will be with us through to the 21st century and will be oriented towards the young and more especially those young people with the poorest record of educational attainments. More women will be at home without paid employment. There will be more job sharing, perhaps even permits to work, a school leaving age of at least 18 (paid for the last two years), less night shift production work but more night-time maintenance work, and 25 hours paid employment per week with little or no overtime will not be unusually low. The likelihood is that these hours will be spread over three days rather than five so that the new leisure time will be taken in large blocks. Retirement will be part-time, then full-time and will be taken between 50 and 65. Computers will have some degree of responsibility for these changes as they will for the changes within the home. As the cabling of homes goes ahead so the computer potential of each home increases. There has been a significant drift towards working from home for typists using word-processors, for programmers using home terminals and for managers. Home working has an unenviable reputation in most countries as a method of paying exceptionally low wages for not very skilled jobs, but this is now changing to a marked degree. Another form of homework will be by the self-employed, especially in creative programming and analysis. Most of these prophecies have been discussed by economists, philosophers, sociologists, futurologists, scientists, and ordinary people; it is both sad and instructive that politicians have not joined in.

As an entertainment centre, shopping and banking centre using Prestel (or its equivalent), work station and centre of social life, the home appears destined to take on new functions. Problems resulting from such changes stare back at an observer from all angles. Nowadays we get most of our social contacts from the workplace. If we spend more time at home how will we meet people, where will friends come from, and will we develop electronic friends, use picture telephones as a substitute for meeting people, or play video telephone bridge as a substitute for kicking one's partner under the table? How will permanent relationships, marriages for example, stand up to the extra strains of partners being in close proximity to each other when one suspects that the reason for their survival has been the relative lack of contact and togetherness. When the diminution of personal stimulation in the new forms of shopping or when using public transport are taken into account too, loneliness or a marked lack of variety in social contacts will become major sources of concern.

At the same time it will be easier, perhaps nicer, to live at home. Domestic robots and controls and systems computers will do both the menial tasks and plan the cheapest uses of energy or food or even travel. Appliances like washing machines, bathroom scales, cookers, do-it-yourself equipment, or even light switches will all become more sophisticated and more reliable – even 'intelligent'. Whilst many factors will be increasing the hours that people spend within the home so the need to be there diminishes. Free time will emerge, time which could be used for educational or socially aware purposes or, on a less high-minded Victorian vein, to enjoy oneself, to travel the world, and to do and see new things.

BARRIE SHERMAN

Discussion points

How do you view the prospect of a 25-hour, three-day working week?

Do you think that a home-based culture would inevitably lead to greater loneliness and marital stress?

How do you feel about the idea of conducting personal relationships via electronic technology, as illustrated in the extract?

Do you feel that society will be able to react quickly enough to the problems resulting from increased leisure?

Try to imagine a typical day in your life in the year 2000. Compare your vision with those of others.

The use of robots

Throughout this century, science-fiction writers have delighted in picturing a world in which robots take over the functions of human beings. It is now beginning to happen in reality. David Bleakley, in his book *In Place of Work . . . The Sufficient Society*, discusses this phenomenon:

> Hand-made by Robots
> Less room for human error
> More room for humans
>
> (Strada car advertisement)

Even bigger developments are forecast in the changing balance of power between robots and people. Scientists are now predicting that a future world war would be computer controlled and directed. A disturbing thought. More disturbing – one suspects that if ordered to arrange the final folly, the robots would have the 'intelligence' to make sure that neutron bombs were employed so favouring the survival of their own species. A case of, 'Robots of the World unite, you have nothing to lose but your humans' . . .

The typical industrial robot, especially when at rest, is indistinguishable from many other pieces of engineering equipment. Where modern robots differ is in their 'thinking' capacity – they can be computer programmed to do an infinite variety of tasks and, unlike human beings, they can be instructed to carry on regardless of time, season or any of the many other factors which complicate production, using traditional methods. In fact . . . it is becoming a matter of industrial pride to boast that people are no longer much involved in the productive process. As one delegate remarked to the 1978 Trades Union Congress, 'They are saying about one company in California's silicon chip valley that it has done so well it is moving into smaller premises'. It is only a small step away to the suggestion that 'man-made' is tantamount to a seal of inferiority.

Nor is the computer revolution confined in application to heavy industry. Robots can be 'told' to mow the lawn, do household chores, educate our children and

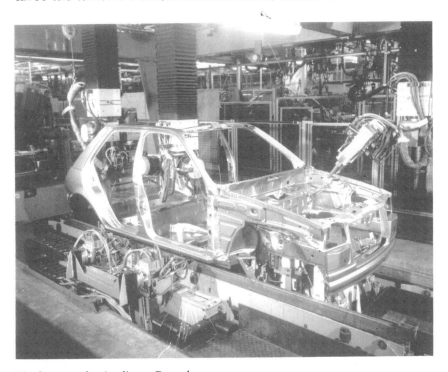

The fiesta production line at Dagenham.

227

control almost any mechanical or electrical system from a toy train to the most complicated of our space machines.

But there is promise as well as threat in this potential. We do not need to create the meaningless leisure of H. G. Wells's *The Time Machine* which was every bit as soul destroying as the monotonous activity in which many millions must engage in modern industrial society. As one American philosopher once reminded us, we can cheerfully eliminate those types of work 'that deform the body, cramp the mind, deaden the spirit'. The exploitation of machines becomes the alternative to the exploitation of people – the Robot becomes a friend and ally.   DAVID BLEAKLEY

Discussion points

Do you find the Strada car advertisement disturbing?

How widespread do you think the use of computers in industry will become?

Do you think that the robot actually will become a 'friend and ally'?

Research suggestion

Anyone interested in modern warfare might undertake research into the various applications of microtechnology to offensive and defensive weapons production.

Ultra Intelligent Machines

For many years, experts have talked of the eventual production of computers which will be intellectually superior to human beings. These will be the 'Ultra Intelligent Machines' of the 21st century.

Christopher Evans, in *The Mighty Micro*, considers the possibilities and implications of their production.

The concept of the Ultra Intelligent Machine (or UIM as it is abbreviated) is a controversial, challenging and, at the same time, slightly frightening one – the more so because it is a logically coherent idea which springs naturally out of our present understanding of computer science. By Good's[3] definition an Ultra Intelligent Machine is a computer programmed to perform any intelligent activity at least marginally better than Man. Intellectual activity, incidentally, excludes such things as enjoying bacon and eggs and admiring good-looking men or women, and includes such things as solving problems, making tactical decisions, exploring logical possibilities and even carrying on interesting conversations. Good points out it

3   Professor Jack Good, originator of the term 'Ultra Intelligent Machine'.

might be necessary to teach the computer some of the principles of aesthetics – a task which is already being attempted on an experimental basis at one or two computer centres – for the computer's conversations might be horribly bland and limited without some understanding of aesthetics. But the most interesting question to consider is what will we do with the Ultra Intelligent Machines when they arrive?

Clearly, the first thing would be to put them to work on some of the numerous problems facing society. These could be economic, medical or educational matters, and also, perhaps, strategic modelling to forecast trends and produce 'early warnings' of difficulties or crises. Weather forecasting, for example, has already been substantially improved through computer analysis, and has great economic significance in parts of the world where the climate is unpredictable and hostile. But as the UIMs improve and expand their capabilities, other areas of interest will fall to their inspection with substantial benefits to mankind . . .

During the 1990s computers will increasingly serve as intellectual and emotional partners . . . In the course of this strange partnership computers will inevitably acquire ways of behaving which allow them to converse with us, exchange ideas and concepts, stimulate our imagination and so on . . . When they do overtake us computers will, in my view, become extremely interesting entities to have around. Their role as teachers and mentors, for example, will be unequalled. It will be like having, as private tutors, the wisest, most knowledgeable and most patient humans on earth: an Albert Einstein to teach physics, a Bertrand Russell to teach philosophy, a Sigmund Freud to discuss the principles of psychoanalysis, and all available where and when they are wanted.

Many people, in particular those who have never had the experience of fiddling with computers, may fail to believe that any machine, no matter how intelligent, could engage one's wholehearted attention for more than the briefest of moments. One can understand the scepticism, and can respond to it emotionally, but it is dangerously misleading. Even in their present lowly state, computers are very interesting to interact with – bearing in mind that I am talking about intellectual interaction and not going on country walks, sailing a boat or falling in love with them. A glimpse of just how interesting they can be often comes when you play chess with them – they are already considered by many skilled players to be more satisfactory competitors than humans. For those who do not play chess, a spell of playing some of the other powerful computer games will provide much the same insight, for they are enormously versatile companions, and pitting wits against them is fascinating to the point of obsession . . .

Progress will be slow at first, for the problems are numerous and complex. Nevertheless, if we so choose, limitless computer effort could be applied, and sooner or later machine intelligence will be not only above that of humans, but also above that of the first UIMs. Then the second generation of UIMs will be available for work and they, too, will be put to general problem-solving and, because of their enhanced IQ, might advance at a dramatic pace. Some Mark 2 UIMs could be assigned to produce further advances in artificial intelligence and a third generation of even smarter machines would result. And so it will go on: the brighter the machines, the more capable they will be of enhancing their own intelligence, and they will begin to leap-frog ahead, each bound being progressively larger than the previous one.

CHRISTOPHER EVANS

In the following extracts from an article in *The Times*, Andrew Moncur reports a meeting at which computer experts followed through the implications of microtechnology to offer their view of the future:

Artificial 'super brains' could take over from the family doctor and make other professional people redundant in under 40 years, Sir Clive Sinclair predicted yesterday.

Sir Clive, head of Sinclair Research and a pioneer in electronics, forecast the arrival of mega-computers, costing no more than a family car and so knowledgeable and quick-thinking that they would supplant the professionals by 2020.

He was looking forward 36 years – the same time span that George Orwell bridged in writing his grim portrayal of 1984 – at a Mensa symposium in Cambridge.

Dr Madsen Pirie, president of the Adam Smith Institute, suggested that the age of the helpless individual dwarfed by the giant, bureaucratic state would be over long before 2020.

Dr Pirie described a family as it might be in 2020. The father is a miner, who took his doctorate in bio-chemistry from an electronic university and whose firm extracts coal products with the aid of coal-eating microorganisms.

The mother works for a special unit organising business conferences, often through audio-visual links. She decided to have two children in her late forties. Her daughter will probably wait until her sixties before she, in turn, conceives. She has already spent a week in China, camping with friends, and has won an award for living under water for 72 hours.

The boy is 14 and has been sexually mature for several years. He is taking a degree in marine biology.

ANDREW MONCUR The Times, 1984

Finally, Michael Shallis, in a chapter of his book, *The Silicon Idol: the Micro Revolution and its Social Implications*, entitled 'Futures', describes what he terms 'the wired society' of the future:

Houses will become places of work and play, eliminating the need for costly transport, because you will be able to talk to your co-workers or friends, by video channel . . .

Money will become bits of information passed round electronically . . .

Two-way channels will enable TV terminals to serve as input as well as output devices. The viewer will be able to comment on and criticise the programme he is watching. Instant polls can be taken on issues, with viewers participating by sending their opinion over the lines to a vote-counting computer. Instant democracy could be extended to serious political decision-making . . .

The new technologies will reduce pollution because the techniques are 'cleaner' than the old mechanised industries. Congestion on the roads and even the spread of motorways will ease as people 'travel' by sitting at home, 'visiting' their friends by electronic communication . . .

Technologies transform, and in these future worlds what transformations will have happened? A goods-dominated society will have become an information-oriented culture. There will be no cash, no paper, little work as we now know it. To read a newspaper will be to scan a TV screen, pushing buttons to flip the pages. To talk to an acquaintance will be to 'see' each other on screens, unable to touch, smell or taste things that otherwise could be shared, the meeting reduced to sight and sound and those not real, but sights and sounds emerging from electronic hardware. Shopping will be done by terminal, goods will be displayed on the customer's screen, selected and paid for automatically and delivered to the door. Exercise can be part of leisure. Factories will be run by robots, offices by computers. Children will be taught by machine; machines will act as doctors, lawyers and consultants. The home will become a new type of place, isolated from nature, defended against the have-nots.

What about those who choose not to participate, who refuse to have an EFT card, who want cash? What about those who want their children taught by people, who want to talk to people face to face, not image to image? What of those who choose not to have a home terminal, will they be able to shop, to discover the news, to vote? Will there be an alternative society parallel to the electronic one, a wired society and a wireless one? Are the futures based on where this technology is leading a form of progress, a cultural growing up, or do they constitute the ingredients of a nightmare? Future outcomes are never what people expect and the two alternatives I have drawn are extremes. The wired society is being advocated strongly, being sought actively; its alternative seems to be neglected. The future will probably consist of ingredients from both possibilities but the concern now should be with the processes of choice.

The technological imperative demands the information society and demands it world-wide. It assumes that developments. such as those outlined here, constitute progress and social evolution to a higher form. Progress, however, implies some purpose, some goals to be achieved; rather than buy 'progress' for its own sake people should first decide what goals they seek and then choose how best to achieve those goals. The futures I have sketched in this chapter would all arise from where computing and communications technologies can take us.

MICHAEL SHALLIS

Discussion points

Do you feel enthusiastic or depressed at the prospect of 'Ultra Intelligent Machines', as described by Christopher Evans?

How do you react to Sir Clive Sinclair's predictions about medicine and the professions in 2020, and to Dr Pirie's visions of family life?

Do you think man is capable of controlling the new technologies, and establishing clear-cut 'goals', rather than allowing technological 'progress' to carry us on to wherever it leads?

Essay titles

a   'Machines are extensions of man's capability; they cannot replace man himself.'

b   What, in your view, are the positive benefits of a branch of modern science?

c   'Progress is not an accident, it is a necessity.'

d   Will science abolish work?

e   Has the age of the inventor passed?

f   How far do you think the computer an indispensable asset to our way of life, and how far do you consider it disadvantageous?

g   To what extent to you think computers and word-processors have diminished the need for numeracy and literacy?

Bibliography

Bleakley, David, *In Place of Work . . . The Sufficient Society*, SCM Press, 1981

Burkitt, Alan and Williams, Elaine, *The Silicon Civilisation*, W.H. Allen, 1980

Burns, Alan, *The Microchip: Appropriate or Inappropriate Technology?*, Ellis Harwood, 1981

Evans, Christopher, *The Mighty Micro: The Impact of the Computer Revolution*, Gollancz, 1979

Macrae, Norman, *The 2024 Report*, Sidgwick and Jackson, 1984

Renmore, C.D., *Silicon Chips and You*, Sheldon Press, 1979

Shallis, Michael, *The Silicon Idol: The Micro Revolution and its Social Implications*, Oxford University Press, 1984

Sherman, Barrie, *The New Revolution: The Impact of Computers on Society*, John Wiley and Sons, 1985

Sieghart, Paul (ed.), *Microchips With Everything: The Consequences of Information Technology*, Comedia, 1982

Simons, Geoff, *Silicon Shock: The Menace of the Computer Invasion*, Blackwell, 1985

Toffler, Alvin, *The Third Wave*, Pan Books, 1980

Advice on writing: preparing and presenting a report

The biggest problem about preparing a report for presentation to other people may well be encountered at the initial stage: finding the information. Let's imagine you are planning to present a report on the use of computers in modern weapons production, and have to start from scratch. Where do you look for information? If your teacher cannot help, the obvious person to ask is a librarian; he or she will at least be able to guide you to the relevant sections in the library. In this case, the section on computers may have a subsection of books specifically on their applications to weaponry. If it doesn't, how do you choose what book to consult? The titles may provide clues to the contents, and a flip through some promisingly-titled books, especially at their indexes, should unearth the information you're seeking fairly quickly. You could also ask the librarian if there are any relevant periodicals, and if the library doesn't actually carry suitable titles, it will at least have the addresses of current periodicals, so that you can send off to a suitable one for information or relevant back issues.

Having found a section of a book which looks useful, it will save you time, if the section is fairly long, to skip-read it, concentrating on the first and last paragraphs of subsections. It may be worth consulting two or three books on the subject of your research, to achieve a fully-rounded picture.

In making your report, it is vital to consider the time it will take to read it, and keep the length within reasonable limits. You should never simply copy chunks out of a book or article. You must consider your audience; they probably have no prior knowledge of the subject at all, and it must be offered to them in an easily-comprehended fashion. The best approach is to assimilate a section of information and write it down as straightforwardly as possible from memory, checking it when complete against the published material, to test for accuracy and completeness. You should include no technical detail without adding an explanation in simple terms. Simplicity and clarity are the main qualities to strive for. Dividing it into sub-sections, dealing with different aspects of the subject, may help your audience to follow the development of your report.

When you have finished writing it, you should read your report out aloud, timing yourself to ensure that it doesn't overrun the time-limit. If it does, of course, you will have to prune it.

When presenting your report, it is absolutely essential to read as slowly as possible, pausing frequently to allow your fellow students to assimilate what you are saying, to make notes and perhaps to ask you to clarify or repeat points you have made.

THE MASS MEDIA

Children in the late 20th century have grown up with the mass media. In Britain, over 90 per cent of households own a television set, and it is watched, on average, for 25 hours a week. Few homes are without daily or Sunday newspapers, and the most popular British Sunday paper has a circulation which is topped only by *Pravda*. The rise of television since the Second World War has brought about a steady decline in the importance of film and radio: the latter, in fact, has become, for most young people, merely an endless supplier of 'rock' music, which is now, in itself, a major mass medium. It is a feature of the media that they feed off one another. Tabloid newspapers constantly report the peccadilloes of 'rock', film and television stars, and for many readers such tittle-tattle provides the primary interest in the papers they buy.

This chapter is concerned with exploring and analysing different mass media. It begins with a pair of exercises in summary skills on newspaper articles about radio. A summary skills exercise on the theme of violence on television can be found in Chapter 4, on pages 43-5.

Summary skills

1   You have been asked to draw up a ten-point publicity statement entitled 'Radio 5: Wooing the Young Back to Radio'. Basing your points on the information and ideas contained in the article which follows, write your statement, using not more than 100 words. The article appeared in *The Times* in August 1990.

(20 marks)

Will the young listen to Auntie?

As BBC Radio 5 prepares to go on air this month, its controller explains how she hopes to give teenage listeners their own voice

Patricia Ewing, the controller of BBC Radio 5, ponders the question of her biggest fear, and finally says it is '. . . that we won't give our listeners the programmes they deserve'.

Observers believe this is something she is unlikely to experience, despite the enormous challenge of bringing sports coverage, youth and education programming and elements of the World Service together to create a loyal audience for the BBC's first new network in 23 years.

The former head of BBC Radio sport and outdoor programming has regularly been putting in 16-hour days ('I'm too busy to be nervous') in the run-up to Radio 5's August 27 launch, on the medium wave frequencies donated by Radio 2, which now becomes a single-channel stereo FM network.

As the last-minute mechanics are sorted out, Ms Ewing remains calmly confident that she can achieve her main goal: to woo the young back to radio.

'Years ago, radio used to offer plays and stories for young children, but there are now two generations that have missed out,' she says. 'We're going to reach an audience that doesn't exist at the moment, with programmes that don't exist at the moment.' Radio 5, in between its ball-by-ball Test match coverage, hourly sports bulletins, schools and Open University programming, aims to foster a wholly new 'youth radio culture' that gives young people their own voice.

The new station's content, unveiled yesterday, goes a long way towards making up for radio's neglect of the young. Less than an hour a week has been devoted to youngsters at home. On Radio 5 they will get four hours a day.

Older children and teenagers who have had few alternatives to pop music stations can listen to a 'youth magazine' live each night from 9.30pm to 11pm, containing a mix of speech, music and lively discussion coming from all over Britain.

Pamela Stephenson, Phillip Schofield, Stephen Fry and Terry Wogan will bring to life children's stories, plays and serials, while Sebastian Scott keeps order as Glenda Jackson and Julian Clary are put on the spot by a teenage audience. Emma Freud will help deal with young people's problems in *The Answerphone*, and Simon Fanshawe presents a live arts programme. Caron Keating examines the European youth scene.

Ms Ewing accepts that, left to their own devices, children will continue to gravitate towards the television, Radio 1 and new commercial radio stations. 'That is why I think we have to be quite good,' she says.

Will children shy away if told by their parents to listen to Radio 5? 'No. I'm more ambitious than that. I want 13-year-olds to tune in to what their parents would not have even dreamt of suggesting. We can be an alternative for youth. They are at an age when they want to be independent. They don't want to do what their parents are doing, which is probably watching TV.'

Clearly, Radio 5 has to give children and youth what they want – 'a voice and no preaching', they have uniformly told Radio 5 planners. 'It takes just one or two to find it and tell their friends. Youngsters have picked up on a programme on Radio 2 or 4 and made it cult listening,' Ms Ewing says.

With schools programming halved from 466 hours in the past academic year to 224 in 1990-91 will the programmes be educationally geared? 'When I went around to schools, the teachers said: 'Don't give us the texts because we've got them; what we need are programmes that relate what is being learnt in class to life.' We want them to see a reason for learning,' she says. Learning, particularly in science, can be linked to the news – a volcano erupting, an earthquake, pollution.

Teachers have already asked Ms Ewing to tell them in advance what novels and plays are to be dramatised so that the relevant texts can be studied that term. Each day the familiar voices of Anita Dobson, Stratford Johns and Sheila Hancock will bring to life subjects from the curriculum.

'I don't believe we'll have it perfectly right at the very beginning,' she says. 'It's a matter of developing it, growing it. Programmes aren't made in isolation.'

MELINDA WITTSTOCK, *The Times*, 8 August 1990

2   You have been asked by the Director of Radio 3 to write a brief report outlining the direct and implicit criticisms of the B.B.C. classical music service (Radio 3) contained in the following article. You should limit your report to 100 words.   (*20 marks*)

Radio's classic battle

Radio 3's elitist image is under attack from a host of would-be rivals. **Edwin Riddell** reports

COMMERCIAL radio is not normally synonymous with classical music. So it comes as a surprise to see the number of experienced independent radio operators queuing up to apply for a classical station in London by today's noon deadline. Up to six bids are now expected for a commercial classical music station in London.

Still more surprising, several of the applicants carry distinct echoes of Rupert Murdoch's Edinburgh tirade on the "elitism" of British broadcasting.

Their target is not, however, à la Rupert, crinoline soaps or strangulated accents. It is rather a growing disenchantment with the whole style and ethos of the BBC's national classical service. It is open season on Radio 3.

"It is very much an exclusive club," says Classic FM's Aidan Day about Radio 3. Day is prospective programme director for Classic FM, one of the groups with several big-star names on board. Classic is backed by Andrew Lloyd Webber's Really Useful Group, now headed by former IBA director-general John Whitney.

As part of their preparation, Classic has carried out specific research into the tastes of the London audience. Among the younger audience, most found Radio 3 "very difficult." When played a tape of what a commercial station with classical music might sound like, the response was "immediately enthusiastic", claims Day.

Classic was a bidder earlier this year when the IBA advertised the first Londonwide FM contract — awarded to London Jazz Radio. Like most of the applicants, it has noted the fact that enthusiasm for classical music and opera has reached unprecedented levels in recent years.

The implicit view that classical music is as much the common man's pursuit as that of the buff promises to be a theme in many of the applications. Among the evidence supporting this view are sales figures from the music industry. While sales of albums have stayed static for a number of years, classical music has steadily increased its sales and share.

The most dramatic increase has been in sales of music on compact disc. The flow of CD classical music releases

on to the market has become a deluge, accounting for some 400 pages in the current Gramophone magazine CD catalogue. Interest, according to one London record megastore, goes through the whole spectrum "from people who don't know anything about classical music to the complete specialists."

The public has been voting with its feet. It is the customer who goes into Virgin or Woolworths to buy Domingo, Pavarotti or classical compilations that the bidders for a commercial station now have in their sights. Few are thought to be Radio 3 listeners.

In response to their demand, Tower Records in London's Piccadilly has just installed a computer browsing system in its classical department. By keying in names of artists or types of music on a screen, customers can call up audio extracts of the available recorded works over their headphones.

It all adds up to a tempting scenario for the IBA. It is recieved wisdom that Classical City Radio — a group chaired by Joan Bakewell, and backed by Liverpool's Radio City and the Guardian-owned Broadcast Communications Group — was among the front-runners at the time of the first London FM franchise, offered earlier

this year. Together with Classic FM, CCR is now expected to join combat with revised applicatons from QFM, a group chaired by IBM chief Sir Edwin Nixon, and Prom FM; and by new bids from the now-separate Diamond FM and London Classical Music Radio groups.

Most of the applicants have kept their real programme proposals close to their chests. All are aware that since the IBA's decision to offer two further franchises, the ground rules have changed. Alongside two other new London-wide FM stations fighting for listeners and cash, they will have to compete for revenue with two services on Capital Radio and a further two on LBC after its launch of two separate speech services on AM and FM.

This is the rub. Experience in the US and Australia suggests that in a crowded marketplace, with many radio services, the dominant stations perform disproportionately better than the minority ones. The prospect that the new London stations will merely divide up a small percentage of the audience while Capital and Radio 1 sail serenely on is hardly inviting.

Which brings us back to the IBA. In a light-touch regime the Authority may not be held responsible for a

238

station which goes bust as a result of excessively ambitious plans in its so-called "promise of performance." But the IBA might be justifiably accused of passing the buck if it fails to take into account the changed nature of the market-place. This time round financial soundness could count for as much as fancy programmes.

With the word out that the IBA is determined to provide popular competition for Radio 3 in London, a close contest is forecast. Don't ask me where they will find their presenters. Radio 3 is not yet about nifty classical jocks with a quip and a timecheck.

It is, of course, many years since the IBA forced commercial sta-

tions to broadcast one hour of classical music a week. It became celebrated throughout the network as The MD's Classical Music Slot — because the managing director usually refused to allocate the show a budget and ended up presenting it himself. Times do change.

EDWIN RIDDELL,
The Guardian,
November 1989

Newspapers

Newspaper organisation

Over the past 40 years, British newspapers have come to be divided into two broad categories: popular (or tabloid) and serious. Control of the press has altered during the same period. Between the wars the newspapers were owned and controlled by wealthy individuals, frequently referred to as 'press barons', like Lords Beaverbrook, Northcliffe and, more recently, Thompson; now they have generally been swallowed up into large corporations, most notably oil companies, whose primary interests lie outside the press.

In the same period also the diversity of political affiliations of the press has largely disappeared, until now there is only one newspaper which consistently supports the Labour Party (the *Daily Mirror*); most of the others support the Conservative Party. All British newspapers, even the one or two more or less independent ones, maintain a fairly rigid editorial line, establishing limits beyond which their journalists cannot step.

The structure within which journalists work is discussed by the journalist Eamonn McCann in an article entitled 'The British Press and Northern Ireland', included in *The Manufacture of News*, edited by Cohen and Young:

Those who have ultimate control over what is printed and what is not are drawn from a relatively tiny segment of society – the owners of big business. Generally speaking, what is printed tends to support their interests.

One of the qualifications for editorship is, naturally, a general acceptance of the owners' attitudes. This is reflected in the editorial 'line' of every paper and it filters through to reporters, sub-editors, etc. A journalist who has covered Northern Ireland for a British daily paper explains:

'You must remember that every journalist wants what he writes to appear, and in practice all journalists know pretty well what their paper's line is, what is expected of them. There is a fair amount of self-censorship. This happens without thinking. No journalist I have met writes what he knows will be cut. What would be the point? If he has a story which he knows will cause controversy back at the newsdesk he will water it down to make it acceptable.'

Most journalists rely heavily on 'official' sources. This explains the sometimes striking similarity of coverage. Stories from 'official' sources will, of course, be eminently acceptable. Moreover, as a former *Mirror* employee writes:

'In a situation like Northern Ireland, our people would have to keep in close touch with the Army Press Office. It would be more or less part of their job to get to know the army press officer as well as possible, and that in itself would affect their judgement a bit. Then one of their bigger preoccupations is not be scooped by a competitor. No one on the *Mirror* would be sacked because he didn't come up with a carefully authenticated and researched piece, written from local hard work. You do get sacked if the rival has a sensation about the IRA.'

Even if a reporter does send through copy which is critical of the establishment and its representatives (e.g. the army), it is at the mercy of the news editor and the sub-editors. These are likely to be the most conservative of all the journalistic staff, with years of grinding practice in what is acceptable to the editor and the management. The average senior sub-editor will, as a reflex action, strike out any sentence which jars his sense of propriety.   EAMONN MCCANN

The influence of newspapers

How influential is the press in affecting the attitudes of its readers? To what extent does a newspaper merely respond to the expectations of the readership at which it is aimed? Contrasting views on the question of newspaper influence are represented in the following two extracts.

The first offers a general view of the British press, arguing that the content of newspapers is dictated largely by the nature and attitudes of their readers. It is taken from a book called *The Politics of the Media* by John Whale.

The tastes of a body of readers may alter over the years. They change as the prevailing climate of ideas changes. They change as a result of what they discover to be appearing in rival newspapers. The *Daily Mirror* would never have begun (in the 1970s) to show photographs of naked women, or to lead the paper with stories like 'I married the monster who raped Miss X', if the *Sun* had not led the way after its change of ownership in 1969. Once the *Sun* had demonstrated that its readers liked that kind of approach, the *Mirror* adopted it too, and the decline in the *Mirror's* circulation was at least checked. Yet it was not an expedient which was open to *The Times*, struggling for new readers at much the same time. Existing readers of *The*

Times would have been outraged at being addressed in that way. The loss would have far outweighed the gain.

It is readers who determine the character of newspapers. The *Sun* illustrates the point in its simplest and saddest form. Until 1964 the *Daily Herald*, and between 1964 and 1969 the broadsheet *Sun*, had struggled to interest working people principally through their intellect. The paper had declined inexorably. Murdoch gave up the attempt and went for the baser instincts. Sales soared. It was an owner's decision, certainly; but it would have meant nothing without the enthusiastic ratification of the readers.

That, in the end, is the answer to the riddle of proprietorial influence. Where it survives at all, it must still defer to the influence of readers. The policy of the *Daily Telegraph*, its selection and opinion of the news it reports, is decided by the editor and his senior colleagues. But there is a regulatory force which keeps the paper's policy from straying too widely or suddenly from pre-ordained paths; and that force is not the proprietor but the readers. They choose the paper for qualities they expect to see continued.

The press is thus predominantly conservative in tone because its readers are. If any substantial number of people seriously wanted the structure of society rebuilt from the bottom, the *Morning Star* would sell more copies than it does. The reason why national newspapers fall tidily into two bundles – popular and posh, with the popular ones all physically smaller than the posh (since the *Daily Express* joined the other tabloids in January 1977) but selling five times as many copies – is that British life remains similarly and obstinately divided. The steady lessening of the economic differences between classes has done nothing to narrow the cultural gap. Certainly there are people who read both a posh and a popular paper, just as there are gradations between the popular papers; both the *Mirror* and the *Sun* aim at readers who are more squarely working-class than the *Express* and the *Mail* do. These things show the complexity of the class pattern, without denying its general lines. The broad shape and nature of the press is ultimately determined by no one but its readers.   JOHN WHALE

The second extract argues a more positive influence by newspapers on readers' attitudes. It is taken from a book called *News Limited* by the journalist, Brian Whitaker.

There are numerous examples of strange effects induced by the media. Probably the most famous was the panic caused by an American radio dramatisation of H.G. Wells's *The War of the Worlds* in 1938. But that was the result of people mistaking the play for reality. On another occasion, as an experiment, British astronomer Patrick Moore pretended to have seen an Unidentified Flying Object near his home. The story he told to his local paper was entirely fictitious, but when it was published several 'witnesses' came forward to confirm the 'sighting'. At a more down-to-earth level, a British newspaper once warned of the possibility of a salt shortage within a few months. The prophecy was fulfilled immediately as people rushed to the shops to stock up.

No self-respecting person admits to being easily influenced. If you were asked: 'Do you believe everything you read in the newspapers?' the only sensible answer would be 'No'. And yet what alternative have we but to believe? We all rely very heavily on newspapers and television for our knowledge of what is going on in the world. So how do we decide what to believe and what not to believe? Partly, it is a question of credibility: does it seem likely that an event has actually happened in the way it is reported? Also, it is a question of reputation: we regard some sources as more reliable than others – often without any good reason. A survey in 1973 showed that only 27 per cent of people who said newspapers were their main source of news also believed newspapers were the most accurate and trustworthy source of news.

Also – rather illogically – we tend to become less sceptical about news reports the further they are removed from our personal experience. So factory workers may dismiss newspaper reports of a dispute in their own factory as a load of rubbish, but not question stories in the same paper that say the Social Security provides a life of luxury for immigrants.

Stories about 'scroungers' and Social Security fiddlers, for example, are common in the popular press. These papers are read by vast numbers of ordinary people, and they influence ordinary people. Stories about 'scroungers' can be effective in several ways. They can:

a make people more willing to accept work for low wages rather than stay on the dole;

b get popular support for keeping state benefits at a low level;

c create divisions between the employed 'taxpayers' and the unemployed;

d encourage people to inform on fiddlers.

And by the simple repetition of such stories, the public begin to accept that 'scroungers' are a major drain on public resources. But if the papers' real purpose was to save money, they would concentrate on the much more serious problem of tax evasion.

BRIAN WHITAKER

The appeal of the popular press

The 'tabloid revolution' was begun by the *Daily Mirror* in the mid-1930s. Stuart Hall and Paddy Whannel, in their book *The Popular Arts*, trace and analyse this phenomenon, with quotations from writings by the former *Mirror* editor, Hugh Cudlipp. In his first book, *Publish and Be Damned*, Hugh Cudlipp described the tabloid revolution led by Guy Bartholomew:

One Monday morning in 1935 the readers were informed, just as they had been in 1934, 1933, 1932 and 1931, that the swans on the lower reaches of the Thames were mating. Three weeks later they picked up their *Mirror* to learn that Queen Ena of Spain had shocked the guests at a dinner at the Savoy by using a toothpick after the succulent savoury and before the dreary orations;

furthermore, that an actress had found it absolute hell to dance at the Dorchester Charity Ball because of her screaming corns. Her husband, a famous actor, threatened to horsewhip the columnist.

From Bath and Bournemouth came letters of protest; from Cardiff and Newcastle guffaws of delight.

The subject-matter of the new *Mirror* was unchanged – queens and duchesses, famous actors and actresses, the Savoy and the Dorchester. What had changed was the slant, the angle of presentation.

We can break the *Mirror* style down into a number of elements. First of all there is the paper's abiding interest in 'life' – in human-interest stories drawn from the marginalia of human existence. Whatever else is happening in the paper, the hum of human gossip is an unmistakable sound in the background. All 'events' in the *Mirror* take place against this backdrop. No deep preoccupation with human nature is reflected here – the technique of the 'human-interest story' is essentially fragmentary, and consistently works against depth of treatment. The style reflects its earlier antecedents – the 'tit-bit' journalism pioneered by Newnes, Northcliffe and Pearson, the magic ingredient of 'Tit-Bits', 'Answers' and 'Pearson's Weekly'. Cudlipp has described those papers as consisting of '. . . the same formula; short paragraphs, half a dozen lines instead of half a column, scraps of jumbled news and information of the 'Fancy That' variety, competitions with prizes, answers to readers' queries, coloured cover, free railway insurance.'

This is a style designed to mirror life's incessant surface flow. 'In the hurrying years,' Cudlipp writes, 'the *Mirror* began to reach out and take up strange handfuls from the brantub of life.'

To the brantub of life was added those other 'human interests' – sex and crime – which have lived in very close proximity to the 'human-interest' story in popular journalism. The third element was the typographic – a revolution in newspaper layout which the *Mirror* pioneered:

> First eye-opener was the transformation of the news pages. Sledge-hammer headlines appeared on the front page in black type one inch deep, a signal that all could see of the excitements to come. Human interest was at a premium, and that meant sex and crime.

Relentless personalisation is central to the paper's technique, a method which tends to reduce all kinds of news to the level of the 'human-interest' story, and to familiarise all world figures, whatever may be their true interests, spheres of work or achievement.

'It was a cheeky pup of a paper,' Cudlipp remarks of the *Mirror* in its formative years. 'In a popular paper we are bound to write of politics in terms of persons not of principles,' he once wrote in a letter to Churchill.

In the mind of the *Mirror*, this liveliness is closely related to the paper's reputation as 'provocative and controversial'. 'Controversy and the *Mirror* was inseparable . . . That was its secret.'

> 'A popular paper has to be more than merely interesting; it must be alarmingly provocative in every issue and abundantly confident of its own prowess and importance.'
> STUART HALL and PADDY WHANNEL

The Falklands crisis in 1982 was an issue on which all newspapers were forced to take sides. The *Daily Mirror* was initially opposed to armed conflict, whilst the *Sun* took the opposite line with a vengeance! The following extract from *Gotcha! The Media, the Government and the Falklands Crisis*, by Robert Harris, traces the *Sun's* handling of the Falklands Crisis, and draws some conclusions about the nature of the popular press, and its significance as a vehicle for news in the 1980s:

When three national newspapers opposed the Government's handling of the Suez Crisis in 1956, they lost readers heavily. The *Guardian* lost 30,000 in a matter of days, though it later recouped them. The *Observer* lost 30,000 in a week, fell behind *The Sunday Times* for the first time and never caught up again. It was the *Daily Mirror* itself which fared worst, losing 70,000 readers. The lesson appeared clear. Supported by Rupert Murdoch, the *Sun* moved swiftly to corner the market in patriotism and to label its rival firmly as a disloyal defeatist.

The *Sun* had already attacked 'the sinking *Daily Mirror* 'as a 'paper warrior' on 2 April, the day of the invasion. On 6 April it struck again. 'At home the worms are already coming out of the woodwork,' taunted the *Sun*.

> 'The ailing *Daily Mirror*, which tried to pretend that there was no threat to the Falklands until the invaders had actually landed, now whines that we should give in to force and obligingly settle the islanders. But our whole experience with dictators has taught us that if you appease them, in the end you have to pay a far greater price.'

'Youths demonstrated outside the Argentinian Embassy in London last night,' reported the *Sun* on 3 April. 'They sang "Rule Britannia", ending with "Don't Cry for me, Argentina, We're going to Nuke you".' 'Sack the guilty men!' ran the paper's editorial on the same day, 'What the hell is going on at Britain's Foreign Office and Ministry of Defence?' To oppose sending the task force was to be 'running scared'; on 7 April 'The Sun Says' fired this salvo:

> 'Out of the woodwork, like the political termite he is, crawls No I Left-winger Tony Benn to demand the evacuation of the Falkland islanders . . .
> And of course, he immediately wins backing from the whining namby-pamby ultra-Left, who always run scared at the first sign of a crisis.'

The following day, the *Sun* printed a two-page spread of photographs of British marines surrendering on the Falklands. 'LEST WE FORGET' was the headline. 'This is why our lads are going to war.'

> 'These were the first moments of humiliating defeat for our brave Falklands few. It was a black moment in our history . . . a wound we cannot forget. But now our troops are on their way . . . to wipe out the memory and free our loyal friends.'

244

The *Sun's* attitude to a negotiated settlement was summed up in a five-word headline on 20 April: 'STICK IT UP YOUR JUNTA'. 'We urge every housewife NOT to buy corned beef produced in the Argentine' was the theme of an early campaign. Two days later the *Sun* reported that 'all over the country, families blacked the "bully" beef to show the South American bully boys what they thought.' 'Angry Sonia Lewis of Hockliffe, Beds', was reported as saying: 'Refusing to buy corned beef is one way we Brits can show the flag.'

Argentinians were 'Argies', a good target for humour. A daily series of 'Argy-Bargie' jokes was instituted, and soon the *Sun* was able to tell its readers, 'Your very own gags have been pouring in'. 'They are so funny that we have decided to give £5 for every reader's Argy-Bargie joke published. Plus a can of Fray Bentos "non Argentinian" corned beef. Today's joke was told to us by Titus Rowlandson, 9, from Brighton . . .' (Titus earned £5 for a joke about two British soldiers wiping out hundreds of 'Argy' soldiers.)

The *Sun's* promotions department was equally busy. On 7 April, 'to give the lads a big morale-booster', the paper began distributing free badges bearing the legend: 'The *Sun* says Good Luck Lads'.

'THE SUN SAYS KNICKERS TO ARGENTINA!' was the banner headline on 16 April. 'Britain's secret weapon in the Falklands dispute was revealed last night . . . it's undie-cover warfare.' The article revealed that 'thousands of women' were 'sporting specially made underwear embroidered across the front with the proud name of the ship on which a husband or boyfriend is serving.' Even Prince Andrew had 'bought several pairs of battle-briefs . . . But Palace officials are keeping mum about who will get them as a Royal gift.' Alongside the story was the inevitable picture of 'delightful Debbie Boyland . . . all shipshape and Bristol fashion' in her 'nautical naughties' embroidered with the name of 'HMS *Invincible*.'

From 11 May every front page bore the slogan 'THE PAPER THAT SUPPORTS OUR BOYS'. The comic-strip headlines continued: 'ARGY JETS SHOT DOWN' (13 May), 'OUR PLANES BLITZ ARGY SHIPS, HOW OUR TOUGH GUYS HIT PEBBLE ISLAND' (17 May), 'ARGIES BLOWN OUT OF THE SKY' (24 May), 'PANICKY ARGIES FLEE BAREFOOT' (3 June), 'HERO BAYONET TROOPS KILL FIFTY' (14 June). Following their peace initiative, the 'contemptible, treacherous Irish' joined the *Sun's* gallery of hate-figures: 'Don't buy Irish golden butter . . . Don't holiday there this summer. It's not much, but it's better than giving succour to our new enemy.' The names of all 33 Labour MPs who voted against the Government on 20 May were printed as a 'Roll of Shame'. 'Enemy quail at the touch of cold steel', reported the *Sun* on 14 June. 'The Argies had no stomach for close-quarters combat and crumbled before the Task Force's full-blooded assaults.' The level of abuse was kept up to the end, even spilling over on to the sports pages during the coverage of the World Cup. 'ARGIES SMASHED . . . They strutted, they cheated and afterwards they bleated. That was the arrogant Argentinians last night. They swaggered on as world champions, and crawled off, humiliated by little Belgium . . .'

Yet if the *Sun* hoped by such coverage to improve circulation, there was no evidence of that by the end of the war. Throughout the country as a whole there was only a tiny rise in the total circulation of all Fleet Street papers: from 14.9 million per day in March to 15.2 million in May (when fighting was at its height), falling back to 15 million in June – an overall increase of less than 1 per cent. In the same period, the *Sun* actually lost sales of 40,000 a day, while the *Mirror* added 95,000. 'We put on 100,000 thanks to a promotional campaign just before the war started,' says Molloy, 'and we managed to keep most of them.' Peter Stephens agrees: 'I don't think anyone prospered or suffered as a result of the war.'

Bearing in mind the precedent of Suez, this was, from the *Mirror's* point of view, an impressive performance. Why was this? The Falklands war was, after all, a much more popular venture than Suez. If papers opposed to military action lost readers in 1956, surely they should have done even worse in 1982?

It seems almost certain that the explanation lies in the expansion of television over the past 25 years. At the time of Suez there were less than 6 million television licence holders in the United Kingdom; today there are around 18 million. By 1971, a BBC Audience Research Unit report found that 86 per cent of the population found television a 'trustworthy' source of news; only 30 per cent 'trusted' newspapers.

The Falklands crisis rammed home the lesson of how powerful a means of communication television has become. When the Ministry of Defence spokesman appeared 'live' on television to announce the latest news from the South Atlantic, the night editor in Fleet Street was receiving the information no more swiftly and in no different a manner from his readers sitting at home. Voice reports from the television correspondents with the task force were arriving back hours, sometimes days, ahead of written dispatches. Throughout the war, as the *Daily Mail* pointed out in its evidence to the Commons Defence Committee, 'most of Britain's national newspapers were largely dependent on taking notes from Brian Hanrahan and Michael Nicholson.'

Given this immediacy, fewer people care any more what the *Sun* or the *Mirror* says. With bingo, the mass-circulation papers of Fleet Street are ceasing to be 'newspapers' in the traditional sense. As bingo can apparently lead half a million readers to change their newspaper in a matter of weeks, it is scarcely surprising that the editorial pages are fast turning into wrapping paper for the day's lucky numbers. Add to this the fact that in recent weeks the *Sun* has sometimes had seven pages of sport and a further five of advertising in a 28-page paper, and the reason why the Falklands war hardly touched circulation may well stand explained.   ROBERT HARRIS

Themes for discussion

What is the political affiliation of each of the British daily and Sunday national newspapers?

Do you think it would be better if there was greater political diversity in the British press?

Do you think that most people take a paper's political affiliations into account when choosing a paper?

Do you think the press would be improved if journalists had greater freedom to report and write what they wanted?

How far do you think newspapers respond to the perceived attitudes of their target readership, and how far do they set out to influence readers' attitudes?

How, and to what extent, do you think papers succeed in influencing their readers?

Why do you think the *Daily Mirror*, followed by all the other tabloid papers, adopted the sensationalising approach analysed by Hall and Whannel? Why haven't the 'serious' papers followed suit?

What do you think is the appeal of the kind of 'human interest' stories favoured by 'tabloid' newspapers?

Why do you think the *Sun* treated the Falklands Crisis in the way illustrated? What is your view of this kind of journalism?

Do you think the *Sun's* Falklands coverage is likely to have influenced a large number of readers?

Why do you think the *Sun* is Britain's largest selling daily newspaper?

What is your opinion of the general standard of the press in Britain?

Research suggestions

Write a report on the work of each of the following:

a   staff reporters
b   correspondents
c   news agencies

Write a report on the ways in which (a) national and (b) local newspapers are financed.

Group assignments

The best way to carry out group research on newspapers is probably to have available a full range of a particular day's papers to work on, individually or in small groups, one paper per person or group.

Here are a few suggestions for analytical work on newspapers:

1   Compare the main front page headlines in each paper, and consider what they reveal about the paper's priorities. Then compare the other front page headlines. This is best done over a number of days, if a significant picture is to emerge.

2   Look at the main front page story in each paper. Estimate the proportion of the page devoted to each of the following: the total item; the headline; the photograph; the story itself. Then work these out as a proportion of the total number of column inches of the page. Discuss the differences between the papers in this respect, and their significance.

3   Compare the main front page stories in each of the papers. Decide which has the greatest national or international importance. Look for this story in each of the other papers, and discuss its position and the amount of space devoted to it, and the significance of your findings.

4   Look at a lengthy news story in each paper, on the front page if possible, and make brief notes, with illustrations, on the following: length of words; length of sentences; length of paragraphs; general style. Discuss the differences which emerge between the papers.

5   Read the front page stories in your paper, and list the stories in the order in which they interest you personally. Compare lists and discuss the significance of your discoveries.

6   Work through the paper, marking each *news* story **H** or **S**, according to whether it deals with 'hard' or 'soft' news. ('Hard' news is that which is concerned with political or economic affairs or social welfare, or which affects a large number of people; 'soft' news is that which deals with events which have no broad significance, such as revelations about the private lives of celebrities, or crime stories.) Work out the percentage of the paper devoted to 'hard' news.

7   Work through the paper, looking for and marking each example you can find of each of the following categories:

national political news and background;	fashion;
entertainment and the mass media;	the arts;
international political news and background;	sport;
financial and industrial news;	advertisements;
gossip stories about celebrities;	photographs;
'human interest' stories;	crime stories;
science and technology;	special features.

Roughly work out the percentage of space in the paper occupied by each category. Compare the percentages in all the papers, and discuss the significance of your findings.

8   Look at one or two political news stories, and one or two editorials, in your paper, and draw what conclusions you can about the political line taken by the paper, and the depth of political analysis it contains. Discuss your findings about each of the papers.

9   Read through your paper and write down examples of emotive language and clichés. Compare the papers in this respect.

10   Analyse the way the news is slanted in the different papers by looking at the position of particular news stories and the space devoted to them, biased uses of language and the use of photographs and interviews.

(Some of these assignments could be extended to take in foreign newspapers as well, if the class contains linguists.)

Individual newspaper analysis

The exercises which follow include detailed written work, which is best done individually rather than in groups.

1   Look at the reproductions of the front pages of all the English Sunday newspapers on page 248. What conclusions can you draw from this collection? Write a detailed statement about the nature of the press in Britain, based on these conclusions.

2a   Collect as many copies as possible of *either* the *Sun*, the *Star* or the *News of the World*. Make a study of several national or international news stories in the copies you have collected. You should attempt to analyse, with illustrative examples, all of the following: the type and complexity of vocabulary employed; the use of slang, cliché, emotive phrases and alliteration; the syntax; the paragraph lengths; evidence of political bias.

2b   Now read the following front page report, from *The Sunday Times* on 9 December, 1990. The article contains about 550 words.

Gorbachev struggles to stave off anarchy

by James Blitz
Moscow

Speculation grew in Moscow yesterday that President Mikhail Gorbachev is on the verge of declaring a state of emergency throughout the Soviet Union, sacrificing perestroika in an attempt to stop the country slipping into anarchy.

Top-level military consultations – amid food shortages, humiliating appeals for foreign aid, and evidence of a lurch by Gorbachev towards authoritarianism – have left diplomats and radical politicians deeply apprehensive.

The fears grew at the end of a week in which leaders of the defence ministry, the interior ministry, the KGB and justice officials have held meetings to consolidate their strength, and Gorbachev has brought hard-line officials into senior military and legal posts.

The Soviet army newspaper, *Krasnaya Zvezda* (Red Star) reported that Marshal Dmitri Yazov, the defence minister, had met top military officers and the law and order chiefs from 13 of the country's 15 republics on Friday. Senior army officers addressed the meeting and, according to the paper, 'emphasised the necessity and real importance of preserving the armed forces so that they can protect the peoples of our country and our fatherland.'

Western diplomats said the emphasis on protecting the Soviet Union as a single state may be another indication that Gorbachev is preparing to use force to stop the rebellious republics seceding. Estonia, Latvia, Lithuania and Georgia have formally announced that they regard themselves as fully independent and are insisting that Soviet troops leave their territory.

Earlier this week two other meetings of military officers suggested that the army is preparing itself for the possible use of force in the repub-lics. On Tuesday and Wednesday, interior ministry officers met 'to anticipate any mass dis-orders'.

Later in the week, a two-day meeting of junior troops from the regular army, the KGB, the interior ministry and the railroad forces took place. Again, there was a hardline atmosphere. 'Let no one doubt,' said Colonel-General I. Shla-ga, the head of the army's political depart-ment, 'that the army, the fleet, the KGB and the interior ministry are loyal to the ideas of socialism, the interest of the country and its security.'

Gorbachev has signal-led in the past fortnight that he is planning tough measures to combat the rebellion of the republics and the chronic food shortage in the cities. The appointment of General Boris Gromov as a deputy interior minister is thought by some to be the most important sign of the new crackdown to come. He is the most popular general in the army and has shown little taste for political or military reform.

Some Western diplo-mats believe Gorbachev is being forced into his new hard line by the generals. About 40 per cent of the armed forces operate in the non-Russian republics and, if the big republics start to break away, the military will find it difficult to manage their redeploy-ment.

Others believe Gor-bachev has no good reason to introduce a nationwide state of emergency. One diplo-mat said: 'I would not be surprised to see the application of martial law in selected areas in the near future . . . But a declaration of military rule over the whole country now would be difficult to understand.'

JAMES BLITZ
The Sunday Times
9 December, 1990

Rewrite the article, in no more than 175 words, for inclusion in either the *Sun*, the *Star* or the *News of the World*. You should employ all the features of the newspaper which you have analysed. (This could be treated as a summary skills exercise, with a one-hour time limit, and a mark out of 40.)

3   Read the following editorials from British daily newspapers in October 1988, and answer the questions which follow. The editorials deal with issues raised by the Appeal Court's decision to lift the ban on the publication of Peter Wright's book *Spycatcher*, which revealed secrets he had discovered while working for the British Intelligence agency MI5.

251

ISSUES

At last, the balance is struck

The tide finally turned yesterday. You do not, normally, expect to find impeccable definitions of press freedom falling from the lips of the Master of the Rolls. Nor do you expect to find a Lord Justice of Appeal describing a Government's argument as 'futile and plainly silly'. But these, and other magical events, came to seem almost commonplace as the Court of Appeal gave judgement on *Spycatcher*. 'Most of the great works of the French Enlightenment were, for good reason, published outside France,' remarked Lord Justice Bingham. 'But the Bastille still fell.'

The key word, yesterday, was balance; the balance between public interest and executive secrecy. And the clear conclusion was that balance had been pushed out of true through the long months of *Spy-*

catcher litigation. No one needs to hail Mr Peter Wright as a good and fragrant egg to see that a world outside Britain which buys over a million copies of his book but forbids newspapers in Britain to detail and investigate his serious allegations is a world that has slewed off its axis. Now, said the three lords a'chiming, the stories should be written, and booksellers should be able to carry stocks without fear. More, for the future (a majority view) the reasonable supposition of iniquity in high and secret places was a public interest, there for investigation and publication. No need to assume that, because the great and good of government claimed all was well, that that was the end of every affair.

Talking of the end of anything in relation to *Spycatcher* is a dodgy

business. The House of Lords may still await. Whitehall's legal coffers never close. But while there is balance, let us stick to it. The free press, said Sir John Donaldson yesterday, 'is an essential element in maintaining parliamentary democracy and the British way of life as we know it.' It is essential not because of any special wisdom or status – but because it is 'the eyes and ears' of the general public. 'The media's right to know and their right to publish is neither more nor less than that of the general public. Indeed, it is that of the general public.' Just (however poorly we sometimes interpret it) so. The judiciary, perhaps, is growing tired and alarmed by the way the Government loses sight of ordinary freedoms, basic public interests. Here, on all sides, is a fundamental moment to pause and take stock.

Dangerous obsession

The Government appears to be dangerously obsessed with the *Spycatcher* affair.

It has now lost its bid to have the book banned from publication in both the High Court and the Court of Appeal. But it

is nevertheless pursuing its case all the way to the House of Lords.

Government motives are perfectly understandable. It is determined to stop the ex-MI5 officer Peter Wright profiting from the sale of secrets

he learned in the Government service and so setting an evil example to other ex-spies on the make.

But enough is enough. Mr Wright's secrets are now available to every rival spy firm in the

252

world. The Government cannot hope to shut this particular door so long after the horse has well and truly bolted.

In the nature of the case, a Government backdown will be no great triumph for press freedom.

Being able to publish Mr Wright's tales out of school does not serve any true public interest.

When you boil it down, Mr Wright is no better than a traitorous turncoat who peddles his charges and innuendoes about his former bosses from the safety of a far country.

Publishing his tittle-tattle is no hard won feat of deeply researched investigative reporting either. It is simply a question of buying and repeating Mr Wright's unsubstantiated allegations.

In fact, by making a major issue out of Mr Wright, newspapers may have unwittingly set back their own cause.

They have antagonised a further section of political opinion in Britain which is becoming significantly critical of press behaviour.

Last week one Bill was put before Parliament demanding a right of reply to newspapers and this week another Bill on privacy is due to be debated.

Press freedom is too important to be hobbled by measures like these. But newspapers need to find better ground than *Spycatcher* from which to fight their corner.

a Comment briefly on the style of each passage.
b Compare the attitudes taken by the two leader writers towards the government's attempts to ban the publication of *Spycatcher*.
c From which newspaper would you imagine each editorial might have been taken? Briefly explain why?

This could be treated as a comprehension exercise, with a 45-minute time limit and a mark out of 25 (10 marks each for questions a and b and 5 for question c.)

Television

Television in Britain

Television as a mass medium is a phenomenon of the post-Second World War era. Its importance can hardly be overestimated. It has penetrated to all but the remotest areas of the globe, and has been largely responsible for the present American cultural domination over much of the world. The saddest effect of this has been to open the eyes of many of the Third World's poor to a lifestyle and level of affluence to which they can never aspire.

Yet television has developed in very different ways in different countries. The development of British television is closely related to the nature of British society, according to Richard Hoggart, in the following extract from his essay 'Mass Communications in Britain':[1]

1   From a chapter of *The Pelican Guide to English Literature*, Vol.7: 'The Modern Age', edited by Boris Ford (Penguin, 1964).

In Russia and China, the mass media are substantially arms of government, with positive and comparatively single-minded functions. In different democracies their use differs, according to the structure and underlying assumptions of each society. We can say roughly that in America the main emphasis is on the commercial use of the means of mass communication – they tend to be aids to selling, or profit-making organisations in their own right. In Britain, which is both a stratified society with a responsible and still fairly powerful Establishment and yet a commercial 'open' democracy, the use of mass communications reflects this piebald character. The British like to use direct governmental controls as little as possible, but their strong tradition of public service and public responsibility causes them (where it is not possible or relevent to support existing voluntary agencies) to establish semi-autonomous chartered bodies under regular, but not day-by-day, government surveillance. This tradition helped to ensure that, once broadcasting had begun to show its powers, in the middle 1920s, a new chartered body was created – the British Broadcasting Corporation – charged with the responsibility for public service broadcasting. After the appearance of television there was considerable pressure for a commercial channel – strengthened by the country's increased prosperity – and so in 1954 the Independent Television Authority was created, to run a second channel from the proceeds of advertisements.   RICHARD HOGGART

The coming of ITV forced the BBC to reconsider its approach to television broadcasting. The main effect was to create competition between the BBC and ITA over audience ratings, so that programmes with a minority appeal were moved to off-peak times, and popular serials, scheduled at the same time each week, became an established feature of the television diet.

The creation of BBC2 in 1964 provided the BBC with the opportunity to expand its service to take in minority and more experimental programmes again, since the second BBC channel was not expected to compete so strenuously for a share of the television audience.

The TV critic, Peter Black, in his book, *The Biggest Aspidistra in the World*, discusses the BBC's view of its role after the creation of BBC2:

The BBC's share of the audience remained what it had been, roughly 50–50; for as Attenborough[2] declared, if its share ever rose above 60, to 70 per cent or beyond, it would signal failure, not triumph. It would mean that the BBC was failing to take advantage of its freedom to balance its output between serving minorities and majorities. 'It would be clear that the schedules were not enterprising enough to devise innovations which initially might be unpopular, nor daring enough in its catering for minority tastes.'   PETER BLACK

Advertising tends to dominate television in some countries, most notably the USA. In Britain an attempt was made to avoid this danger when

2   David Attenborough, then Head of BBC 2, writing in 1972.

254

commercial television was introduced, as is shown in James Curran and Jean Seaton's book, *Power Without Responsibility:*

The American system of programme sponsorship, in which advertisers pay for individual programmes, was rejected when commercial television started in Britain on the grounds that it gave advertisers direct power over programme content. Instead, only 'spot advertising' was permitted. Advertisers could only buy time slots between or within programmes. At first, advertisements were limited to an average of six minutes per hour. Later, when it was seen that this led to an accumulation of advertisements in peak viewing times, which had above average amounts of advertising, it was decided to limit advertisements to no more than seven minutes in any one hour.

The decision to adopt restricted spot advertising had been hailed as a victory for public service broadcasting. Spot advertisements were seen as guaranteeing the independence of programme making from the influence of advertisers. Spot advertising would protect the editorial integrity of commercial television.

JAMES CURRAN and JEAN SEATON

The dream machine

If it is used with intelligence and discrimination by producers and public, television is uniquely equipped, in the immediacy and vividness of its sensory appeal, to help break down the barriers of misunderstanding between peoples. In Marshall McLuhan's much-quoted phrase, it has turned the world into a 'global village'. It can even have a significant impact on the course of world events. The day-by-day American television coverage of the Vietnam War, in the 1960s and 1970s, exposed the carnage and horror of that war with such stark vividness that the war became unacceptable to a large body of the American people.

Used without intelligence, however, television tends to produce inertia or worse. It enslaves millions of undiscriminating addicts. It can even, at its most insidious, blur the line between reality and fantasy. These negative aspects of television are discussed in the following extracts from Peter Conrad's book, *Television: The Medium and its Manners:*

Commercials

As well as enticing us to lust for hardware instead of human bodies, consumerism boasts of its victory over economic necessity by striving to make us hungry when we don't need to eat. This is why television has so charmed a generation with the junk food it advertises. We watch television between meals, when we oughtn't to be thinking about food, but the medium exploits our suggestibility by encouraging us to slaver at the chocolate bars, potato crisps and popcorn it's selling. Consuming these unnutritious victuals isn't eating so much as the repletion of a bored and querulous vacancy, as indeed is watching television. One of the mixtures of toffee and chocolate advertised on British television presents as its chief virtue the time it

255

takes to chew. Disconsolate queuers at a bus stop snap at their chocolate bars and gobble them up at once. The chap armed with the correct brand is still contentedly toiling over his when – presumably hours later – the bus arrives. This is a kind of eating which, like gaping at television, is a substitute for doing anything, a condition of inane passivity. The original technological revolution was about saving time, shortcutting labour; the consumerism which is the latest instalment of that revolution is about wasting the time we've saved, and the institution it deputes to serve that purpose is television. The ads are always admonishing us to stop working. A dishwasher volunteers to relieve us of our chores, saying, 'Sit, America – we'll do the washing up'. But what do we do while we're not washing up? Television's answer is smugly self-referring: we watch television, and on it we see the dishwasher uncomplainingly toiling on our behalf.

Soap operas

Stardom on television is experienced by its beneficiaries as a limitation and an ignominy not, as in the movies, an access of monarchical power or an ascension to the company of divinity. The television star is someone who has been made the victim of a stereotype, and who feels cramped and depreciated by its strictures. He longs to shed the image which has supererogated his own reality, and battles frantically to break out of the box. Henry Winkler, donating the Fonz's scuffed leathers to the Smithsonian, resents the programme to which he owes his celebrity and irritably corrects infants who yell, 'Hi Fonzie!' at him, explaining that his name is Winkler.

The type may, as in the case of *Dempsey and Makepeace*, seem benign, but the stereotype is malignant, and its most pathetic victims are the actors on the soap operas. They're required by their contracts to conduct their private lives as extensions of the fiction : morality clauses empower the producers to dismiss a performer if he or she violates the sudsy probity which the serials defend. Yet at the same time they're punished in their own persons for the malfeasances of the characters they play. The soap actors have a sorry history of bruises and buffetings, administered by a censorious public. Margaret Mason, when playing Linda in *Days of Our Lives*, had a carton of milk poured over her in a supermarket by a consumer outraged at the character's perfidy; Eileen Fulton, playing the bitchy Lisa in *As The World Turns*, was clubbed with a handbag by another viewer who shrieked while beating her, 'I hate you!' Paranoia is an occupational ailment for these people. When Rachel Ames as Audrey was flirting extra-maritally in *General Hospital* she was accosted and abused by a man who claimed that his wife had been so upset by her vicious goings-on that she'd almost suffered a heart attack. When her character was on trial for murder, Rachel Ames was convinced that shop assistants were punishing her by refusing to wait on her. In spite of their protests, these actors have been subsumed by their roles.

News

Television's deftest alteration of content to match its hermetic, transistorised form occurs with the news. As we watch, reality is remade as televisual fiction. For, rather than reporting the news, television's presumption is to invent it. The news on television isn't hearsay, relayed to us by an impartial messenger. It happens at the medium's instigation, for the cameras are no longer obsequious witnesses but agents of provocation. The demonstrators raise their voices and their clenched fists when the cameras arrive. The newsman won't scruple to incite a media event if it seems reluctant to occur. Gary Paul Gates – in his account of CBS television news, *Air Time* – described an adventurer who, hastening to New Jersey to film what he hoped would be a prison riot, found only a mild ruckus, which had already been pacified. The prison authorities at first refused to admit the cameras, knowing they could easily reignite the protest. Eventually they relented, but still would not allow the crew direct access to the prisoners. The news team therefore went sedately about its business, preparing to film some indifferent and inactive convicts. Then, when all was ready, the reporter in charge signalled to the prisoners with a raised arm and a single extended finger in a gesture of scabrous disdain. They of course co-operated by staging a noisy riot for the cameras.

PETER CONRAD

Television news

Whilst a 'tabloid' newspaper can present a trivial but titillating discovery about the private life of a popular entertainer as its main front page feature, national television news generally concentrates on events of genuine significance.

Since its foundation, the BBC has maintained a reputation for providing an exceptionally unbiased news service. However, selection is an essential part of television news presentation, since only half a dozen or so items can be dealt with in any single news bulletin. In its selection of which items to include in a news broadcast, hidden bias is manifested. In her essay 'Fourth Channel: Third World', from which the following extract is taken, J. Ann Kammit analyses this hidden bias in British television news coverage of Third World affairs:[3]

Television tends to be interested in the stories, not the issue. Therefore most programmes and reports on the developing world are eye-catchers focusing on the drama of disasters – floods, famine, earthquakes and disturbances such as wars and coups. This is further accentuated by the news, which normally only refers to the Third World when there are catastrophes or political conflicts. This gives an extremely negative impression of developing countries and their populations.

3 Included in *What's This Channel Four? An Alternative Report*, edited by Simon Blanchard and David Morley (Comedia Publishing Group, 1982).

The real drama affecting Third World countries is the drastic poverty and exploitation which forms the permanent economic and social context for the mass of the population, who are only occasionally affected, if at all, by the more newsworthy hurricanes. But the many programmes which deal with the immediate effects of such disasters naturally concentrate on those most affected – the poor – helping to establish the overall impression that all Third World people are desperately poor. Those of us who have benefitted from travel or study know this not to be the case. As in our own society, most underdeveloped countries do have wealthy, sometimes very wealthy, élites and often a sizeable middle class. This is not to argue of course that we should not be concerned most with the poor and oppressed, but that we should see their poverty in context.

However, media treatment, like many development policy documents, tends to make frequent reference to Third World countries or nations rather than particular social groups. This is an effective means of depoliticising issues, leaving aside crucial questions about the simultaneous existence of extreme poverty and substantial wealth, and the social, political and economic structure which explains that poverty.

The view of 'the Third World problem' which underpins the perceptions and analyses of most programme makers, and particularly news reporters, reflects the ideological structures of our own society. Thus TV programmes are informed by the dominant model of so-called development theory, which still holds sway in most of academia and schools education. This model of the causes (ignorance, ill health) of Third World poverty, and of the remedies (modernisation, increased aid) has been persistently challenged within development studies over the last decade.

J. ANN KAMMIT

Cable television

Cable television is likely to widen viewing choice enormously. It has been available in North America for many years. In his book, *Television in the Eighties*, Rex Moorfoot describes cable television in the USA, and discusses its possibilities for Britain:

The cable viewer has his choice extended – he can choose from relays of the networks, local stations and locally produced community programmes and access programmes. The local programmes will range from earnest features of one kind or another to the most risqué access programmes, for example, in New York regular interviews conducted in the nude, men and women sitting comfortably on a hearth rug in front of a blazing fire. For the remainder of channels, the cable operator, wherever he is, will select a dozen or so of the 40 programme services distributed by satellite to the whole nation. Most are 24-hours-a-day services: four news channels, one sport, one weather, three religious, one black, one Spanish, and one Jewish; three popular music channels, three cultural channels, specialist channels for women, children and health; and 'super-stations' such as WTBS, Ted Turner's

24-hour independent channel from Atlanta, Georgia, which provides family entertainment based on feature films and sport. These cable services come free to the viewer, supported for the most part by advertising.

There is little doubt that the development of cable television, based on thirty channels and available in half the homes in Britain, would have profound effects on the acquisition and scheduling of programmes. It could lead to 'generic' television, national channels distributed by cable for local relay, not by satellite as in America. These could include a news channel, a sports channel, a weather channel, a 'pop' channel, a music and arts channel, an educational channel, and others. New organisations could come into being to provide these generic services.

REX MOORFOOT

Deregulation: the TV franchise

The most contentious issue in the 1989 Broadcasting Act was that of the TV franchise. The government argued that its 'auctioning' of the new commercial channel to the highest bidder would raise the quality and variety of British television, since no bid would be allowed without the promise of 'sufficient' good programmes.

The Consumers' Association was not convinced, as the following extract from a *Times* article in April 1989, shows:

Controversial government plans to award ITV franchises to the highest bidder could lead to more soap operas and game shows in the 1990s and less choice for viewers, according to a Consumers' Association report published today.

Far from resulting in better, more varied programmes, the Government's proposed shake-up of broadcasting could result in a worse service for viewers.

Mr Stephen Locke, the Consumers' Association's head of policy research, says: 'There is a real risk that all programmes will tend to converge on a single type, like soaps or chat shows, which can be guaranteed to command a 'safe' level of ratings.

'People are highly satisfied with the present system. We are sceptical about the need to change the way ITV franchises are awarded.'

The consumer watchdog's findings also lend support to the criticisms made last week by Sir Richard Attenborough, chairman of Channel 4, who warned the television industry of the dangers posed by 'market-place' economics. The Association says market forces are an 'entirely inadequate guarantee' of consumer interests and cannot be relied on to provide consumers with what they want from universal (not subscription) television channels financed by advertising.

Mr Locke says: 'Advertisers, not consumers, are the main players in the market. They are, of course, concerned to see high audience ratings for individual programmes.

'But they have no real interest in maintaining a varied, high-quality programme schedule. The contract is between the company and the advertisers: not between the viewer and the television company.

'A company making the highest franchise bid it can afford will have to make the profit gap between what it earns in advertising and what it spends on programmes as big as possible.'   from *The Times*, 10 April 1989

Themes for discussion

The Television Act (1964) requires 'that nothing is included in the programmes which offends against good taste or decency or is likely to encourage or incite to crime or to lead to disorder or to be offensive to public feeling'. Do you think there is too much sex and/or violence on British television? Can you think of any programmes which you have seen recently which infringe any of the prohibitions in the Act?

Do you think the distinction between the behaviour of heroes and villains in crime series is clear enough? Does it matter?

Do you think British television is sufficiently broad and enterprising in its scope? What kinds of programmes would you like to see more, and less, of?

Do you think Channel 4 has broadened the scope of television?

Do you see any advantages in the British system of financing television programmes partly through licence fees rather than wholly by advertising? How would you feel about the BBC introducing advertising?

The avowed purpose of television in Britain is 'information, education and entertainment' (Television Act). How much of each is reflected in a typical evening's viewing? How much of each do you think the typical viewer watches? Do you think most people discriminate sufficiently in their television viewing?

To what extent do you think television increases passivity and unsociability?

Are there any television programmes that you try never to miss? What are they?

What is the appeal of 'soap operas'? Do you consider any of them to be successful artistically? Why do you think some people become involved in the lives of 'soap opera' characters to the extent illustrated by Peter Conrad?

Do you think British television presents the news in an unbiased way? Do you think it is too parochial in its choice of news items?

Do you think news bulletins should be more positive, and concentrate more on success stories (e.g. good industrial relations) and less on conflict (e.g. strikes)?

Why do you think television (and the mass media generally) fails to follow up situations once their initial news value has waned? Do you think it ought to produce more follow up items?

In what ways do you think poor people in the Third World are influenced by seeing television programmes showing life in the West?

Do you think television could/should do more to educate people about the crisis in the Third World and the global environment?

Do you think cable television is a welcome development?

How do you feel about the auction of the new TV franchises to the highest bidder?

Questionnaire

After reading the guidelines for preparing and presenting a questionnaire on page 134, it could be of value to produce a questionnaire on television viewing habits. Here are some specimen subjects on which questions might be set:

- the number of hours of television watched each week on average;
- whether a television programme or a book is preferred on a particular theme, such as an adventure story;
- whether TV is watched mainly for amusement, relaxation or education, or for no special reason;
- if radio is ever preferred to TV in the evenings, and the sort of radio programmes listened to;
- if there are any TV programmes which the interviewees try never to miss, and what they are.

(Some of the questions could be correlated, to work out, for example, if people who watch large amounts of television discriminate as much as those who watch less.)

Assignments

1   With the help of a copy of a listings magazine, such as *Radio Times* or *TV Times* for a particular week, work out the proportion of broadcasting time in the evenings devoted to 'Serious' and 'Light' programmes, following discussion to establish the distinction. This could be undertaken in groups, working on different channels and blocks of time. The findings can be correlated, and percentages worked out.

2   Using your listings magazines, draw up a chart of the number of hours per day or evening, over the period of a week, which each channel devotes to each of the ten following categories of programme:

news and news magazines	'soap operas'
current affairs	comedy
documentaries	quiz shows and other light
drama	entertainment

> music
> film   sport
>
> Work out percentages for each channel and draw conclusions.

3   Watch an instalment of a 'soap opera' or an episode of a weekly crime or
    drama series, and make notes on each of these features:

    The characters: Were they convincingly drawn, or merely stereotypes?
                       Were their reactions to situations realistic on the
                       whole?
                       Were you able to get involved with the characters and
                       situations?
    The dialogue: Was it convincing?
    The story: Was it realistic, amusing or exaggerated?
                       Did it contain any interesting insights into life?

    You should note down any episodes or incidents which particularly
    illustrated any of these features, positively or negatively.

4   Make a study of fictionalised violence on television, over several days,
    noting the number and instances and the types of violence portrayed.
    The best way to organise this work would be for students to volunteer to
    watch particular programmes advertised in a listings magazine, so that
    the entire range of programmes in which fictionalised violence is likely to
    feature is covered.

5   Watch the evening news bulletin on each channel, over a period of three
    or four days. List each item, and work out the proportion of domestic
    and international news on each channel. Work out the proportion of
    items involving conflict, and involving violence. Compare the selection
    of items on the different channels. Were you aware of bias in any of the
    news coverage?

Advertising

Social effects of advertising

Advertising is massively big business, and is the only mass medium from
which no one in the Western world can escape. A whole new pseudo-science
of 'motivational analysis' has grown up over the past few decades, seeking
ways of persuading us to buy one company's product rather than another's.
Since, for all practical purposes, there is nothing to choose between different
brands of toothpaste, soap powder, petrol and thousands of other consumer
items, advertising is inevitably concerned largely with the creation of
imaginary differences between brands, which in turn leads to all kinds of
distortion and deception on the part of the advertisers. As J.A.C. Brown put
it: 'It is obviously impossible to appeal to common sense by truthful

advertising which relies on giving factual data if the brands from which the customer is expected to choose are alike in all essential qualities.'[4] What are the implications of this?

The psychological and social effects of advertising in Western society are discussed by Frank Whitehead in a chapter of the book, *Discrimination and Popular Culture*, edited by Denis Thompson.

In recent years the advertising world has turned increasingly to the twin techniques of market research and motivational research, in order to make more efficient its empirically-gained knowledge of how best to work upon human frailty.

It can be argued that the constant appeal to discreditable impulses is unlikely to have much effect except on those who are already abnormally susceptible. We may agree that it is the self-indulgent who will respond with most alacrity to slogans about chocolates with 'less-fattening centres', or to the stomach-powder manufacturer's encouragement to 'Eat what you like – without suffering for it'. On the other hand advertising agents are united in their conviction that sheer weight of repetition can be amazingly effective (hence the remarkably long life meted out to such slogans as 'Players Please' or 'Guinness is Good for You'); and it should be remembered that what we are exposed to is a combined assault by many different advertisers, all converging to direct their appeal to a small number of well-proved human weaknesses. Thus although it may be only the exceptional motorist who falls in at all fully with the implications of the invitation to 'Put a Tiger in your Tank', nevertheless this particular extreme example works in consort with a host of other advertisements for petrols, cars, and motoring accessories to establish an unquestioned assumption that what every motorist longs for above all (on our overcrowded roads) is speed, engine-power, and acceleration. Road safety is not apparently considered a strong selling-point for motor-cars.

For the most part, advertising acts (and is content to act) as a reinforcement of already existing tendencies, but even so it seems likely that the multiplicity of small pressures work together to effect significant shifts in the total pattern of socially accepted values. In countless ways often unnoticed we are led to accept as common ground a world in which the key to happiness is the possession of the newest model of car, dining-room suite, refrigerator, and television set, in which any malaise can be neutralised by recourse to a branded anodyne or laxative, and in which the chosen reward for a hard day's work is to 'treat yourself' to a luxury you can't afford because you feel you 'deserve' it – or even 'owe it to yourself'.

The tendency to reinforce impulses which are socially undesirable is only part of the problem. Even more insidious may be the advertiser's growing ingenuity in linking his product with ideas and images which are in themselves innocuous, pleasurable, even commendable. In consequence of this the concepts of sexual love, manliness, femininity, maternal feeling are steadily devalued for us by their mercenary association with a brand-name – as though the real human values they

4   J.A.C. Brown, *Techniques of Persuasion* (Penguin, 1963).

represent can be purchased by rushing out and buying a new shaving lotion, a new deodorant, even a new washing-machine. Mother-love seems to be the target most favoured by practitioners of this tactic, and the following example is only a little more nauseating than most of its kind:

> 'When there's love at home, it shows. It shows in the smile of the mother who gives it. It shows in the happiness of her family who are secure in it . . . It shows in the fact that she chooses Persil for their clothes.' FRANK WHITEHEAD

The rationale of advertisers

Advertising costs large companies millions of pounds. How can the expense by justified? In an essay entitled 'Understanding Advertisers' [5] Kathy Myers reveals some of the underlying assumptions, approaches and justifications of the advertising industry:

For a product to become a brand it needs to establish and maintain a position in the market over a defined period of time. Market stability ultimately depends upon repeat purchases.

Ralph Horowitz put the case for manufacturer's investment in advertising as follows: 'The role of advertising is to diminish uncertainty. Advertising sets out to secure a predetermined level of demand for a given future and to diminish fluctuations around that predetermined level.' The ability to predict total revenue from advertised products is crucial if manufacturers are to accurately plan future output, product development and capital investment.

It is therefore the need to take the trial and error out of selling that motivates advertisers to create a clear picture of the audience they are selling to and what role or function the product could play in people's lives.

Attention to the 'needs' and 'desires' of the consumer informs every level of marketing strategy: the design of the campaign, the kind of media exposure given, the amount of exposure, the choice of packaging, distribution, etc. The advert which we see is only one part of this highly co-ordinated marketing offensive.

From the advertiser's point of view, women's magazines are a highly reliable way of reaching the female consumer. Readership profiles are available for each magazine on the market.

One unquantifiable benefit to advertisers is that magazines provide a 'hospitable environment' for the digestion and assimilation of advertised information. Glossy, colourful and eye-catching, women's magazines are reputed to have a 'keep' value. They may be read at leisure, used for reference, shown to friends or left about the house. Publishers and advertisers believe that these magazines provide a source of information, advice, solidarity and companionship, and that women have grown to

5 Included in *Language, Image, Media*, edited by Howard Davis and Paul Walton (Basil Blackwell, 1983).

trust the opinions voiced. It is a credibility jealously guarded by editors and highly valued by advertisers, for both groups feel that some of the journalistic credibility is carried over into the advertisements. The magazine environment as an essential ingredient of advertising success was the message of an IPC advert for their Women's Group of magazines. The copy quoted a Saatchi and Saatchi spokesman on the subject of Anchor Butter:

'While our TV advertising is promoting the use of Anchor Butter in the family, we are looking to posters and women's magazines to reinforce our branding for us. We want the housewife to be absolutely certain that Anchor is the name she can rely on for real butter goodness, and we are confident that in the relaxed, intimate environment of women's magazines our message carries complete conviction.'

Conflicts within agency strategy are reflected in the system of beliefs which validate the industry as a whole. On the one hand, members of the advertising profession see advertising mythically as consistent with the needs of a democratic egalitarian society: it helps to make the consumer aware of available market 'choices'; it 'educates' the consumer into 'product benefit' and so on. But the vision of advertising as a democratic information service is distorted by the fact that it is the job of each individual agency to promote one product at the expense of competing products. The apparent contradiction between these two aspects of commercial philosophy is rationalised in terms of the 'Darwinian' survival of the fittest product. In the Western economy, where 95 per cent of the new products introduced onto the market each year fail to maintain a market position, successful marketing and advertising is felt to be essential to give products a competitive chance.

KATHY MYERS

Themes for discussion

Why do companies spend so much money on advertising?

How do you think people in general are influenced by advertising?

Can you think of any ways in which you personally have been influenced by advertising?

What influence do you think advertising has on people's lifestyles, attitudes and aspirations? How important a part does it play in Western culture?

Do you think that advertising has a tendency to cheapen and debase language?

Are there any aspects of advertising which you feel should be legislated against?

Research topic

Write a brief report on the advertising code of practice in Britain.

Assignments

1 Collect a range of newspaper and magazine advertisements and analyse the appeal of each. Try to find an example of an advertisement appealing to each of the following basic urges and anxieties:

    greed   ease and comfort   health fears
    security   maternal feelings   sex appeal
    identification with famous people   snob appeal
    fear of nonconformity and urge for acceptance.

2 Analyse some of the advertisements in more detail. Consider:

The picture: Is it appropriate to the product? If not, what urge is it appealing to?

The slogan: Is it a logical, verifiable statement?

The copy: Does it concentrate on presenting facts which will help the reader make an informed decision? Does it make any claims or statements which cannot be verified? Does it use inappropriate pseudo-scientific language? Does it use an inappropriate or exaggerated style?

Does the advertisement as a whole link the product with irrelevant drives, and make questionable statements?

3 Decide what kind of people the advertisement is appealing to, on the basis of your analysis.

4 Look at a selection of recorded television commercials. Analyse the appeal of each, in similar terms to those suggested above.

5 List the commercials in order of effectiveness, and discuss what makes an effective television commercial.

6 Make a collection of advertisements from each of the following: a 'quality' Sunday newspaper colour supplement; a 'tabloid' newspaper; a women's magazine. Look at some of the advertisements in each, and try to draw some conclusions about the kinds of appeals and audience each is aimed at.

7 Look at a range of advertisements for the same type of product, e.g. cosmetics, cars, beer, chocolates, shampoo. Decide whether the basic appeal is similar in each, and if not, why not.

8 Collect some advertisements which link products with irrelevant urges.

9 Make a collection of meaningless slogans and statements in advertisements.

10   Make a collection of inflated, inappropiate phrases used in advertisements.

Film, video and censorship

For centuries, censorship has been a contentious issue. In Britain, all films have to be passed for public exhibition by the British Board of Film Censors. In the extracts which follow, from an interview with Beverley Brown in a 1982 issue of *Screen* magazine, the Secretary of the Board, James Ferman, discusses film censorship and the dangers of video 'nasties':

When I joined the Board in 1975, censorship was extremely controversial. The Board was going through a difficult period largely as a result of a number of contentious films which came out in the early 1970s – *Straw Dogs*, *Last Tango*, *Emmanuelle*, *The Devils* . . . And there had of course been a sudden trend for sex films, beginning with sex education films in the early 1970s and going on to soft porn films of which *Emmanuelle* is the most obvious example. This meant that the local authorities suddenly found themselves involved in a very controversial business, while the newspapers found that there was a lot of good copy in censorship. The film industry in its turn – to be fair to the newspapers – often traded on that, because controversy was good for the box office.

It has generally been thought that the OPA[6] refers only to pornography, but it's not just hard-core pornography, it's anything that may be depraving and corrupting to a significant proportion of those who are likely to see it. It includes the advocacy of drug-taking, the portrayal of horror or violence as a 'turn-on'. In other words, there may be something which is not pornographic in the common sense of the term, in that no genital organs are on display on the screen, but the wicked behaviour portrayed is presented as a 'turn on', an encouragement to behave in an anti-social or seriously harmful manner.

There is a tradition in this country that, on the whole, we restrict seriously offensive or potentially offensive sexual material by confining it to clubs or semi-private situations. This is the British solution. It's not a solution which any other country has developed, but if we can accommodate the club licensing system to that tradition then on the whole it will prove more acceptable, and clubs and public cinemas could still retain their character as different social spaces.

I think the Board's view has always been that there was room in our society for a kind of film which would not be widely shown but shown only to those who seek it out. Provided that it did not encroach on the consciousness of those who had no wish to know about it, through indecent or disturbing advertising – advertising is very important, the ads for *Driller Killer* on video are very worrying, and advertising also affects how people come to see the film or video itself – and provided it was not depraving or corrupting.

6   Obscene Publications Act.

I think it's fair to say that no film made before 1970 had a serious tendency to deprave and corrupt by today's standards. But since then there has been a tendency to indulge in an exploitation of evil for its own sake: 'We are now going to show you the nastiest, most unpleasant thing you've ever seen – and if this isn't strong enough for you, next week we'll show you something even stronger,' putting the idea into people's minds, that is, actually inciting them to find evil attractive, saying, 'We want to put you in the position of the rapist, we want you to watch this from the standpoint of a man who is enjoying participating in it.'

The problem is that the way films work is not necessarily a direct incitement. The law talks of a tendency to deprave and corrupt, which is exactly what it is. There's very little evidence that if you see one rape film, it will incite you to rape, but if you see two, six, ten? Out of 402 films in 1976 we had 58 which included scenes of on-screen rape. Some were quite serious films, but most were exploitation trying to make the audience enjoy the rape as male spectators. I don't think you can say that any one of those films is a direct incitement, but they gradually erode the taboo against it, they gradually teach a male audience – at least American porno films do – that women don't really mind rape, that they will respond to it as a liberating experience. I think it's a tendency, the cumulative impact of a whole genre of film.

In a *Newsweek* programme on pornography, Gene Abel, the New York researcher, found that in showing rape images to normal men, measuring their physiological sexual response, the erotic content was the main factor and the physical response decreased when the violence factor was increased. With convicted rapists, on the other hand, it was the other way around; and this is the problem with these recent 'slasher' films – which are in fact all heavily censored in Britain, more than the critics notice – that violence and rape itself is presented as a 'turn on'.

And, again, I think we must remember that films are not isolated experiences, people go to the cinema repeatedly. The generation 16 to 25 used to go a couple of times a month, or used to when they had money. Now they're hiring video, and seeing far worse things, with the added factor that they don't even have to see the 'film as a whole' – they can just skip the boring dialogue and spool through to the rape or the brutality, and see it again and again.   JAMES FERMAN

Discussion points

Do you think that scenes of explicit sex and ultra-violence should be banned from the cinema? How would you draw the line between what is acceptable and what is not?

Why do you think people watch 'video nasties'? Do you see them as a reflection of any trends in our society? What do you think is the probable effect of films which present rape and other forms of sadistic cruelty as a 'turn on'?

Essay titles

a 'Advertising and affluence are closely related.'

b 'A good newspaper is a nation talking to itself.' What are your views on what constitutes a good newspaper?

c 'Television dulls the senses and prevents rebellion.' Do you agree?

d You have been asked to produce two pieces of journalism, one for a quality newspaper and one for a tabloid newspaper, on the topic of solutions to pollution problems. Using the same basic information for both, write the two articles. Give each piece a title, and make it clear which newspapers you are writing for.

e Do British newspapers have anything to do with 'news'?

f How far do newspapers influence views in society and how far do they merely reflect them?

g In what respects do you think standards in television may be in decline?

h Consider the treatment by the mass media of any *one* important recent issue.

i To what extent do national newspapers reflect all shades of public opinion?

j What is the appeal of soap operas, and how do you react to them?

Bibliography

Black, Peter, *The Biggest Aspidistra in the World: a personal celebration of fifty years of the BBC*, British Broadcasting Corporation, 1972

Cohen, Stanley and Young, Jock, *The Manufacture of News: Deviance, Social Problems and the Mass Media*, Constable, 1976

Conrad, Peter, *Television: The Medium and its Manners*, Routledge and Kegan Paul, 1982

Curran, James and Seaton, Jean, *Power without Responsibility, the Press and Broadcasting in Britain*, Methuen, 1985

Glasgow Media Group, *Bad News*, Routledge and Kegan Paul, 1976. *More Bad News*, Routledge and Kegan Paul, 1980

Hall, Stuart and Whannel, Paddy, *The Popular Arts*, Hutchinson, 1964

Harris, Robert, *Gotcha! The Media, the Government and the Falklands Crisis*, Faber & Faber, 1983

Moorfoot, Rex, *Television in the Eighties: The Total Equation*, British Broadcasting Corporation, 1982

Smith, Anthony, *The Newspaper: An International History*, Thames and
    Hudson, 1979
Thompson, Denis (ed.), *Discrimination and Popular Culture*, Penguin, 1964
Whale, John, *The Politics of the Media*, Manchester University Press, 1977
Whitaker, Brian, *News Ltd: Why You Can't Read All About It*, Minority
    Rights Group, 1981

Advice on writing: choosing a question

The right choice of question on a language essay paper is of fundamental
importance. If you realise after half an hour that you do not know enough
about your chosen subject to continue writing authoritatively about it, then
you cannot expect to do well. A reasonably detailed plan, with a paragraph
scheme, should prevent this from happening. Your plan should enable you
to establish quickly whether you can write convincingly about the subject
for the length of time allocated. Scrapping an essay after five minutes'
unsuccessful planning is better than struggling to think of ideas when it is
too late to start a different essay. During the planning stage, you should try
to think out exactly what the examiner is looking for, and make sure that
you have sufficient information and ideas about the topic you have chosen to
write an effective answer. We will look at some specimen essay questions,
and consider how you can decide when a question is best avoided.

It is quite likely that at least one of the questions on a general language
essay paper will concern a comparatively current issue. We will look at one
or two such questions, and discuss what the examiners are likely to be
expecting.

The issue of terrorism has been prominent in the news for some years. Let
us therefore take the question: 'Can terrorism ever be justified?' If you have
read newspaper reports and analyses; and watched television news and/or
documentary programmes about IRA bomb attacks, then this might be a
good question to attempt. However, if this is the only example of terrorism
that you can think of, then your answer is certain to be too narrow. A
discussion of the Libyan terrorist attacks in the mid-1980s and the American
response to them, and of the Lockerbie disaster, would show, for instance,
that you are also aware of terrorism as an international problem.
Furthermore, if you have only a vague knowledge of the situation in
Northern Ireland, then you are unlikely to be able to write convincingly
about it. Your essay would be further broadened by a discussion of 'state
terrorism', rather than merely concentrating on the horrors of isolated bomb
attacks. You would also be expected to show some awareness of the
justifications (however dubious you might consider them) for terrorism, and
not assume that terrorists are simply lunatics who enjoy killing people.

Similarly, if the question you chose read: 'Weapons of war are obsolete.

We should abolish them.', you would be expected to focus on a range of aspects of war; its necessity or otherwise in different circumstances would have to be discussed, as well as the practical feasibility of abolishing weapons. It would obviously be relevant, in the light of the ending of Soviet control over Eastern Europe, and the subsequent planned destruction of the Soviet and American nuclear arsenals at the beginning of the 1990s, to discuss the question of whether or not nuclear weapons are obsolete, and could ever be entirely abolished. However, if you focused too heavily on this one aspect of the question you would score poorly. The Gulf War in particular, and some of the more limited civil and other wars which are always going on, would also need to be discussed, to give your essay the necessary breadth.

Vagueness is one of the most serious failings in language essays. If you write in generalities when the question invites specific illustration, you will lose quite a lot of marks. If the question, for example, was, 'Do we owe a greater debt to the artists than to the scientists?', you would be expected to cite a reasonably wide range of both. If you can only think of one or two writers whom you happen to be studying in literature, then you will merely be displaying your ignorance. Again, if the question was, 'Given a Time Machine, to which past age would you like to return, and why?', you would be expected to display a fairly detailed knowledge of life in your own chosen era. If your historical memory is sketchy, then it would be best not to attempt the question. Similarly, if the question was, 'Modern dramatists apparently enjoy expressing violence; they should look for more positive values in our society', then you would be expected at least to display a knowledge of the works of a variety of dramatists who express violence, and ideally be able to cite one or two whose messages you consider positive.

Vagueness can be a fatal flaw in essays on the press. To answer a question which reads, 'To what extent do national newspapers reflect all shades of public opinion?', you would be expected to be aware of the political affiliations of the main national papers; an answer which did not refer to specific papers would be bound to lose marks. Likewise, the question, '"A good newspaper is a nation talking to itself." What are your views of what constitutes a good newspaper?' could not be answered adequately without some analysis of at least one specific paper.

You must make sure, therefore, that you fully understand the implications of a question before attempting to answer it, that you can discuss it in depth, and that you can illustrate your answer adequately, if illustrations seem to be called for.

FOUR THEMES IN
BRIEF

In this chapter, four more themes are suggested, in addition or as alternatives to the eight already explored in depth. Written exercises and ideas for planning a discussion or debate are provided on each. The themes are: politics; science; youth, marriage and old age; and drugs.

1 Politics

With a topic as wide as politics, all that can usefully be done is to suggest a few approaches to discussion.

Reading a political article

A good way to develop political awareness is to take a political article in a newspaper and to analyse it in terms of political phraseology and ideas. The article which follows appeared in *The Times* in October 1990, and deals with the issues of German reunification, the problems facing East Germany after achieving its freedom from Soviet domination, and the implications of a single German nation for the European community.

   The article and accompanying questions are designed for use in a discussion session rather than as a written comprehension, and are intended to highlight issues: the answers are not, in general, meant to be found in the article itself.

With all its might, Germany can be a power for good

On the eve of unification, **Helmut Schmidt**, former West German chancellor, sets out his hopes – and anxieties

East Germany's craving for freedom from communist dictatorship first became clear to the 5 world on 17 June, 1953, when Soviet troops crushed the uprising in East Berlin. Thirty-six years were to pass before 10 the Brandenburg Gate was finally forced open, the Wall pulled down and the killing zone neutralised. Such was 15 our joy that tomorrow's celebrations of unification can only be an echo of those momentous events of last November. 20 None the less, 3 October will be an important date for the future because reunification alters significant aspects 25 of our foreign defence, and domestic and international economic policies. New opportunities present themselves, but 30 at the same time there are grounds for concern.

There is so much to do in what was the GDR. During a visit last 35 month, thousands of people expressed anxiety to me about the power still exercised by former members of the secret 40 police and ex-

Communist party career politicians running the factories, co-operatives and government offices. 45 Because of the falling sales of East German goods, companies are threatened with closure, with a consequent loss of 50 jobs. Already unemployment is approaching a million.

Who owns what is in practice unclear. The 55 mayor of a town simply does not know how much of the land is at local government's disposal. There is a genuine 60 cash crisis in both the public and private sectors. Local treasurers doubt whether they will be able to meet their 65 wage bills during the next quarter. Much of the money Bonn is pumping eastwards is flowing back as East 70 Germans buy West German goods.

Although there is a danger of psychological setbacks and political 75 disillusionment, I believe there will be an upswing during 1992 at the latest and that East Germans will reach West German 80 productivity levels and

standard of living by the turn of the century. The quality of housing will lag behind far longer, 85 however, and the federal government needs to show greater urgency in improving roads, railways and telecommuni-90 cations.

If anyone still believes that the financial aid required can be raised through the issue of gov-95 ernment bonds, he is mistaken, particularly in view of the Gulf crisis and Bonn's huge obligations to the Soviet 100 Union.

Despite these demands on our resources, and the competing claims of financial aid to Poland, 105 Hungary and Czechoslovakia, many politicians and journalists abroad take for granted that Germany, with its 60 110 million people, will have achieved dominant economic and financial power by the end of the decade.

115 This assumed economic power, in turn, fuels the fear that Germany will be tempted to a new arrogance in foreign 120 policy and an exertion of

273

our will over the European Community and its politicians. Because of our treaty with Moscow, 125 some fear that Germany might try to have a foot in both camps, West and East, throwing our great weight first to one side 130 then to the other.

Such anxieties are certainly exaggerated, but they exist, in London, Paris, Warsaw and else-135 where, and Germany has to take them into account as a political fact of life. Those particularly fearful of the Mos-140 cow treaty should recognise that without it, there would have been no unification, and Soviet troops would have 145 stayed in East Germany indefinitely.

In the past, West Germany has stood up to both the Soviet Union 150 and the United States over nuclear weapons. In future, clashes of interest are more likely with medium-sized 155 European powers, notably Poland, and will require delicate handling. All German-Polish problems are, and will 160 long remain, overshadowed by memories of Auschwitz and the tragic history of our bilateral relations stretching back 165 for more than two centuries. Added to these today are negotiations about exit visas for 170 ethnic Germans, Polish financial demands, and recognition of the Oder-Neisse Line. In dealing

with any weaker country, we Germans need to 175 show not only tact and understanding but generosity.

Relations with France, an equally important 180 neighbour, are no longer as firm and co-operative as they were in the early 1960s, at the time of Adenauer and de Gaulle, 185 or during the seven years I worked with Giscard d'Estaing. Although German and French 190 interests clashed at times, neither side ever lost sight of the vital truth that without trust and close cooperation 195 between the two, there can be no peace in Europe, no common security, no European integration and no prog-200 ress in the EC, which is vital for Europe's future political and economic stability. Although these truths have not been for-gotten completely by 205 Bonn or Paris since 9 November last year, they have been neglected.

That brings me to rela-210 tions with Britain. When I first became involved in politics after Hitler's war, I was an Anglophile – the result of my 215 schooling in Hamburg, where I was born. But since the late 1950s, when I was disappointed by the way the British 220 remained on the sidelines of the EC, I have leaned strongly towards Franco-German cooperation. Given the concern 225 expressed in Britain about the economic muscle that Germany is expected to exercise in future, my heartfelt wish 230 is to make one thing clear to British readers. If the ecu is not introduced as the single common currency in the EC, 235 the mark will indeed become Europe's dominant currency, which I would consider most undesirable.

So I appeal to you: see to it, along with us, that we create an independent system of European central banks with the ecu as 245 the EC's one and only currency. A common market with 11 or 12 currencies is the most uncommon market that 250 world economic history has ever seen.

The constitutional and internationally recognised reunification of 255 Germany ends a long, difficult and painful phase of our post-war policy. The years ahead, however, confront us 260 with even more difficult tasks. We have to ensure that Germany stays on a foreign-policy course that does not disturb our 265 neighbours, but strengthens and justifies their trust in us.

European countries with democratic constitutions and a market 270 tutions and a market economy are pinning their hopes on the future influence of the EC. The British and the Germans 275 should therefore bring all their political and economic power to bear in the Community. All the other countries of 280 Europe, even the Soviet Union, are hoping along with the EC member stares that a continuation of the Helsinki process 285 will achieve increased cooperation.

At the end of this terrible 20th century, my people have been given 290 another great chance. We shall be able to take it if, as well as solidarity with the people of the old GDR, we remember the 295 need for solidarity with our neighbours. I pin my hopes and trust on a steadfast continuation of the policies that West 300 Germany has so far pursued.

HELMUT SCHMIDT, *The Times*, October 1990

1   What does Helmut Schmidt mean by 'communist dictatorship'? (lines 2–3) What were the essential features of the Communist system in East Germany?

2   What was 'the Wall'? (line 12) What was the significance of its being 'pulled down'? (line 12)

3   What was 'the GDR'? (line 33)

4   What is the reason for the fears of the people of East Germany about 'former members of the secret police and ex-Communist party career politicians'? (lines 38–42)

5   Why is unemployment rising in East Germany? (lines 50–2)

6   Why is it unclear 'who owns what in practice' (lines 53–4) in East Germany?

7   What does Schmidt mean by 'Bonn's huge obligations to the Soviet Union'? (lines 98–100)

8   Why are Poland, Hungary and Czechoslovakia competing for aid? (lines 103–6)

9   What does he mean by 'a foot in both camps'? (lines 126–7)

10 What does he mean by saying 'All German – Polish problems are . . . overshadowed by memories of Auschwitz'? (lines 158–62)

11 What is the 'ecu'? Why is its creation preferable to the mark becoming 'Europe's dominant currency'? (lines 236–7)

12 What is 'a market economy'? (lines 270–1)

13 What is 'the EC'? (line 273)

14 Why does Schmidt say that 'even the Soviet Union' is hoping for a continuation of the process of 'increased cooperation' in Europe? (lines 280–6)

15 Why do you think Schmidt talks of 'this terrible 20th Century'? (lines 287–8)

Topics for discussion

There are plainly any number of approaches to a discussion of politics. Exploring particular issues can be a valuable way of developing a political perspective, but the goal of being able to read political reports in newspapers with some degree of understanding is probably as valuable as any. The suggestions which follow have this end in view.

British politics

A debate, in which individuals or pairs present a general case for the main British political parties' current policies.

A discussion of the different parties' policies with relation to specific issues, such as defence, privatisation and nationalisation, workers' participation in industry, law and order, etc., following research by individual students.

Research and/or discussion of current political vocabulary, such as: 'left' and 'right' in a party and general political sense; mixed economy; the 'market'; monetarism; Keynesian economics; proportional representation; Marxist; capitalist, etc.

World politics

A discussion of the major world political systems: anarchism, capitalism, centralist communism, democratic socialism, fascism. A useful approach might be to take a political map of the world, and discuss the political systems in operation in different areas and countries.

A discussion concentrating on the differing political systems in selected areas, e.g. Central America, the Far East. In the former case, individual students could research the current politics of Nicaragua, El Salvador, Honduras and Costa Rica; in the latter the systems in India, China, Indonesia and Taiwan could be discussed and compared.

As a follow up or an alternative to this kind of approach, discussion could centre on more general political abstractions such as: the meaning and value of 'democracy', the concepts of 'freedom' and 'liberty', the uses and limitations of bureaucracy, etc.

Essay titles

a   'Power tends to corrupt, and absolute power corrupts absolutely. Great men are always bad men.'

b   'When people contend for their liberty, they seldom get anything by their victory but new masters.'

c   In pursuing higher living standards, do we overlook the quality of life?

d   Discuss the case for the complete revision of the electoral system in Great Britain.

e   'As society becomes more complex we have more government and less freedom.' Is this inevitable?

f   'Liberty must be limited in order to be possessed.'

g   'The principal concern of politics is the allocation of resources.'

h   Is 'equality of opportunity' attainable or is it only an ideal?

i   'Democracy is the tyranny of the majority.' How do you respond to this assertion?

2   Science

A detailed understanding of scientific theory and its practical applications cannot be expected of arts students. However, it is not unreasonable to assume an awareness of the major scientists and inventions in layman's terms, and discussion of these, as well as a more philosophical consideration of the value and limitations of science in terms of its practical applications in human affairs, would be valuable.

A comprehension/summary exercise on a radical feminist analysis of the nature of scientific activity should serve as a useful lead-in to discussion.

Comprehension, comment and summary skills

The article which follows appeared in *New Internationalist* magazine in April 1988. Read it carefully and answer the questions. You are advised to spend about one and a half hours on this exercise.

a   Explain and comment on the links which the writer asserts in lines 26–97 between scientific activity and masculinity.   (*8 marks*)

b   Explain the parallels which the writer draws between 'the attack on nature by the scientists' and 'the rape and exploitation of women in misogynist cultures'. (lines 113–7)   (*6 marks*)

c   How do you react to the final paragraph?   (*5 marks*)

d   By detailed reference to the language used, and the presentation of the arguments, show the extent to which you consider the article to be biased.   (*9 marks*)

e   Magazine articles generally assume a certain kind of readership. By reference to the details of the passage, and especially to its register, vocabulary, tone and political stance, deduce what kind of audience the article is aimed at. *(12 marks)*

f Summarise the writer's theory about genius in not more than 50 words. *(10 marks)*

(50 marks total)

Science on the couch

Why is science dominated by men? What draws them to it? Judy Gahagan argues it has more to do with virility than the creative search for knowledge.

'It's a boy!' read the telegram from nuclear physicist Edward Teller announcing his pride and joy – the successful detonation of the first hydrogen bomb. His choice of image was apposite: a telling hint of what makes mad, male science tick.

Science begins in the mind, of course, keeping company with all the fantasies, conflicts and symbols of the human psyche. When it emerges it is permanently shaped by these things. This is why much of the prestigious science produced over the last three centuries in Western Europe has been obsessed with virility and fertility.

The domains of science are themselves arranged in a prestige hierarchy according to their 'hardness'. Those subjects – such as particle physics – which are most abstract, have least contact with matter, which 'penetrate' furthest into Nature, are the 'hardest' and therefore the most prestigious. Biology and psychology, which observe living beings interacting with their natural environment, are the 'softest'. This hierarchy has nothing to do with complexity, profundity, progress, even importance. It has everything to do with virility.

Hard science has triumphed in an age of capitalism and materialism. Because it masquerades as the apotheosis of pure reason, few have been inclined to poke around inside its psyche. But as we approach the apocalypse, brought about by its proudest achievements, many reckon it's time to get this god onto the analyst's couch.

Once inside that psyche, we are confronted by three major ideas that have been around for several centuries, and underlie all scientific activity. The first is the division between mind and matter. Since the time of Francis Bacon, (male) mind has sought to penetrate (female) matter.

Related to this idea is the assumption that the scientist's purpose is to control or exploit nature, as opposed to caring for, measuring, conserving – or just simply understanding it. And rounding off the trio is the way each scientific discovery glorifies its author's ego, in a way that, say, running a nursery school could never do. And so the race to be first, to claim paternity, is on. Thus is prestigious modern science relentless, aggressive and competitive.

But before we can look at the minds of individuals, we have to explain how these three ideas came to hold such sway within science's collective psyche. Many people have suggested they arise from a fear and hostility towards fem-

278

inine principles that is thought to gnaw away at *110* the vitals of the masculine unconscious (and not so unconscious). They see the attack on nature by the scientists *115* as parallel to the rape and exploitation of women in misogynist cultures. This hostility, they argue, is *170* rooted in a fundamental *120* of biology. The story runs thus: the female's role in creating life is visible and unchallengable. Motherhood can- *125* not be disputed and makes the primary family unit a matriarchal one. The male is excluded from this primal *130* creative process – and his resultant envy and insecurity are terrible. It can only be assuaged by creating secrets and *135* miracles for himself or by exerting total control over women. The assuagement takes many forms. One form is the *140* widespread and brutal enforcement of virginity to ensure biological paternity. A considerably less oppressive *145* method is found among many indigenous peoples, where the men have secret societies and ceremonies which allow *150* them special communion with nature, and from which women are strictly excluded. (Australian aboriginal *155* women comment scathingly that 'men make secret ceremonies, women make babies'.) But the form we know

160 best is men's modern quest to produce fantastic, dangerous and futile technologies in an effort *165* to gain control over life itself.

This quest has the effect of both dominating over and escaping *170* from everything associated with femininity. Scientists have a reputation for being obsessive, working 17 hours a day in conditions of mental *175* and physical isolation. Such dedication earns our approval, and we understand that it is essential for scientific *180* progress. But is it? Why should this flight from life be seen to be the real hallmark of the genuinely committed *185* scientist?

And what of the passion to be the undisputed author of a discovery, the father of the brain- *190* child, to be first? In reality there is no hurry at all. In fact, if there had been a bit less urgency about nuclear research, *195* scientists might have got around to contemplating just where the radioactive garbage was going *200* to go. Indeed, the whole course of science might have been different had all scientific papers been published anonymously, *205* solely in the service of knowledge.

The mysterious nature of scientific research, its isolation and the secrecy *260* so often surrounding it, *210* also help feed the myth of genius. The genius is a

person with a different kind of intellect, blessed with extraordinary gifts *215* and powers. Or so we've always assumed. But recently psychologist Robert Weisberg has been examining the evi- *220* dence for this assumption. And he has discovered that the processes needed for solving problems like the structure of *225* DNA, the mechanism of evolution, the behaviour of particles, are no different from those involved in putting a new lock on *230* the front door or investigating which signals an autistic child responds to most positively.

To qualify as genius, a *235* scientist will indeed have above average fluency in certain logical, spatial or mathematical operations. But more important than *240* these is their fascination, or obsession, with a subject. This means they often persist with a single problem for years. *245* Using biographical and historical documents, Weisberg demonstrated convincingly how perfectly ordinary were the *250* processes leading to 'great' discoveries. Only the obsession with the subject and the passion to be first were distinc- *255* tive to the genius. Yet both are, as we have seen, potentially lethal characteristics.

All this leads to a con- *260* clusion: that true science must emerge from feminine and masculine qualities. Every institution

that isolated men from
265 the creative care of children, that alienates them
from the feminine in
themselves and other
people, helps to set in

270 motion a monstrous per-
version of human intel-
lect, rather than a crea-
tive search for know-
ledge.
Judy Gahagan is a free-

*lance writer and former
psychology lecturer based
in London.*

from the *New Interna-
tionalist*, April 1988

Discussion and analysis

List the most significant scientific discoveries of the century. What makes each of them important?

List as many famous scientists as you can, and name their discoveries.

What was life in Britain like before the development of modern science?

What are the negative effects of scientific discoveries?

Should scientists be expected to take account of the social and moral implications of their research?

On the whole, has the development of science been a good thing for the human race or not?

3   Youth, marriage and old age

This may seem a rather artificial linking of what are, in reality, separate themes. They can of course be treated separately, but since each is in itself a relatively minor social issue in terms of a written English language examination, it may be convenient to deal with them all in a single discussion session. A comprehension on marriage will serve as the preliminary written exercise.

Comprehension and comment

Read the following passage, and answer the questions that follow. You are advised to spend about one and a half hours on this exercise.

The most neurotic, the most difficult marriages, those with a lot of anger and frustration, are not those that dissolve most easily. In fact, outwardly bad marriages often last till death. It is the easy marriages, those with less pathology, that often separate so smoothly they scarcely seem to have been joined.
5   In fact, marriage until death seems an absurd route to choose for an easy life. An absurd route to choose for other goals – not necessary for sex, indeed in the long term inimical to it; very difficult for equal and mutual growth; deep relationships are quite possible outside it (one of the messages of Ingmar Bergman's *Scenes from a Marriage* was that the couple could only be genuine friends once they were apart.

10 Only then did they understand each other). Indeed, one quite possible explanation of the state of marriage today is that a great many people are entering it who are quite unsuitable to something so strenuous. A hundred years ago far fewer people were able to marry, largely because of their financial situation. About one-third of women under 44, for example, were not married in the Victorian era. Today about

15 95 per cent of males and females have been married by the time they reach 45.

What then is the point of monogamous marriage till death? Guygenbuhl-Craig, the Swiss Jungian psychiatrist who made all these observations, derived the facts from the married people he treated in his practice. In his book *Marriage – Dead or Alive*, he looks at an archetypal marriage, that of Hera and Zeus. To the Greeks, this

20 was marriage. It was extremely stormy – usually about Zeus's incessant infidelity (though Hera was by no means faithful herself). At one time Hera tied Zeus up so completely that helpers from Tartarus had to free him. At another, he had her hung from the rafters of heaven. She was furiously jealous and would exact appalling revenge against his lovers. When he seduced Io, Hera turned her into a

25 cow. This wasn't enough, so she loosed upon Io a gadfly, a gigantic insect whose stings drove her mad. In complete panic, raving with fear, Io as cow raced through large parts of the world. Many wives have longed for such powers.

This myth holds a clue to what marriage is about. It is about the Jungian view of salvation.

30 Salvation is distinct from well-being. Well-being means comfort, freedom from anxiety, sexual relief, companionship. Salvation has to do with the meaning of life far beyond comfort. It is about facing up to suffering and death. Jungians have a word to describe the search for salvation – 'individuation'. Guygenbuhl-Craig says that individuation can be described exactly, in detail. This is not true. It is a mystical

35 concept which is rather fuzzy and that is its strength. It can only be described in terms of the kind of things it involves, and by reference to myth and metaphor. It means not just finding out about, but working through, the forces in our subconscious: in a man, the powerful aspects of the feminine which are part of him; in a woman, the active masculine aspects; dark forces of destruction and cruelty

40 which are also part of our natures. This last is particularly difficult, and all ages try and avoid it (putting it on to the devil, for instance, or, like us, on upbringing or social forces or 'capitalism', 'communism'). This process is, in fairy stories, a journey. But individuation is both the journey and the goal – the process of working through the self and the achieved reconciliation. It is like the life of Christ, where the life and

45 its end were together the message.

Marriage till death is a pathway to salvation, a process of individuation. Because there is no avenue of escape it is an extremely unusual path. Here it resembles the strictest of enclosed medieval orders, or the vocation of a hermit. 'In this partially uplifting, partially tormenting evasionlessness lies the specific character of this path.'

50 It is absurd to expect that marriage should be 'happy'. It is the way of salvation, and in myth the road to heaven leads through hell. Because it is a way of salvation marriage is an endless series of exalted high feelings and deep low ones, a continuous belt of ups and downs. It has happy moments of course, many of them, but also suffering and sacrifices.

55   Sacrifice always plays a major role in the myths of salvation. It is true that with Abraham and Isaac, God accepted a goat, but many myths have a tendency to comfort. The point was that Abraham had to be ready to sacrifice. In Christianity, the central myth of the last 2,000 years, sacrifice is cardinal. In any road to salvation there is a profound need to sacrifice oneself, a feeling one should pay the price. It

60   goes without saying – you have only to look – that great sacrifices are demanded by marriage. The long-term confrontation of marriage is only possible if one or both partners renounce something important. This sacrifice is necessary to the personality. It is quite wrong for friends or therapists to say no one should have to go on giving affection to someone cold, no one should have to make such sacrifices.

65   That situation is the marriage. Their sympathy is misplaced. Dante crossed hell, but he reached heaven. The successful marriage, the endured marriage, leads to the deepest kind of existential satisfaction.   JONATHAN GATHORNE-HARDY

Note: Your answers should be *in your own words* as far as possible.

a   Consider the meaning of the sentence 'it is the easy . . . seem to have been joined'. (lines 3–4)   (*2 marks*)

b   Explain, in your own words, what the writer means by saying 'marriage until death seems an absurd route to choose for an easy life'. (line 5)
                                                                    (*4 marks*)

c   Why do you think the writer mentions the myth of Hera and Zeus?
                                                                    (*3 marks*)

d   What do you understand by the term 'individuation'?   (*5 marks*)

e   Consider the significance of the references to: (i) the devil and (ii) the life of Christ.   (*5 marks*)

f   What do you think that the writer means by saying that marriage 'resembles the strictest of enclosed medieval orders, or the vocation of a hermit'? (lines 47–8)   (*5 marks*)

g   Why is the 'sympathy' of 'friends or therapists' in the final paragraph 'misplaced', according to the writer?   (*4 marks*)

h   Give the meaning of the following words and phrases as they appear in the passage:
     (i)   inimical (line 7);
     (ii) strenuous (line 12);
     (iii) incessant infidelity (line 20);
     (iv) myth and metaphor (line 36).   (*6 marks*)

i   Comment on the view of marriage expressed in the last two paragraphs.
                                                                    (*8 marks*)

j Comment on the effectiveness of the author's prose style in this passage, looking in detail at his language and syntax.   (*8 marks*)

(*50 marks total*)

Youth

A discussion of the theme of youth may usefully take in youth culture. Here are some forms of preparation:

A history of post-war fashions and ideologies amongst young people might provide an enjoyable project to undertake.

A more time-consuming but more creative approach to youth culture would be for a group of students to present a history of rock music since the mid-50s. A cassette could be prepared, illustrating the changes in popular music, to be accompanied by an analysis of the movements and trends in fashion and philosophy which went with these musical styles. Different students might perhaps work on different eras. A strict time limit must be established at the outset, however, if this project is not to last for ever! The following books might be useful for research into the music and movements of the 1950s and 1960s:

  Colin, Nic, *Awopbopalubopalopbamboom: Pop from the Beginning*,
  Paladin, 1970
  Gillett, Charlie, *The Sound of the City: The Rise of Rock and Roll*,
  Souvenir Press, 1983
  Melley, George, *Revolt Into Style: The Pop Arts in Britain*, Penguin,
  1970

More formal discussion might take in such questions as inner-city riots, the effects of unemployment on young people, or, on a more personal level, young people's experiences of the 'generation gap' and the problems of adolescence. Four books which deal with these issues through the eyes of teenagers are the following:

  Cashmore, E. Ellis, *No Future*, Heinemann, 1984
  Fisher, Susie and Holder, Susan, *Too Much Too Young?*, Pan Books,
  1981
  Lawton, Anthony, *Parents and Teenagers*, Allen and Unwin, 1985
  McCormack, Mary, *The Generation Gap: the view from both sides*,
  Constable, 1985

The family

Any discussion of the family will inevitably enable you to talk from personal experience. The theme can be considered purely on a personal level, without any prior preparation, dealing with such questions as:

  What is the best age at which to marry?

283

Should marriage be a lifelong commitment?
Under what circumstances should partners consider divorce?
Are extra-marital affairs ever right?
Should both husbands and wives work if they have young children?
Should children be brought up in a strict or a liberal family environment?

Research can again be useful to back up discussion of the family. It may be interesting to look up comparative divorce statistics, and statistics of the ages at which men and women married in different eras and areas. More detailed research could be undertaken on such subjects as alternative methods of child rearing (such as the Israeli Kibbutz system) and differing concepts of marriage in different countries. The following books may be of interest:

Bernard, Jessie, *The Future of Parenthood*, Calder and Boyars, 1975
Bettelheim, Bruno, *Children of the Dream: Communal child rearing and its implications for Society*, Paladin, 1971.
Gathorne-Hardy, Jonathan, *Love, Sex, Marriage and Divorce*, Jonathan Cape, 1981
Skynner, Robin and Cleese, John, *Families and how to survive them*, Methuen, 1983

The magazine *New Statesman and Society* frequently carries articles on the family.

Old age

Old age is becoming an increasing social problem in Western society, and, once again, research will considerably aid discussion. An illuminating exercise would be to compare the numbers of people over retirement age in Europe, with those under school-leaving age in Latin America or other areas of the Third World. A discussion of the significance of these statistics would provide a useful introduction to the problem.

Further research could be undertaken into such matters as the National Health Service provisions and services for old people, methods of preparing people for retirement, and the problem of senility.

A more personal response to growing old might be evoked from reading stories about old people, such as 'Uncle Ernest', in Alan Sillitoe's *The Loneliness of the Long Distance Runner* (Granada, 1985) or listening to songs such as 'Bookends' (and the accompanying 'Voices of Old People') from Simon and Garfunkel's *Bookends* album (CBS, 1968). A collection of stories and extracts about old people is to be found in a book called *Old Age*, in the Routledge and Kegan Paul *Themes* series, published in 1972.

Books of general interest on the theme are as follows:

Greengross, Sally (ed.), *Ageing, an Adventure in Living*, Condor, 1985
Hellie Huyck, Margaret, *Growing Old: Things you Need to Know About Ageing*, Prentice Hall, 1974

Hobman, David (ed.), *The Social Challenge of Ageing*, Croom Helm, 1978

Essay titles

a 'Fashion dictates the way we live.'

b Is there a 'generation gap'?

c Do you agree that personal happiness is best found in long-term relationships?

d Is the family out of date?

e Medical advances have to a large extent prolonged life. Do you think this is entirely an advantage?

f It used to be said that it was a woman's business to get married as soon as possible, and a man's to keep unmarried as long as he could. Is this a fair view of marriage?

g The duties, responsibilities and pleasures of the family.

h We do not respect the old; they are no longer wise.

i How will we cope with the problems of living to an average age of 100 years?

j Melanie Klein said: 'However good are the child's feelings towards both parents, aggressiveness and hate also remain.' How do you react to this statement?

4 Drugs

This is obviously one of the most sensitive of all social problems to discuss in a class situation. The passage which follows serves as a historical introduction to the subject, as well as a summary skills exercise.

Summary skills

Write a summary of the following passage in not more than 230 words (the passage contains about 680 words). Your summary should be in clear, connected English, and the number of words used should be indicated at the end. You are advised to spend about one hour on this exercise.   (*40 marks*)

Even if heroin and cannabis could have been banished, it had become clear by the 1970s that they would immediately have been replaced by other drugs. Some had already established themselves – occasionally with the active help of governments, or of the medical profession, or both.

When the amphetamines – 'pep pills' – were first marketed in the 1930s, doctors had begun to prescribe them for patients who felt tired or lethargic; and later as a slimming aid. During the war they proved a help to men in the forces who were required to stay alert on duty; and when it ended, vast quantities of them, surplus to requirements, were dumped on the open market . . . But then it was realised that, injected intravenously, the amphetamines could produce an explosive bout of euphoria; and as they were cheap and easily available, they were soon being extensively used for that purpose, with destructive effects on the health of some of the addicts, ranging from brittle finger-nails to ulcers, chest infections, liver disorders, and cerebral haemorrhages. Governments banned sales, except on prescription; but so many people had acquired the habit of taking the drug, and so many doctors were willing to indulge them, that the black market was rarely short of supplies. Taking amphetamines, in Brecher's estimation, ranked 'among the most disastrous forms of drug use yet devised' – particularly in Sweden, where the attempt to impose total prohibition led only to a rise in the price, encouraging illicit manufacture and smuggling, and leading to a spectacular growth in the number of addicts . . .

Cocaine also made a come-back. 'Sniffing' had enjoyed a vogue in the United States in the 1920s; in his *Drugs and the Mind*, Robert S. de Ropp surmised that the original 'dope friend' peddled cocaine, rather than heroin. But it was expensive; the amphetamines, far cheaper and more easily obtainable, for a while replaced it. When the amphetamines proved an unsatisfactory substitute, cocaine began to return to favour in American cities. Its high price was less of an impediment to sales than it had been in the depressed 1930s, and provided an incentive to smugglers. With the raw materials, coca leaves, abundant and cheap, this left an ample margin to perfect smuggling techniques, and to bribe Customs or police. Once the cocaine had been brought in, there was no difficulty in selling it. What Plate called the iron law of drug marketing, 'supply determines demand', came into operation; whenever it was available, cocaine became . . . the drug of choice, not only among whites but ever increasingly among affluent black drug users as well . . . Among Latin Americans in New York, cocaine is often the preferred drug of entertainers, expensive prostitutes, very successful businessmen, and certain religious sects for whom cocaine use is literally an act of faith. And among white drug users, cocaine is especially popular with rock stars, writers, younger actors and actresses, and stock-brokers and other Wall Street types . . .

And even if all these drugs could have been brought under some control – by, say, the discovery of some instrument on the lines of a geiger counter, capable of infallibly detecting them – it would not have solved the problem. Apart from synthetic variants, there were numerous substances which, though not sold as drugs, could be used for that purpose – and frequently were. Benzine and glue had long been sniffed 'for kicks', and with the advent of the aerosol can, it was found that there were endless alternatives; 'literally hundreds of easily accessible sources', the Le Dain Committee found, including paints, paint removers, lighter fuel, and dry-cleaning fluids: 'it was recently observed that 38 different products containing

such substances were available from the shelves of the service station's highway store in Ottawa'. In the circumstances, the Committee pointed out, effective restriction was hardly practicable, 'except at considerable inconvenience to a large segment of the population'; and, as the large segment of the population was unlikely to accept that inconvenience, the existence of these 'substances' created a problem 'which clearly calls into question the potential of the crimino-legal system in controlling drug use'.
BRIAN INGLIS

Further reading

Inglis, Brian, *The Forbidden Game: a Social History of Drugs*, Hodder and Stoughton, 1975

Lamour, Catherine and Lamberti, Michael R., *The Second Opium War*, Allen Lane, 1972

Manning, Mary, *The Drugs Menace*, Columbus Books, 1985

Nowlis, Hellen, *Drugs Demystified*, Unesco Press, 1975

Wyatt, John, *Talking About Drugs*, Wayland Publishers, 1973

Videos

A variety of videos and films are available on drug abuse and its dangers. There are police officers in most areas of Britain who can be contacted to show drug films at schools and colleges, and this may be the best visual approach to the issue.

The following videos may be of particular use:

Drugwatch – a programme in four parts:
  Part 1: Getting Started (19 minutes)
  Part 2: Getting Hooked (14 minutes)
  Part 3: Getting Off (8 minutes)
  Part 4: Avoiding It All (17 minutes)
How Much Can You Drink? (Horizon, 48 minutes)
Suckers (David Bellamy on smoking, 23 minutes)

Essay title

The abuse of drugs.

Advice on writing: preparing for the exam

Writing at Advanced level in English language ought to be a reasonably stimulating and enjoyable experience. It should combine intellectual rigour and creativity, and practice in writing should enhance the precision and accuracy of your expression. Let us end with a few concluding observations and suggestions about English language writing in general, and preparation for an exam in particular.

Whatever question you choose for continuous writing in exam conditions, you will be marked according to three essential criteria: content, presentation and expression. The quality of ideas, information and/or imagination which you display, in other words the content of your writing, is of absolutely prime importance. It is to be hoped that the discussion and analysis and subsequent essay practice provided in this book will help with the content of your essays. The essay you write in the examination must also be well presented, in other words clearly and effectively structured and paragraphed, as the first two chapters stress. Thirdly, it must be effectively and accurately written.

The examiner will hope to find fluency and clarity, and ideally vividness of expression, in your writing. He or she will also look for formal accuracy, which means correct spelling, a suitable register, and accurate sentence structure and punctuation. Since professional writers frequently break the rules and write ungrammatically for effect, this may seem over-formal. James Joyce, after all, avoided punctuation altogether in the last 60 pages of his masterpiece, *Ulysses*, and used his own method of indicating dialogue when he *did* punctuate. The justification is, of course, that you have to prove that you can apply the rules accurately before you are allowed to break them!

You must, therefore, work at the formal accuracy of your writing. You must try to ensure that you always write grammatically accurate sentences. Every sentence you write must be a complete statement, with subject(s) (noun or pronoun) and finite verb(s) (verb(s) with a past, present or future tense). You must try to punctuate as accurately as possible. Commas are a particular problem for most people, and it might be a good idea to learn and practise the rules for the use of commas. Dialogue is notoriously difficult to punctuate accurately, and you must make sure that you always separate the actual spoken words from the verbs of saying (she said, he shouted, etc.) with punctuation marks. Apostrophes are frequently left out or misused, and you should make sure that you are confident about their use, and check, when you have finished writing, that you have put them in correctly. The semicolon is a sophistication of punctuation which it might be worth your while to master.

Spelling is a particular problem for some people. There are some words (like argument, tragedy, 'alot' for 'a lot', 'infact' for 'in fact') which are extremely commonly misspelt. If your spelling tends to be a bit shaky, it would be a good idea to write down, in a small notebook, correct versions of words you have spelt wrongly in written work, and reread the correct spellings frequently. Only by seeing how words *look* will you imprint the correct version on your memory. However, you should not allow uncertainty about the spelling of difficult words to inhibit you from using them (as long as you are certain of their meaning!). You will be penalised for misspelling common words, but not for attempting more unusual ones. The most important requirement is for you to create a sense of personal engagement in what you are writing, and attempt to write as expressively as you can.

Finally, a word about timing. In all examinations, timing is crucial. If you have two quite different exercises on the same exam paper, such as an essay and a summary skills exercise, it might be best to decide the order in which you are going to tackle the questions before you go into the exam room. A case can be made, in the situation just described, for starting with the summary exercise, on the grounds that it is easier to wind up an essay in a hurry than a summary. In a comprehension exercise it might be best to leave questions which carry few marks till last, unless you are confident that you can answer them quickly.

With regular practice there is every chance that your writing will improve, as long as you learn from your mistakes.

APPENDIX

Specimen answers to passages for summary in Chapter 4, pages 42–47

1   The normal child, if he has confidence in his parents, is extremely disruptive, testing the strength of the family set-up to establish a framework before settling to play. This is because the young child's sense of reality and selfhood is undeveloped. A stable, loving family is essential for natural development. If the framework is lacking, he is disturbed, and seeks the stability he needs for mental health and the development of independence in his wider family, friends and school. The anti-social child seeks further afield for this essential stability.   (90 words)

2   Most people recognise the usefulness of critical training in the arts, feeling that, although appreciation should be sufficient, it will remain superficial unless backed up by analytical study, and that untrained appreciation tends to lead to mere self-assertion rather than real involvement in the arts. The capacity to explain our preferences in the arts to ourselves and others is valuable, since generally it deepens our awareness of art.

Critical training may, however, lead to desensitisation, so that while we learn to understand and evaluate artistic works, our natural pleasure in them is dulled through an over-concentration on correct interpretation. But this is a necessary risk, and critical evaluation is one means of developing our humanity.   (115 words)

3   Educationalists frequently claim that there is too much violence in the mass media. The issue is complex. Violence and death have always featured in great art, and a distinction must be drawn between their treatment in serious programmes and those designed for a mass audience. Essentially, there are too many badly-produced programmes relying on violence at peak viewing times, and competition for viewing figures almost certainly exacerbates the problem. Although only emotionally disturbed children are likely to actually learn violence from watching any particular programme, the repeated

exposure to violence on television actually causes ordinary children to regard violence as normal and acceptable. If there are insufficient programmes expressing positive values, this acceptance is strengthened. Gratuitous lingering on violence increases the effect, and far too many programmes rely for their emotional impact on the scenes of violence, rather than on any message which the programme might be presenting.   (149 words)

4a   Based on a novel by E.M. Forster.
Directors: Ismail Merchant and James Ivory.
Cast: Judy Dench plays Eleanor Lavish, a novelist.
Helena Bonham-Carter plays the heroine.
Maggie Smith, Denholm Elliott and Simon Callow take other leading roles.
Several elderly English actresses play ageing English ladies.
Screenplay: Ruther Prawer Jhabvala.
Setting: Florence, and later, England.
Film is a period piece.
Shows great care with costumes and interiors.
Forster's chapter headings used to introduce scenes.
Later scenes contain tea-parties and portrayal of social embarrassment.

b   It concerns some English people whose visit to Florence early this century brings them spiritually to life. The romantic imagination of a female novelist and the barely concealed passion of another female character are portrayed.
    It is also about social pressures constricting people, and the conflict between the splendour of Florentine architecture and the pettiness of English social life. There are moments of violence. The English scenes include tea-parties and episodes of social embarrassment, including an interrupted nude bathing scene. The film is partly a pastiche of film versions of the Edwardian era.   (94 words)

c   The film has a genteel graciousness which is highly effective. It is a conscious period piece, and such great care is taken with costumes and interiors that it seems almost museum-like. The Edwardian scenes are superbly constructed. The extreme care with which the directors attempt to capture precise details of the era, and the novel, gives the film a feeling of artificiality. However, every scene contains brilliant visual effects. The use of chapter headings is effective, though these tend to interrupt the flow of the action. The balance and control of the directors add power to passionate scenes. The tension of the film comes partly from the contrast between the magnificent setting of Florence and the carefully captured English dialogue, and there are some superb scenes of social embarrassment in the English scenes. The casting and acting of both major and minor parts is superb.   (146 words)